SOUTH ASIA
IN THE NEW DECADE
Challenges and Prospects

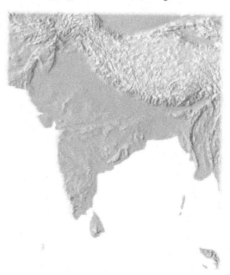

SOUTH ASIA
IN THE NEW DECADE
Challenges and Prospects

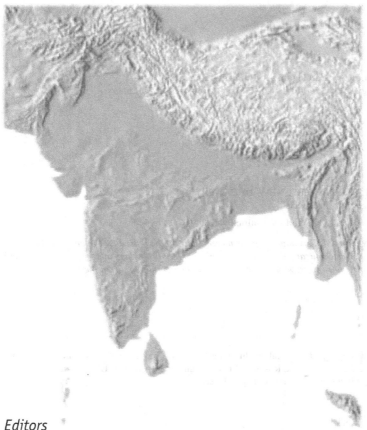

Editors

Amitendu Palit · Gloria Spittel
National University of Singapore, Singapore

 **World Scientific**

NEW JERSEY · LONDON · SINGAPORE · BEIJING · SHANGHAI · HONG KONG · TAIPEI · CHENNAI

Published by

World Scientific Publishing Co. Pte. Ltd.

5 Toh Tuck Link, Singapore 596224

USA office: 27 Warren Street, Suite 401-402, Hackensack, NJ 07601

UK office: 57 Shelton Street, Covent Garden, London WC2H 9HE

British Library Cataloguing-in-Publication Data
A catalogue record for this book is available from the British Library.

SOUTH ASIA IN THE NEW DECADE
Challenges and Prospects

ISBN 978-981-4401-06-7

In-house Editors: Sandhya Venkatesh/Nithin Jayan

Typeset by Stallion Press
Email: enquiries@stallionpress.com

Printed in Singapore.

Preface

The second decade of the current millennium, much like its predecessor, has begun on a somber note. The sobriety is largely on account of the economic reverses suffered by the world in 2008, whose effects have continued to linger in various regions, most notably Europe. In a world where not only markets but industrial processes are intricately linked, economic downturns — particularly one as severe as that witnessed in 2008 — have become more lasting and catastrophic than analysts imagined them to be. The anxieties over national economic prospects and preservation of household and per capita incomes have not remained confined to the Western hemisphere alone. They have travelled far and wide and impacted South Asia, which, despite being less integrated with global commercial traffic than other parts of the world, has nonetheless begun experiencing the effect of global business swings more than it used to a decade ago.

No other South Asian country symbolizes synchronicity with global trends as much as India does. From being a robust high-growth economy for most part of the last decade until the onset of the economic crisis, India has lately slipped into a phase of marked contraction in economic activity. It is difficult to say whether the region's largest economy, which is a U.S. \$1 trillion plus commercial giant figuring among the world's top ten economies, will be able to shake off its slumber notwithstanding the sluggishness in the global economy. What is, however, clear is that the Indian economy cannot expect to find solace in the argument of "decoupling", which many analysts advocated following the global financial crisis. The hypothesis underlines emerging market economies, particularly large Asian economies such as China and India having developed growth momentums of their own, as insulated from what happens in the rest of the world. India has become a distinct part of the global and regional business cycles, as have other countries of South Asia depending upon their respective integrations into world trade and investment cycles. A critical challenge for India and other economies of the region in the medium term would be to ensure that their national economic prospects much as they are affected by global developments do not peg them back in a manner that is unsustainable.

Challenges for India and other countries in the region in the decade stem from both external and internal spheres. In addition to the negative externalities produced by a depressed global economic outlook affecting prospects for trade and investment, South Asia continues to remain vulnerable to spill over from political turbulences in the neighborhood. One of the biggest concerns in this respect is the outcomes of the "Arab Spring", which have produced multiple civil uprisings and violent political upheavals across large swathes of the Arab World to the West of South Asia. South Asia's concerns over these developments are not confined to the difficulties which its countries are likely to face in accessing energy, or livelihood concerns of the fairly sizeable South Asian expatriate population in the Arab world. They also relate to realignment of policies toward new regimes and governments in a manner that does not aggravate instabilities at home and abroad. Strategic dilemmas of the South Asian countries become even more complex given the prolongation of involvement of extra-regional actors such as the U.S. in the Arab world, as well as the growing strategic presence of China. Balancing multiple objectives in a volatile and unpredictable scenario is never easy. South Asia's west surely does not show signs of making it easy in any respect.

The intractable and chronic challenges, however, remain within the region. The region has lived with these challenges for several decades. While the fundamentals of the challenges have hardly changed, the nature and intensities have varied over time, and continue to do so even now. The end of several years of ethnic conflict in Sri Lanka has been replaced by political calm. But whether a harmonious process of social and cultural assimilation or integration — the lack of which was largely responsible for fomenting the ethnic conflict — has been put in place is not certain. Accommodation of greater plurality within a well-defined state framework is a major challenge facing Sri Lanka. Till the issue is successfully resolved, South Asia's most socially developed economy is unlikely to take the giant economic leap, which its progressive and outward-oriented policies should have fashioned decades ago. But while Sri Lanka at least conveys an impression of political tranquility, however superficial, westward in the region, Pakistan and Afghanistan continue to be rocked by sectarian violence and extremist tensions. As the next Parliamentary elections in Pakistan draw close, the country continues to remain embroiled in political instability with the incumbent government finding it increasingly difficult to manage various tensions. Pakistan's woes in recent times have been compounded by a series of natural calamities that have rocked its fragile and staggering economy. Concerns about Pakistan have now enlarged from short-term worries about the country's economic recovery and new elections to bigger apprehensions about the ability of the Pakistani state to successfully mitigate ethnic, political and institutional tussles in the long-term and ensure the country and its economy's stable progress in future. Pakistan's security and strategic prospects are intricately linked to the developments in Afghanistan, where hopes of gradual demilitarization and increasing occupation of the vacated space by civil society, continues to be pitted against extremist perceptions.

The rather unfortunate aspect of South Asia's tryst with nation-building and harmonious socio-cultural assimilation in the contemporary era has been the low fulfillment of promises and hopes following far-reaching political restructurings. The elections held in Bangladesh around four years ago ushered in a new government with a resounding mandate. The government, which was expected to improve governance and public service delivery by providing the much-desired political stability and social harmony, appears to have veered off course after the initial couple of years of positive performance. The elected government in Nepal led by the Maoist communist group continues to struggle to integrate the erstwhile "rebels" into the civil society mainstream and balancing power within a constitutional framework accommodating plurality. Indeed, the later years of the last decade had witnessed spirited revival of democratic processes in the region with fresh elections being held in Pakistan, Afghanistan, Sri Lanka, Bangladesh and Nepal — all of which had elicited hopes of durable positive outcomes and the strengthening of democratic institutions. The hopes appear to have faded away as most countries in South Asia continue to search for the elusive plurality in their national frameworks which would accommodate multiple aspirations and ambitions. The critical question at this juncture is whether democracy in South Asian countries has matured to the extent that it can facilitate the search for such frameworks.

Democracy — in a different way — has been in focus in India as well. Unfortunately, the focus has not been in a particularly positive light with the fractured electoral mandates, coalition governments — both at the centre and in several provinces — and diverse interest groups exerting their individual and specific influences on policy-making and governance in distorted and counter-productive fashion. India's ability to push ahead on economic policies has been severely hampered by the pervasive "policy paralysis" — a state of almost complete inertia in kicking-off pending economic reforms. The incumbent government in India got elected for a second term in 2009 with the promise of delivering better on several fronts particularly public service delivery. However, the last three years have hardly witnessed much improvement in this regard. Instead, the government has been engaged more than full-time in warding off a valiant civil society on charges of nepotism, poor governance and corruption. India's limited success over the last couple of years in achieving economic progress and failing to establish credible standards of transparency in governance exemplifies the fairly conspicuous disappointment on part of the people in South Asia from the manifold democratic choices they have made in the recent past.

Fighting chronic ills is destiny that South Asia can hardly avoid. The current decade will continue to remain a period during which South Asia's public policies will need to stay firmly focused on achieving the human and social development targets set under the Millennium Development Goals (MDGs). Different countries of the region have differing varieties of shortfalls in this respect. As a region, however, South Asia falls significantly short of the required landmarks. Given that the region is the most populous part of the world, low achievements on MDGs by South Asia means lack of access to basic needs and inferior quality of living for a significant chunk of the global population. Be it environment, education, health, drinking water, or sanitation, the imperatives for the region is distinct and occasionally alarming. There are some aspects of sustainable development that have increasingly assumed serious proportions for the region compared with perceptions a decade ago. The most notable of these are the outcomes of climate change, which has manifested in grave dimensions for a small island country like Maldives, increased vulnerability to natural disasters for much bigger countries like Bangladesh and Sri Lanka and made weather patterns, particularly rainfall volumes sporadic leading to uncertainties about agricultural prospects. The region's efforts to move to more environment-friendly, less carbon-intensive modes of production by using more biofuels has to overcome the larger challenge of food security and livelihood issues for marginal populations in most members.

The papers in this collection address several of the challenges looming large before South Asia and the prospects of the region in successfully mitigating these challenges. Given the multiplicity of complex issues preponderant in the region, it is impossible to have all the challenges analyzed specifically with due regard to their country-specific distinctions. The collection does not claim to have achieved this impossible task even remotely. What it however claims to have brought together is a diverse range of scholarly perspectives on various aspects of some key challenges facing the region. These challenges vary from the complexities produced by growing interface between China and India from an orthodox security perspective to contemporary societal reflections of riots and ethnic tensions, the multilateral standpoints, the increasingly pervasive role played by nontraditional media in influencing debates and opinions within the region, outstanding issues of governance and sustainability and the success (or the lack of it) of the region in integrating with the rest of the world through economic means. This volume is a notable addition to the growing body of multi-disciplinary academic literature on South Asia and we hope the readers will be benefited from the thoughtful and often unique insights which the papers offer.

Amitendu Palit
Gloria Spittel
5 June 2012

Acknowledgment

The success of the Sixth International Conference and the publication of this edited volume are indebted to the participation of the authors and their thoughtful contributions. We are thankful for their participation particularly to the Deputy Prime Minister of the Republic of Singapore Mr Teo Chee Hean and Mr Jaspal Singh Bindra, CEO Standard Chartered Bank for taking time off their considerable busy schedules to attend and contribute to the conference.

We are grateful to Max Phua, Sandhya Venkatesh, Nithin Jayan and the rest at World Scientific without whom the publishing of this book would not have been as smooth. Finally, but surely not the least, both the conference and the publication of this book would not have been possible if not for the support of the staff at ISAS. We especially thank Ambassador Gopinath Pillai, Chairman ISAS; Professor Tan Tai Yong, Director ISAS; Johnson Davasagayam, Senior Associate Director, ISAS; our colleagues at ISAS — Sithara Doriasamy, Jacqueline Goh, Kamarunnisa Shaul Hameed, Kirby Khoo Kian Sim, Hema Kiruppalini and our ex-colleague Christopher Stonaker — for their generous support.

Contents

Introduction

South Asia in the New Decade: Challenges and Prospects

Teo Chee Hean

Introduction

South Asia is a strategically important region. Located astride the key sea lanes of the Indian Ocean and home to more than a fifth of the world's population, it is easy to see how South Asia is poised to play a key global role in the 21st century. Economically, the region has already begun to display its potential. South Asia has seen a strong rebound in its economic growth since 2009, and is slated to grow around 7% in 2010 and nearly 8% in 2011, one of the highest rates in the world. The resilience of Foreign Direct Investment (FDI) into the region amidst the global economic crisis, the quick resumption of capital inflows into South Asian stock markets since 2009[1] and frequent visiting of leaders from key countries are indicators of its economic potential and of keen interest in South Asia.

In 2010, South Asia's regional body, the South Asian Association for Regional Cooperation (SAARC) celebrated 25 years of establishment during the summit hosted by Bhutan in April. Alongside South Asia's prospects and triumphs are also major challenges, including recovery from natural disasters such as the devastating floods in Pakistan after exceptionally heavy monsoon rains. It is a daunting task to provide a detailed and comprehensive picture of the region and of the various countries that

---

[1]The World Bank South Asia Economic Update 2010: Moving Up, Looking East. (p. 20).

comprise South Asia over the two days of this conference, let alone within a single speech; I begin by addressing the challenges before discussing the prospects and the way forward for the region.

Challenges Confronting South Asia

South Asia's diversity lies in many facets; it has flourishing mega-cities, as well as conflict-torn zones, billionaires and business tycoons as well as impoverished masses. It has one of the world's most populous countries sitting beside some of its smallest ones. More fundamentally; social, ethnic and religious cleavages cut across the region — often through the various states themselves. The vast diversity of South Asia's human landscape is matched only by the variety of challenges its nations face, across domains ranging from economic, social, environment and security.

Economic and social development

Foremost amongst the challenges is economic development, in particular, inclusive economic growth necessary to improve the lives of the people in South Asia. Many in South Asia live below the poverty line, and are in need of basic healthcare, education, drinking water, food and sanitation — challenges that will be exacerbated by climate change and environmental challenges. With a projected economic growth rate of around 7% in 2010 and nearly 8% in 2011 combined with foreign interests and investment the foundation for economic growth is quite stable, the challenge lies in the dispersion of wealth across society and the prioritization of social healthcare and education programmes.

Security and environment

Regional stability in South Asia continues to be affected by the India–Pakistan relationship. While bilateral relations remain tense, and erupt occasionally, both sides understand the need to sustain the relationship bearing in mind the huge consequences if they were to reach boiling point. In addition to the tense India–Pakistan relationship, there are other areas that pose pressing governance and security challenges for the region. Some of these are nontraditional security threats including transnational crime and terrorism, ethnic-religious violence, illegal migration, small arms proliferation, drug trafficking, the spread of infectious diseases and climate change.

Indeed, it is a nontraditional security threat that arguably may have the greatest long term impact on the region. Environmental fluctuations, such as changes in the temperature, or in the volume of rainfall, often have serious consequences for the densely-populated South Asian countries. In May 2010, a record heat wave claimed hundreds of lives in India.[2] The worst floods in Pakistan's history have significantly affected nearly 20 million people since July 2010.[3] In October 2010, high waves and storm surges caused by a tropical cyclone in Bangladesh forced 150 thousand people to flee their homes.[4] The impact of such environmental or natural disasters is likely to be intensified by climate change — global warming will threaten the very existence of small island states in the Indian Ocean, and affect the flow of major rivers that span several countries — posing a continued and pressing threat to regional stability.

Prospects for the Region

Despite these challenges, there are positive prospects for the region; however it is extremely important that states recognize the need to seriously address these challenges. They should be aware of the limitations of trying to deal with these issues by themselves without the benefit of coordinated action with their neighbors. Globalization has helped to break down walls within the region, as well as between South Asia and the rest of the world. South Asian nations are increasingly adopting liberal economic policies, and have begun opening up their markets. The increased economic trade within the region should be used as a benchmark for further regional cooperation in areas such as poverty alleviation, food security, and physical connectivity. To this extent, the regional body SAARC has made some headway in developing frameworks for regional cooperation of these areas.

---

[2]The Guardian, Hundreds die in Indian Heatwave (30 May 2010), http://www.guardian. co.uk/world/2010/may/30/india-heatwave-deaths.

[3]UN Office for the Coordination of Humanitarian Affairs estimate (as of 18 August 10).

[4]ABC News, Thousands homeless after Bangladesh storm surge (7 October 2010) http://www. abc.net.au/news/stories/2010/10/07/3032469.htm.

Undoubtedly the diversity inherent in South Asia also means that each of the nations has its own specific blend of challenges and, in turn gives rise to different prospects and policy options for the future. Nevertheless, there are success stories which can be shared and used across the region as a benchmark.

India

India, as the largest South Asian country, plays a significant role in shaping South Asia's destiny. A rising economic and geopolitical powerhouse, India generates more than 80% of the region's GDP. While it is still grappling with many challenges, it has made impressive advances in the economic realm; its IT and services sectors are world-renowned and the Indian government is undertaking the difficult reforms necessary to sustain growth. India also has demography to its advantage. More than half of India's population is below 25 and more than 65% is below 35. This projected demographic dividend will place India in a good position to be a major growth engine for Asia, lifting and energising its neighbours. However, a large young population can be a boon or blight, depending on whether the potential of that population can be developed, harnessed and realized. Access to good education is the key determinant. Investment in education, or lack of it, is cumulative, and impacts and affects the prospects of the people for many years. This is true too for other countries in the region. India's adult literacy rate of 34% lags behind that of fellow BRIC nation, Brazil, which has an adult literacy rate of 90%.[5] By some estimates, for India to maintain its economic growth in a global marketplace fuelled by the knowledge economy, it would need to approximately double its number of students in higher education by 2012.[6] Nevertheless, India has the potential to do very well for itself.

Sri Lanka

Sri Lanka having emerged from a decades-long civil war is enjoying an economic revival. In 2010, it was the second-fastest growing Asian economy after China, a fact not lost upon the IMF, which recently upgraded Sri Lanka

---

[5]UNDP, *Human Development Report* 2009.
[6]CSIS, *South Asia Monitor*, May 2010.

to middle income emerging market status. Like Brazil, Sri Lanka enjoys an adult literacy rate of just over 90%. Sri Lanka's gross enrolment ratio,[7] which gives an indication of school attendance, is also comparable to that of China. What is particularly noteworthy of Sri Lanka's growth is the narrowness of its gender gap. In the *Global Gender Gap Report 2010* published by the World Economic Forum, which measures gender-based disparities on economic, political, education and health-based criteria, Sri Lanka was the only South Asian country to rank within the top 20.[8] Closing the gender gap is not just an issue of gender equity, it is also one of harnessing the available human resource potential while uplifting the potential of the next generation. The most important determinant of a country's competitiveness is its human talent — the skills, education and productivity of its workforce. In any country, women account for half of the available talent base and have a key role in nurturing the next generation.[9]

Bangladesh

Bangladesh has made steady economic improvement with an economic growth rate between 5%–7% annually over the last decade. It has sharply reduced poverty rates while making impressive progress in a range of educational and health indicators. The government has started the process of transiting the economy from a predominantly agrarian one to one that is industrial and service-focused. The textile and garment manufacturing sector in Bangladesh is thriving, especially for small, export-oriented companies. This sector has become critical to the country's exports and growth. Bangladesh is also a pioneer in microcredit schemes, providing small loans to encourage employment and to alleviate poverty. The Grameen Bank Project and its founder Dr. Muhammad Yunus, were honoured with the 2006 Nobel Peace Prize for their work in Bangladesh. The project has

---

[7]UNDP, *Human Development Report* 2009. The gross enrolment ratio (GER) or gross enrolment index (GEI) is a statistical measure used in the education sector and by the UN in its Education Index. In the UN, the GER is calculated by expressing the number of students enrolled in primary, secondary and tertiary levels of education, regardless of age, as a percentage of the population of official school age for the three levels.

[8]Sri Lanka was ranked 16 out of 134 countries.

[9]WEF, *Gender Gap Report* 2010.

been a source of inspiration for similar projects in more than 40 countries around the world.[10]

Pakistan

Pakistan shares the potential of its neighbors even though it faces challenges posed by extremist violence. Pakistan is an important front for overcoming the global threat posed by extremist terrorism. The restoration of order and security has to move in tandem with social and economic development. There have been some encouraging results from military operations in the Northwest Frontier Province and South Waziristan since July 2009, providing some measure of confidence in the government's ability to cope with its challenges. However, progress depends also on whether and how the current situation in Afghanistan develops. While Pakistan's economy has suffered a setback due to the recent flooding, it has also seized the opportunity to recover. In the first week of November, Pakistan accepted an EU trade package that will grant Pakistan exclusive enhanced market access to the EU market, which is its major trading partner.[11] The EU will suspend tariffs on 75 key Pakistani products, including textiles, thus facilitating the reopening of textile industries in flood-affected areas and creating new jobs.

Moving Forward — Enhancing Regional Cooperation

Although South Asia has enormous long-term potential, in the short term, significant challenges remain; particularly in the area of regional security. In order for realization of South Asia's potential, regional agreements within the South Asian region and beyond are necessary.

South Asia regional cooperation

Greater regional cooperation will contribute to regional development on two fronts. Firstly, increased regional cooperation will aid in the addressing and overcoming of transnational challenges such as the threat of terrorism,

---

[10]The Grameen Bank: Banking for the Poor. http://www.grameen-info.org/.

[11]Daily Times, PM for early approval of EU trade package for Pakistan, (2 November 2010). Details found in The European Commission, Pakistan's flood-hit economy set for major trade boost from EU Commission proposal (7 October 2010), Press release.

criminal activity or climate change. Second, regional cooperation will also provide the South Asian nations an avenue to exploit their potential in trade and development. Such shared interests will provide the impetus for greater cooperation between South Asian countries and their people.

Many commentators, analysts and pundits point to the existing divisions in South Asia and are subscribers to the view that these differences are irreconcilable. However, if the South Asian nations are determined, it is possible to forge ahead through confidence building measures and by the development of shared interests. Intractable differences can be mitigated to prevent them from escalating while more attention is given to concentrating on cooperating in areas of mutual interests and benefits. This is well illustrated by the two largest countries in Asia, China and India. Although disagreements abound, both sides are managing their differences and seeking cooperation in areas where there are shared interests and mutual benefit. Bilateral trade between India and China has risen rapidly from U.S. $15 billion in 2005 to U.S. $41 billion in 2009, making China India's largest trading partner. Dramatic as this increase in trade may appear, some studies suggest that only a quarter of the trade potential of South Asia has been exploited, with intra-regional trade amounting to only some 5% of South Asia's total trade. By comparison, intra-regional trade makes up a quarter of ASEAN's trade figures. If differences and mutual misgivings could be set aside, greater intra-regional trade and economic cooperation amongst South Asian countries could facilitate direct people-to-people exchanges and engender an atmosphere of trust and cooperation. This could enable further regional cooperation across a variety of areas that could collectively bring peace and prosperity to the region. Ultimately, the aim must be to progressively widen the confluence of shared interests, to ensure that everyone benefits.

South and Southeast Asia cooperation

There is also further potential for mutually beneficial engagement between South and Southeast Asia. South Asia and Southeast Asia share cultural, religious, historical and geographical affinities. There is also an increasing confluence of interests between South and Southeast Asia. As the balance of global economic and geopolitical weight shifts to Asia, South Asia, Southeast Asia and Northeast Asia will be seen as a huge contiguous growth area accounting for half of the world's population, with a growing middle class driving demand for goods and services. Between our two regions, there are also common interests in tackling challenges such as terrorism, transnational crime, the spread of infectious diseases, and ensuring maritime security and freedom of navigation in key sea lines of communications like the Indian Ocean.

There are plenty of opportunities for South Asian countries to develop their relations with Southeast Asian countries. Trade and investment cooperation is one area where closer links can be forged. Since 1992, India has been "Looking East" and trade between India and Southeast Asia has grown more than fifteen-fold from U.S. $3 billion in 1992 to U.S. $47 billion in 2008. Security cooperation is another area. Here, South Asian and Southeast Asian countries have ample opportunities for further cooperation through forums like the ASEAN Regional Forum[12] and the Shangri-La Dialogue. There is also significant scope for people-to-people ties to grow, whether through tourism, education, cultural exchanges, or conferences like this one.

South Asia has tremendous potential for economic growth, security development and social stability but it also faces many challenges. I have briefly discussed these prospects and challenges. South Asia's growing economic and geopolitical importance is already making news waves, this will only grow in importance once the nations of the region mitigate their differences and cooperate into realising South Asia's potential. South Asia's growth trajectory will be one of the defining stories of our time. I expect the many speakers lined up in this conference will provide insights into how this trajectory is developing. I hope that this conference, now in its sixth year, will provide practical opportunities to exchange views and forge useful ties. Given the strategic weight of the region and its potential, this conference is thus both apt and timely, calling us to consider both the challenges and prospects ahead for "South Asia in the New Decade."

---

[12]India, Pakistan, Bangladesh and Sri Lanka are members of the ARF.

Chapter 1

India and China:
Competitive Coexistence in the Asian Century*

Rory Medcalf [†] and Ashley Townshend [‡]

1. Introduction

The relationship between India and China has long been one of the most understudied great power complexes in international affairs.[1] While this has changed in recent years, the newly fashionable nature of the subject is not necessarily bringing greater clarity to our understanding of Sino–Indian relations. An increasingly common argument posits that India and China, as rising Asian and global powers, are natural competitors whose proximity and zero-sum interests are creating tensions that will make it extremely

---

*This chapter is based on a presentation by Rory Medcalf at the 6th International Conference on South Asia held by the Institute of South Asian Studies, Singapore, on November 11, 2010.
[†] Program Director, International Security Program
Lowy Institute for International Policy
New South Wales, Australia, and
Senior Research Fellow, Indian Strategic Affairs
University of New South Wales, Australia
[‡] Rydon Scholar in Government and M.Phil. Candidate in the Faculty of Oriental Studies at the University of Oxford.
[1] It should be noted that, there is a paucity of English-language scholarship presenting Chinese perspectives on Sino–Indian relations. Although this chapter seeks to offer a balanced assessment of the India–China relationship, it relies on the work of Western and Indian scholars.

difficult to avoid sustained strategic rivalry.[2] This has become a prominent view among many strategic analysts, scholars and journalists. The evidence, however, is considerably more mixed.

Strategic competition appears likely to overshadow cooperation in India–China relations. Yet a relationship with strong elements of competition can also be one of coexistence. As for rivalry — a more hostile form of competition that entails long-term risks of military conflict — the record at this stage remains inconclusive. On the one hand, leaders in New Delhi and Beijing deny that serious bilateral animosity exists, although such rhetoric is a predictable feature of great power diplomacy. On the other hand, the myriad of often divergent goals and unresolved tensions suggest that competition will trump cooperation in Sino–Indian relations. Nevertheless, firm conclusions about strategic rivalry — a situation in which competition between two states dominates their external policy agenda — are harder to reach.

This chapter contends that while India and China are not fully-fledged strategic rivals, a degree of strategic competition will remain ingrained in bilateral relations in the foreseeable future. Such tensions, moreover, are at risk of deepening over time. Given that both states share a number of important interests and face wider challenges than each other's strategic ambitions, the relationship between Asia's two rising giants is unlikely to descend into a straightforward contest for dominance. Rather, a state of "competitive coexistence" will continue to characterize India–China relations whereby issue-based cooperation will take place under an overall climate of strategic mistrust. Whether this competition can be managed, reduced or allowed to worsen will depend, in large part, on the quality of diplomacy and trust-building efforts between the two rising powers. A decline in rivalry remains possible but not inevitable.

---

[2]For prominent accounts of the Sino–Indian rivalry thesis, see Emmott, B (2008). *Rivals: How the Power Struggle Between China, India and Japan Will Shape Our Next Decade*. London: Penguin; Kaplan, R (2010). *Monsoon: The Indian Ocean and the Battle for Supremacy in the 21st Century*. New York: Random House; Holslag, J (2010). *China and India: Prospects for Peace*, pp. 67–76. New York: Columbia University Press; Bajpaee, C (2010). China–India relations: Regional rivalry takes the world stage. *China Security*, 6(2), 3–20; and A Himalayan rivalry (August 21, 2010). *The Economist*, pp. 17–20.

The following analysis proceeds in four parts. Part one explores the potential for cooperation in India–China relations by examining several common challenges that have led to limited collaboration between New Delhi and Beijing. Part two offers a conceptual framework and set of indicators for analyzing strategic rivalry. It evaluates the competitive aspects of the India–China relationship across four key areas of potential tension: conflicting geopolitical interests; military modernization and force posture; economic competition; and soft power. Part three highlights a number of ongoing challenges within Sino–Indian relations, including complications arising from the interests of third-party states, and suggests policy-oriented ways these issues could be addressed. The final part of this chapter examines whether smaller nations like Australia and Singapore might have a role to play in assisting India and China to develop a more stable relationship.

2. Harmonious Giants?

While few analysts fully subscribe to the "Chindia" thesis, there is some substance to the prediction that Sino–Indian relations in the 21st century will be underscored by cooperation and mutual benefit.[3] Indeed, India and China share a range of interests and challenges which may, over time, serve as a foundation for greater cooperation, compromise and policy alignment. In the domestic arena, New Delhi and Beijing will continue to face massive population bases, rising resource needs and the associated challenges of poverty alleviation, development, public sector reform, environmental sustainability and internal stability.[4] As sustained economic growth is a prerequisite for addressing each of these concerns, India and China have a common interest in preventing their wider geopolitical concerns from impeding the national accumulation of wealth.

---

[3]The term "Chindia" was allegedly coined by Goldman Sachs executive, Jim O'Neil, in a 2001 report entitled "The World Needs Better Economic BRICs". For a selection of works on the Chindia thesis, see Baru, S (2009). India: Rising through the slowdown. In *Strategic Asia 2009–10: Economic Meltdown and Geopolitical Stability*, A Tellis, A Marble and T Tanner (eds.), p. 217. Washington: National Bureau of Asia Research.

[4]On the shared challenges faced by India and China and their mutual imperative to cooperate, see Siddharth Varadarajan, Time to reset the India–China relationship (December 15, 2010). *The Hindu.*

Over the past decade, mutual economic need has transformed India and China into substantial trading partners for the first time in modern history.[5] In 2008, China overtook the United States to become India's largest trading partner and, during President Hu Jintao's 2010 visit to New Delhi, the two states set a bilateral trade target of U.S. $100 billion by 2015.[6] Accordingly, India and China are, to a limited degree, assisting each others' economic rise.[7] It is even conceivable that a time may come when a threat to China's economy will be viewed as a threat to the Indian economy as well — although it is difficult to envisage this level of interdependence applying equally in the other direction, owing to India's large trade deficit with China and China's enmeshment with U.S., Japanese and European economies.[8]

Given their domestic imperatives for rapid economic growth, a key objective of Indian and Chinese strategic policy is the maintenance of a stable international environment — that is, a world system conducive to trade and internal development.[9] Yet as both states are situated in turbulent neighborhoods — replete with fragile states, protracted insurgencies, contested sovereignty claims and unresolved boundary disputes — the stability of recent years may be difficult to sustain. It remains to be seen whether India and China can transform the shared challenges of terrorism, separatism, piracy, organized crime, pandemics, resource insecurity and environmental degradation into a foundation for sustained bilateral cooperation.

In their identity and worldview, India and China again share similar characteristics. Both societies exhibit rising sentiments of popular

---

[5]Anil Gupta and Haiyan Wang, Why China and India need each other (May 27, 2010). *Bloomberg.com.*

[6]India and China set $100 bn trade target by 2015 (December 16, 2010). *BBC News.*

[7]For an optimistic account of the mutual interests in the Sino–Indian economic relationship, see Khanna, T (2007). *Billions of Entrepreneurs: How China and India are Reshaping their Futures and Yours.* Boston: Harvard Business School.

[8]For a negative assessment of India's trade imbalance with China, see Mohanty, S (2010). Sino–Indian trade ties: An uncertain future. *China Article*, No. 3053. New Delhi: Institute for Peace and Conflict Studies. See also, Trade to top China–India talks (December 10, 2010). *Businessworld.*

[9]On India and China's need for a stable international environment, see D. S. Rajan, India–China connectivity: No need to over hype, Paper No. 3889 (South Asia Analysis Group, 2010); Charles Freeman, Memorandum to President Hu Jintao (January 18, 2011). *CSIS Commentary*; and Foreign Secretary Nirupama Rao, Perspectives on Foreign Policy for a 21st Century India, keynote address at the 3rd IISS-Indian Ministry of External Affairs Dialogue, London (February 22, 2010).

self-confidence and nationalist pride informed by strong feelings of historical injustice and a desire to overcome the legacies of colonialism and Western interference. In China, a key aspect to this narrative concerns the Middle Kingdom's emergence from a "century of humiliation" and its bid to become a great power.[10] Many Indians, for their part, wish to see New Delhi assume its "rightful place" at the top table of global diplomacy, while their policy elites are rediscovering the subcontinent's wider maritime region with a sense of historical entitlement.[11]

However, while both India and China believe they are reclaiming a place of greatness, in reality their strategic ascendency is relatively untested. Not only is the sheer human scale of their economic rise without historical precedent, but the crowded, rule-governed and immensely interconnected global stage upon which both states are rising is a fundamentally different international environment from that in which previous great powers have risen. If policymakers in New Delhi and Beijing are able to resist the jingoistic demands of their media and netizens,[12] it is possible that a confluence of similar worldviews and economic interdependence will enable India and China to address many of their mutual interests in a reasonably cooperative manner.

On security issues, the two states have taken some modest steps toward dialogue and cooperation. In 2007, India and China established an annual defense dialogue which has identified shared concerns about terrorism and piracy.[13] To be sure, most of their bilateral military activities —

---

[10] See, Erickson, A, L Goldstein and C Lord (Summer, 2010). China sets sail. *The American Interest*, 5(5), 27–34; and Ross, RS (Fall, 2009). China's naval nationalism: Sources, prospects, and the U.S. response. *International Security*, 34(2), 60–72.

[11] See Cohen, SP (2002). *India: Emerging Power*, pp. 51–54. Washington: Brookings Institution Press; and Scott, D (2006). India's "grand strategy" for the Indian Ocean: Mahanian visions. *Asia-Pacific Review*, 13(2), 97–129.

[12] For an excellent account of the role of netizens in Chinese foreign policy decisionmaking, see Jakobson, L and D Knox (2010). *New Foreign Policy Actors in China*, pp. 41–46. Solna: Stockholm International Peace Research Institute.

[13] Since 2008, the navies of India and China have participated in parallel anti-piracy missions off the Gulf of Aden. During the second annual defence dialogue held in New Delhi, 2008, both states agreed in principle to coordinate efforts to fight terrorism and violent religious fundamentalism. A week before the talks, India and China undertook the joint exercise "Hand-in-Hand" to build interoperability in counterterrorism operations. See, India, China join hands to fight terrorism (December 15, 2008). *Thaindian News*; and Indian, Chinese troops show "team spirit" during joint army exercise (December 8, 2008). *Thaindian News*.

predominantly joint exercises and port visits — have been minimalist in their aims and execution. Practical cooperation and policy coordination have been little more than aspirations. Nevertheless, defense officials from India and China have managed to develop limited relations amidst a climate of mistrust. For instance, while New Delhi moved to suspend high-level defense talks following China's 2010 political provocation over the status of Kashmir, military-to-military dialogue is set to resume in the wake of Prime Minister Manmohan Singh's visit to China in April 2011.[14] Moreover, several bilateral military drills have taken place — including counterterrorism training on each others' soil — and, after a three-year hiatus, bilateral exercises are likely to resume in 2011.[15]

On issues of global governance, policy alignment between New Delhi and Beijing appears slightly more robust. At the 2009 United Nations Climate Change Conference in Copenhagen, China, India, Brazil and South Africa loosely coordinated their negotiation strategies in order to protect developing economies from trade barriers and binding carbon reduction targets.[16] A trilateral foreign ministers' dialogue was established between India, China and Russia in 2005, although this forum remains a long way from becoming a viable mechanism for coordinating the interests of approximately 40% of the world's population.[17] India's observer status in the Shanghai Cooperation Organization (SCO), China's matching position in the South Asian Association for Regional Cooperation (SAARC), and both states' involvement the East Asia Summit (EAS) and annual BRICS Summit offer further opportunities for India and China to cooperate and even jointly lead at a regional level — despite the fact that neither country has so far seemed eager to exploit these prospects.

---

[14]On the visa-related Kashmir dispute which led New Delhi to suspend bilateral defence talks, see India–China ties hit by visa row (August 27, 2010). *Al Jazeera.*

[15]See Manu Pubby, India, China to revive joint army drills (January 12, 2010). *Indian Express.*

[16]See Saibal Dasgupta, Copenhagen conference: India, China plan joint exit (November 28, 2009). *The Times of India.*

[17]R. N. Das, Russia–China–India trilateral: Calibrating a fine balance (November 15, 2010). *IDSA Comment.*

3. Assaying Rivalry

Despite the opportunities for Sino–Indian partnership, there are inherent limits to bilateral cooperation. Indeed, some of the attributes which both states share — such as their export-driven economies, energy insecurity and increasingly nationalistic middle classes — may imperil cooperation and exacerbate tensions, especially when added to their long-unresolved territorial disputes over Arunachal Pradesh and Aksai Chin.[18] While it may not be analytically neat, the many contradictions in India–China relations mean that elements of cooperation will endure, perhaps even deepen, alongside growing strategic rivalry. We may define this situation as "competitive coexistence".[19]

Before considering the competitive impulses in Sino–Indian relations, it is necessary to specify what we mean by "strategic rivalry". Strategic rivalry is an extreme form of interstate competition. It is a condition in which the antagonisms of two states become a defining feature of their foreign policies, affecting everything from defense and diplomacy, to economics, trade, development assistance and soft power. In most instances, strategic rivals consider one or more of their fundamental national interests to be threatened by each other. Indeed, their inability to resolve contentious issues of strategic importance leads rivals to regard each other with deep-seated mistrust, whether or not this perception is fully justified. Strategic rivalry also involves a contest for regional and/or global hierarchy in which both protagonists struggle to gain political influence in third-party states. While relations between strategic rivals can undergo periods of issue-specific cooperation, such states are willing to shape and constrain each other's decisions through the threat or use of military force.[20]

Drawing on these criteria, we can identify four areas of tension that may serve as an analytical framework and set of indicators for assessing the

---

[18] See, Yuan, J (Summer, 2007). The dragon and the elephant: Chinese–Indian relations in the 21st century. *Washington Quarterly*, 30(3), 134–139.

[19] For a similar argument, see Scott, D (2008). Sino–Indian security predicaments for the twenty-first century. *Asian Security*, 4(3), 244–270.

[20] For a detailed analysis of the components of interstate rivalries, see Colaresi, MP, K Rasler and WR Thompson (2007). *Strategic Rivalries in World Politics: Position, Space and Conflict Escalation*, p. 4. Cambridge: Cambridge University Press.

extent to which India and China are strategic rivals: conflicting geopolitical interests; military modernization and force posture; economic competition; and soft power. While one would not expect bilateral antagonisms to be present in equal measure across all areas simultaneously, a degree of competition on each issue is a prerequisite for a relationship of strategic rivalry.

3.1. *Conflicting geopolitical interests*

Are India and China seeking to predominate in overlapping areas of geopolitical interest? Is each state competing for influence in third-party states and multilateral organizations? Do officials in New Delhi and Beijing regard strategic competition between India and China as a primary concern of their respective foreign policies?

Despite their disputed borders, India and China do not currently define their principal geopolitical objectives as being directly opposed. Even as the growing integration of the Asia-Pacific and Indian Ocean regions is creating a grand "Indo-Pacific" strategic system,[21] India and China continue to have relatively distinct areas of primary geopolitical interest. In India, foreign policy elites are predominantly concerned with strategic issues in South Asia and the Indian Ocean. These include the conventional and nuclear deterrence of Pakistan, the maintenance of Jammu and Kashmir as sovereign Indian territories, the struggle against Islamic terrorism emanating from Pakistan, the stabilization of Afghanistan and the security of Indian Ocean sea-lanes.

To be sure, India has recently expressed concerns over the growing prevalence of Chinese commercial port facilities and PLA-Navy (PLAN) warships in the Indian Ocean — a region across which roughly 90% of Indian crude oil imports is transported each year.[22] There is a growing struggle for political influence in some of the smaller states of the Indian Ocean where India, in order to forestall Chinese diplomacy, has stepped up its security and infrastructure assistance to such nations as Mauritius, Madagascar and the Maldives. Nevertheless, these initiatives remain far

---

[21] See Cook, M, R Heinrichs, R Medcalf and A Shearer (2010). *Power and Choice: Asian Security Futures*, p. 31. Sydney: Lowy Institute for International Policy.

[22] The figure for Indian oil imports is based on 2005 data from the International Energy Agency (IEA). See IEA, *World Energy Outlook* 2007 (Paris: International Energy Agency, 2007).

from a full-blown contest for regional dominance. Indeed, despite India's growing role in East Asian diplomacy and its deepening economic, political and defense relations with many Asian states — including a nascent strategic partnership with Japan — New Delhi has yet to extend India's primary sphere of geopolitical interest further east than the Strait of Malacca.[23]

China, for its part, remains primarily focused on the power balance in Northeast Asia. Its declared maritime interests remain concentrated in the South China Sea and the Western Pacific. In this region, Beijing's strategic interests include neutralizing superior U.S. military power, preventing Taiwanese independence (by force if necessary), prosecuting China's large maritime sovereignty claims against Japan and various Southeast Asian nations, and avoiding both a new Korean war and regime collapse in Pyongyang. As a result, most Chinese officials do not currently perceive India as a primary threat to national security, even if some Chinese maritime security analysts worry that the Indian navy could blockade China's energy supply routes with an "iron chain" centered around the recently upgraded tri-services military facility on India's Andaman and Nicobar Islands.[24] Moreover, while the nuclear arsenals of New Delhi and Beijing are designed, in part, to deter mutual aggression, both their postures are relatively restrained and display little sign of a bilateral arms race.

It may, in fact, be on land where Sino–Indian geopolitical interests are most likely to clash in the short term. Many analysts have argued that China's reluctance to resolve its border differences with India is due, in large part, to its anxieties over retaining control of Tibet. Beijing remains troubled by the activities, rhetoric and very existence of a resilient community of

---

[23]While India has deepened security partnerships with East Asian states through initiatives such as the annual Malabar naval exercises, New Delhi's Asian focus is mainly concerned with the extent to which East Asian power shifts are affecting the wider Indian Ocean region. The expansion of India's maritime horizons to include, but not surpass, the Malacca Straits has been made clear in a number of official documents — such as the *Indian Maritime Doctrine* (2004) and *New Army Doctrine* (2004) — as well as statements by Prime Ministers Atal Bihari Vajpayee (2003) and Manmohan Singh (2004). For further detail, see Scott, India's "Grand Strategy" for the Indian Ocean, pp. 110–115. On recent developments in the India–Japan strategic partnership, see Takenori Horimoto, "The Japan–India nuclear agreement: Enhancing bilateral relations? (April 15, 2011). *Asia Pacific Bulletin*, No. 107.
[24]See Holmes, JR, AC Winner and T Yoshihara (2009). *Indian Naval Strategy in the Twenty-First Century*, pp. 133–135. New York: Routledge.

Tibetan exiles in India, and is presumably eager to shape the succession of the Tibetan spiritual leadership when the current Dalai Lama passes away.[25] Accordingly, the existence on Indian territory of the Tawang monastery — a location of great significance in Tibetan Buddhism which could play an important role in the religious succession — poses an ongoing problem for what Beijing views as the maintenance of domestic order. It does not appear coincidental that China's willingness to talk seriously with India about resolving the border disagreement waned even further following the protests in Lhasa in 2008.

In multilateral organizations and regional institutions, relations between India and China have a competitive edge. In 2005, during the establishment of the EAS, Beijing attempted to exclude India in order to maximize its own political influence within the forum.[26] New Delhi's exclusion of China in the India-led Indian Ocean Naval Symposium (IONS) — a biannual gathering of 26 regional navy chiefs — denotes a similar effort to restrict China's involvement in security affairs west of Malacca. Similar wrangling has occurred in the SCO and SAARC where China and India initially sought to prevent the other from gaining observer status in what each considered its own regional forum.[27] In light of these diplomatic skirmishes, the behavior India and China display at the EAS, IONS and newly formed ASEAN Plus Eight Defense Ministers' Meeting (ADMM+8) may become a useful barometer for Sino–Indian rivalry.

3.2. *Military modernization and force posture*

Are the large-scale military modernization programs in India and China motivated by the exigencies of bilateral rivalry? Is either state's force posture designed with the primary aim of coercing, deterring, fighting or otherwise constraining the strategic options of the other?

---

[25] Kaveree Bamzai and Sandeep Unithan, Hidden dragon, crouching Lama (February 4, 2011). *India Today*.

[26] Mohan Malik, China and the East Asia summit: More discord than accord (February 2006). *Asia-Pacific Center for Security Studies*. Online: http://www.apcss.org/Publications/APSSS/ChinaandEastAsiaSummit.pdf.

[27] For a detailed analysis of Sino–Indian relations in regional institutions, see Singh, S (Spring/Summer, 2011). Paradigm shift in India–China relations: From bilateralism to multilateralism. *Journal of International Affairs*, 64(2), 1–14.

From Beijing's perspective, both questions may be answered in the negative. To be sure, Beijing has troops deployed along the disputed border and, in 2010, upgraded its road-mobile nuclear arsenal to include solid-fuelled CSS-5 medium range ballistic missiles (MRBMs) that can reach much of India. However, while it can be assumed that such capabilities were deployed to strengthen bilateral deterrence against New Delhi, these represent only a small proportion of the PLA's rapidly modernizing military arsenal.[28] Indeed, the PLA remains predominantly focused on safeguarding and expanding Beijing's strategic interests in the Taiwan Strait, the South China Sea and the wider Western Pacific. This has involved preparing for possible confrontation with the United States and its East Asian partners by acquiring attack and ballistic-missile submarines, land- and sea-based cruise missiles, modern warships and sophisticated command, control and information systems.[29] All of these denote a PLA acquisition program and force posture that is geared more toward military options in maritime Asia than a land war with India. Of course, the PLAN's so-called "historic missions" abroad — including ongoing anti-piracy operations in the Gulf of Aden and the deployment of air and sea capabilities to evacuate Chinese nationals from the Middle East in early 2011 — could encroach upon Indian interests in New Delhi's traditional sphere of influence.[30] Yet, Beijing's limited capability to project power at long ranges combined with its predominantly East Asian strategic focus will restrict its capacity to be a major threat to India, at least for another decade.

India, on the other hand, is already making a number of acquisitions and deployments based on its concerns about China's expanding strategic weight and reach. Over the past five years, much of India's ambitious naval modernization program has been based on a strategy of securing New Delhi's place as the principal maritime power in the Indian Ocean.

---

[28] On recent upgrades of the PLA's nuclear capabilities, see *Annual Report to Congress: Military and Security Developments Involving the People's Republic of China, 2010* (Washington: Office of the Secretary of Defense, 2010), pp. 34–35; and Hans M. Kristensen, DF-21C Missile deploys to central China (September 28, 2010). *Federation of American Scientists Strategic Security Blog.* Online: http://www.fas.org/blog/ssp/2010/09/df21c.php.

[29] *Annual Report to Congress*, pp. 1–9.

[30] See C. Raja Mohan, Sino–Indian rivalry in the western Indian Ocean (February, 2009). *ISAS Insights*, No. 52.

Apart from the United States, China is the only other conceivable long-run contender for this role. In particular, New Delhi's acquisition of advanced warships, nuclear-powered submarines and long-range surveillance aircraft appear explicitly designed to outmatch future PLAN capabilities in this region.[31] Similarly, India's recent moves to buttress troop deployments in Arunachal Pradesh are motivated by New Delhi's longstanding anxieties about a land conflict with China.[32]

Nevertheless, these developments do not indicate that India's strategic community has reached a consensus in regarding China as a primary external threat, whatever the grim assessments of some prominent individuals.[33] The Indian navy's 15%–18% slice of the defense budget demonstrates a less than wholehearted commitment to competing with China as a maritime power. Beijing, for its part, allocates about a quarter of its military spending to the PLAN. While border deployments have recently increased, troop numbers on both sides have fallen dramatically since the last major India–China confrontation in 1987. Moreover, while India's conventional superiority against Pakistan would suggest that New Delhi's nuclear arsenal is intended to deter Beijing, if India was genuinely involved in strategic rivalry with China, it would be racing to develop a credible second-strike capability to threaten targets deep within China. So far, this effort has proceeded slowly and unevenly. Indeed, while there has been recent progress on this front — including India's launch of a "technology demonstrator" for its planned ballistic-missile submarine in July 2009 — an effective sea-launched deterrent remains many years away.[34] The pace and effectiveness with which India completes this quest will reveal much about the extent to which rivalry is on the horizon.

---

[31] On Sino–Indian naval modernization and strategic developments in the Indian Ocean, see Townshend, A (2010). Sino–Indian maritime relations: Managing mistrust in the Indian Ocean. In *Strategic Snapshot*, Vol. 6. Sydney: Lowy Institute for International Policy.

[32] See Edward Wong, Uneasy engagement: China and India dispute enclave on edge of Tibet (September 9, 2003). *New York Times*; and Subir Bhaumik, India to deploy 36,000 extra troops on Chinese border (November 23, 2010). *BBC News*.

[33] For an excellent account of the different ways Indian strategic thinkers perceive China, see Joshi, S (2011). Why India is becoming warier of China. *Current History*, 110(735), 156–161.

[34] See C. Raja Mohan, India's nuclear navy: Catching up with China (July, 2009). *ISAS Insights*, No. 78.

At present, New Delhi has more urgent security concerns than the longterm implications of a powerful China. India's security establishment remains heavily focused on Pakistan and has, in the wake of the devastating 2008 attacks in Mumbai, enhanced efforts to prevent terrorists from striking soft targets inside India. China's longstanding support for the Pakistani military means that Indian threat perceptions about Pakistan cannot be entirely separated from concerns about China. Still, India's most immediate threats may be internal. Civil unrest has worsened in Kashmir since Indian central and state government authorities squandered the opportunities for improved governance following credible elections in 2002 and 2008. Moreover, 2010 witnessed a worsening of the Naxalite (Maoist) violence in central and eastern India, an enduring problem which has been described by Prime Minister Singh as India's "biggest internal security challenge".[35] As a result, India has allocated substantial resources to fix its counterterrorism and counterinsurgency capabilities — none of which are designed for strategic rivalry with China.[36]

3.3. *Economic competition*

To what extent do India and China perceive their bilateral economic relations as zero-sum? Does each state regard the other as an economic competitor in global markets? Are India and China willing to sidestep market mechanisms in order to constrain the economic opportunities of the other?

Relatively unscathed by the global financial crisis of 2008–2009, India and China continue to forge a lucrative trade partnership. While bilateral trade stood at a mere U.S. \$270 million in 1990, by 2010 India–China trade revenue reached U.S. \$62.74 billion (up 42% since 2009) — a figure which some predict will surpass U.S. \$120 billion by 2012.[37] This has been underscored by a high-degree of complementarity in Sino–Indian

---

[35] See Fred Burton and Ben West, A closer look at India's naxalite threat (July 8, 2010). *STRATFOR.*

[36] See *The Military Balance* 2010 (London: International Institute for Strategic Studies, 2010), pp. 335–336.

[37] See, respectively, A Himalayan rivalry, p. 17; China Economic News in Brief: Sinopec LNP Project; Vegetable Oil Imports; Tianjin Sewage Treatment Plants; Sino–Indian trade (March 24, 2011). *China Daily*; and India's bilateral trade with China to cross \$120 bn (November 20, 2010). *The Navhind Times.*

exports.[38] Whereas India is currently known for services and raw materials, China's exports have been predominantly in manufactured goods — a point frequently cited by proponents of the "Chindia" thesis.[39] The potential for positive-sum trade ties has prompted optimistic rhetoric from leaders in both states. As Prime Minister Singh has often stated, "India and China are not in competition … there is enough economic space for both … countries to realize … [their] growth ambitions".[40]

In a hint of what government-driven bilateral economic cooperation might look like, between 2005 and early 2006 Beijing and New Delhi briefly coordinated efforts to secure new energy projects. India's Oil and Natural Gas Corporation (ONGC) and the China Petrochemical Corp (Sinopec) secured joint energy contracts in Sudan, Syria, Columbia and Iran. But these entities, and the two states more widely, remained fiercely competitive in other markets.[41] For instance, China continued to outbid India in larger energy deals in Angola, Nigeria, Myanmar, Kazakhstan and elsewhere; while New Delhi's enthusiasm for a bilateral energy partnership waned in 2006 after the then Union Cabinet Minister for Petroleum and Natural Gas, Mani Shankar Aiyar, lost his portfolio for apparently unrelated reasons.[42]

As concerns about energy security underscore each state's push for naval modernization, it is unlikely that shared dependence in hydrocarbon imports will unite China and India. More broadly, while India and China do not currently view each other as economic rivals, many argue that their trade interdependence is unsustainable and that there exist a number of latent grievances in the economic relationship. Above all, there is a large imbalance in bilateral trade which causes considerable resentment in India.

---

[38]Malone, DM and R Mukherjee (2010). India and China: Conflict and Cooperation. *Survival*, 52(1), 148.

[39]See Holslag, *China and India*, pp. 67–76.

[40]PM says India and China are not in competition (November 23, 2009). *Deccan Herald*.

[41]See Indrajit Basu, India, China pin down $573 m Syria deal (December 22, 2005). *AsiaTimes Online*; and Siddharth Srivastava, India, China work out new energy synergies (September 26, 2006). *AsiaTimes Online*.

[42]On China's successful attempts to outbid Indian companies in energy deals, see Vibhuti Haté, India's energy dilemma (September 7, 2006). *South Asia Monitor*, No. 98; Elizabeth Mills, Keep friends close but enemies closer: Changing energy relations between China and India (July 10, 2009). *Harvard International Review*; and Behera, LK (2005). Oil politics: India's failure in Kazakhstan, *India and the World — Articles,* No. 1885. New Delhi: Institute for Peace and Conflict Studies.

While China is India's largest trading partner, accounting for roughly 6.5% of Indian exports in 2007, India ranks ninth as a source of Chinese imports, leaving New Delhi to capture just 2.9% of Chinese trade flows in the same year.[43] While India's exports to China have since picked-up, growing at 75% in early 2010, its trade deficit with China surged to U.S. $19.2 billion in March 2010.[44]

Owing to these disparities and concomitant concerns about the security implications of some Chinese state-led investments in India, New Delhi has instigated a number of trade restrictions — limiting Chinese investment in Indian telecoms, rejecting Chinese bids for port facilities in Mumbai and Vizhinjam, barring Chinese companies from bidding for sensitive offshore oil and gas projects, and tightening visa arrangements for Chinese migrant workers.[45] China has been accused by New Delhi of dumping in textiles, toys, automobile components and chemicals — controversies which make the notion of an India–China free-trade agreement even more remote than it appears at present.[46] These problems aside, as both India and China diversify their economies and exports, it seems reasonable to expect that trade complementarity will decline, causing them to increasingly compete for similar markets and industries.[47] A shift toward heightened competition in the economic sphere may thus simply be a matter of time.

3.4. *Soft power*

Do India and China use soft power — that is, the attractiveness of their respective societies, ideals and policies — to compete for regional and global influence?[48] Is soft power employed as a strategic resource to counter each other's normative appeal?

---

[43] Holslag, *India and China*, p. 76.

[44] Wei Gu, Trade should leave China and India both winners (December 14, 2010). *Reuters*; and Nupur Acharya, India–China trade deficit could reduce on renminbi appreciation — RBI Study (April 15, 2011). *Dow Jones Newswires*.

[45] Bajpaee, *China–India relations*, pp. 8–9.

[46] See Ananth Krishnan, India–China anti-dumping row escalates (August 7, 2009). *The Hindu*; and Holslag, *India and China*, pp. 77–80.

[47] Holslag, *India and China*, pp. 70–76.

[48] For a definition of soft power, see Nye, J (2004). *Soft Power: The Means to Success in World Politics*, p. 2, x. New York: Public Affairs.

As two of Asia's oldest and most revered civilizations, India and China are historic competitors for cultural influence and societal gravitas. This ideational contest appears to be resurfacing in a contemporary form, with divergent political systems and social values augmenting distinct cultural qualities. What is less clear is the extent to which each state is actively and effectively deploying its soft power to buttress its reputation against the other's international image. Perhaps, the dominant view of Sino–Indian soft power competition posits that democratic India will ultimately prove more successful than China in attracting external admiration.[49] Given its liberal values, market economy, open society and democratic institutions, it is not surprising that India trumps China in polls analyzing how foreign nationals perceive both states' relative performance in governance and human rights.[50] Moreover, via a large and influential diaspora and a burgeoning media industry, Indian perspectives are increasingly transmitted to the world.[51] To be sure, these same networks also disseminate damaging images of India's unruly polity, widespread corruption and cumbersome bureaucracy. This was exemplified by the negative reportage of New Delhi's 2010 Commonwealth Games which paled beside the 2008 Beijing Olympics as a showcase of efficiency, skill and quality control.[52] Even so, the so-called "New India's" mood of enterprise, youth and openness is likely to bolster India's reputation and help it to overcome such hurdles.[53]

China, for its part, has invested far more strategically than India in trying to define its international image. For much of the past decade, Beijing's

---

[49]See, for example, Kaplan, *Monsoon*, pp. 97, 185–186; and John Lee, India's edge over China: Soft power (June 17, 2010). *Businessweek*.

[50]See Whitney, CB and D Shambaugh (2009). *Soft Power in Asia: Results of a 2008 Multinational Survey of Public Opinion*, pp. 9–10. Chicago: Chicago Council on Global Affairs.

[51]See Malik, A and R Medcalf (2011). India's new world: Civil society in the making of foreign policy. In *Lowy Institute Analysis*. Sydney: Lowy Institute for International Policy; and Shashi Tharoor, Why nations should pursue "soft" power (November, 2009). *TED Talk*. Online: http://www.ted.com/talks/shashi_tharoor.html.

[52]See Lee, J (2010). Unrealised potential: India's "soft power" ambition in Asia. *Foreign Policy Analysis*. Sydney: Centre for Independent Studies; and Ashish Kumar Sen, Problems plague India's Commonwealth Games (September 21, 2010). *The Washington Times*.

[53]For an excellent account of India's internal strengths and lingering challenges, see Nilekani, N (2008). *Imagining India: Ideas for a New Century*. London: Allen Lane.

so-called "charm offensive" has sought to project an unthreatening impression of China's rise through lavish international broadcasting, condition-free investment, foreign development assistance, multilateral engagement, humanitarian aid and often astute diplomacy at the United Nations and elsewhere.[54] However, while many states in Africa and Southeast Asia were initially impressed by China's entreaties, since 2008 these reputational gains have been undermined by Beijing's hardening stance on a range of issues — from maritime assertiveness and sovereignty claims in the South China Sea, to security crackdowns in Xinjiang, Tibet and against a number of prominent dissidents. English-language state broadcasting and the hundreds of Confucius Institutes worldwide do not appear to be dramatically improving Western or Asian perceptions of China.[55] While India's reputation may have been battered by the 2010 Commonwealth Games, China has suffered more fundamental damage as a result of its heavy-handed response to foreign protests during the 2008 Olympic torch relay.

It is too early to conclude whether India and China are making extensive use of their soft power to compete with each other for influence, let alone to assess which state is currently winning. However, were a full-blown soft power competition to develop, it would most likely include: an explicit use of foreign aid and cultural diplomacy to counter each other's influence; large-scale Indian investment in international state broadcasting; and the mobilization of diaspora worldwide to oppose each other's interests in third countries.

4. Preventing Instability under Competitive Coexistence

The varying levels of strategic competition across four key areas of great power tension suggest that the Sino–Indian relationship is one of competitive coexistence. Asia's two largest military powers are not, at present, fully-fledged strategic rivals. On the contrary, Beijing's predominantly

[54] See Zheng, DE (2009). China's use of soft power in the developing world: Strategic intentions and implications for the United States. In *Chinese Soft Power and its Implications for the United States: Competition and Cooperation in the Developing World*, C McGiffert (ed.), pp. 1–9. Washington: Center for Strategic and International Studies.

[55] See, for instance, Pew Research Center, strengthen ties with China, but get tough on trade: Public's global focus turns from Europe to Asia (January 12, 2011). *Survey Report.*

U.S.-focused strategic community appears, at times, indifferent to the strategic anxieties of India's defense establishment. If sustained, this seemingly apathetic approach to India — which many in New Delhi interpret as a sign of China's lack of respect for India as a great power — could heighten Indian anxieties and further exacerbate bilateral tensions. For the moment, however, most Indian policymakers seem to be content with making only gradual adjustments to the military capabilities that would enable India to deter a more assertive China.[56]

Although strategic rivalry is not inevitable, India and China should not be complacent about the need for measures to stabilize bilateral relations. The current situation of competitive coexistence offers an opportunity to establish patterns of dialogue, predictability and mutual understanding before underlying tensions worsen. Building stable expectations and a degree of trust through careful diplomacy and confidence-building measures — such as the establishment of a leader-to-leader hotline in early 2010 — could assist both states in managing future discord.

This will not be straightforward. Many voices in both states will see a fundamental clash of interests on the horizon and will argue that the best Beijing and New Delhi can hope for is to build mechanisms to manage an inevitable confrontation. Indeed, some will even argue that their nation's priority should be to prepare for rivalry, including in the military sphere. Even if policymakers in China and India were to recognize the merits of bilateral confidence-building and cooperation, the reality is that these two great powers are rising in a complex international environment where their bilateral relationship cannot be separated from wider strategic dynamics. Four such strategic challenges should be considered in some detail: the role of the United States; the Pakistan–China–India triangle; maritime security in the Indian Ocean; and the India–China nuclear dynamic.

4.1. *The role of the United States*

Relations between India and China will continue to be shaped by the wider Indo-Pacific strategic system in which both states are embedded. Among the

---

[56]On the ruling Congress party's aversion to large-scale defence expenditure and military competition with China, see Cohen, SP and S Dasgupta (2010). *Arming Without Aiming: India's Military Modernization*, p. 28. Washington: Brookings Institution Press.

most defining characteristics of the regional power balance will be the extent to which New Delhi becomes a truly strategic partner of the United States or, somewhat less likely, a member of an informal U.S.-led balancing coalition against China.[57] Since President George W. Bush and Prime Minister Atal Bihari Vajpayee launched their strategic partnership in the first few years of the 21st century, relations between Washington and New Delhi have grown dramatically closer and more comprehensive, involving multi-billion dollar defense deals, expanded military-to-military ties, the controversial 2005 civilian nuclear energy deal and a number of high-profile state visits.[58] During this same period, an expansion of the annual "Malabar" exercises — a series of U.S.–India naval war-games which have often included Japan and, occasionally, Singapore and Australia as well — has highlighted India's growing potential within a regional network of American partners and allies. In this context, Japan has emerged as the most eager of Washington's Asian allies to cultivate India as a balance against the Chinese power.[59]

While claims about the birth of an Asian NATO are overblown, it is true that India and the United States share a common goal in hedging against potential Chinese assertiveness.[60] Not surprisingly, Beijing views the U.S.–India partnership as evidence of a growing attempt to contain China's rise.[61] The initial response by Chinese policymakers appeared to involve an attempt to compete with Washington for favor in New Delhi — a theory which helps explain the improvement in Sino–Indian relations between 2002 and

---

[57] On the post-Cold War emergence of a U.S.-India strategic partnership, see Burns, RN (2007). America's strategic opportunity with India. *Foreign Affairs*, 86(6), 131–146. On the prospects for a U.S.–India balancing coalition against China, see Gordon, S (2009). Sino–Indian relations and the rise of China. In *Rising China: Power and Reassurance*, R Huisken (ed.), pp. 59–61. Canberra: ANU E-Press.

[58] On deepening relations between the U.S. and India, see Cohen and Dasgupta, *Arming Without Aiming*, pp. 165–171; and Mohan, CR (2011). India, China and the United States: Asia's emerging strategic triangle. In *Strategic Snapshot*, Vol. 8. Sydney: Lowy Institute for International Policy.

[59] For more information on the India–Japan strategic partnership, see the *Joint Declaration on Security Cooperation Between Japan and India*, signed in Tokyo on 22 October, 2008. Online: http://www.mofa.go.jp/region/asia-paci/india/pmv0810/joint_d.html.

[60] See, Carter, AB (2006). America's new strategic partner? *Foreign Affairs*, 85(4), 42–43.

[61] See D. S. Rajan, China: Media Fears Over India Becoming Part of Western Alliance, Paper No. 2350 (South Asia Analysis Group, 2007).

2004, including China's recognition of Sikkim as part of India and the establishment of direct air links.[62] However, since roughly 2005, China has indicated its displeasure at burgeoning U.S.–India relations by toughening its stance on other bilateral issues — such as seeking to block India's EAS membership and reasserting its claim on Arunachal Pradesh.[63]

Balancing its growing strategic alignment with the United States and its need for stability and engagement with China will be among New Delhi's toughest diplomatic tasks. Perceptions about China's growing assertiveness — whether against India or China's other Asian neighbors — are likely to continue to push New Delhi closer to Washington. At the same time, India will be wary of any agreement that implies, even informally, any alliance entanglement. It is intriguing to consider how the United States might perceive and respond to a significant worsening or improvement in Sino–Indian relations. Some observers claim that the burden will fall on Washington to play a stabilizing, perhaps even peace-making, role between New Delhi and Beijing.[64] By contrast, the Chinese view tends to assume that Asia's rising giants would get along much better if America's influence was somehow marginalized. The reality is likely to be more complicated than either of these narratives. What is clear, however, is that decisions in Washington and India's partnership with the U.S. will profoundly affect the direction of Sino–Indian relations. Chinese fears about a U.S.–Indian alignment may well heighten its security concerns about India. But, as the 1962 war demonstrated, Beijing and New Delhi are perfectly capable of ruining their bilateral relationship without external involvement.

4.2. *The Pakistan–China–India triangle*

China's longstanding support for Pakistan remains a serious concern for policymakers in New Delhi. India has long viewed this as Beijing's intention — enhancing Islamabad's military and nuclear capabilities contains

---

[62]Before talks, a CBM: China puts Sikkim in its India map (May 6, 2004). *The Indian Express.*

[63]See, Jo Johnson and Richard McGregor, China raises tension in India border dispute (12 June, 2007). *The Financial Times.*

[64]Kaplan, RD (2009). Center stage for the 21st century: Power plays in the Indian Ocean. *Foreign Affairs*, 88(2), 31–32.

Indian power in South Asia and, in turn, divides New Delhi's strategic focus so that it cannot concentrate its forces against China. Rather than having a stabilizing effect, Beijing's support for Pakistan has helped Islamabad perpetuate its security competition with India — including by enabling state-backed militants and terrorists to strike soft targets in India under the protection of a nuclear umbrella.[65] As the 2002 India–Pakistan crisis demonstrated, such attacks run the risk of sparking a wider confrontation or full-scale war between New Delhi and Islamabad, with real prospects for nuclear escalation.

For Indian strategists, China's role in assisting Pakistan's nuclear weapons and missile program is the ultimate sign of bad faith in Sino–Indian relations. Indeed, if India and China are to have a relationship of even moderate strategic trust, Beijing will need to clearly place its relations with New Delhi ahead of those with Islamabad. This will mean curtailing its military assistance to Pakistan and recognizing the existing Line of Control as a basis for resolving the Kashmir dispute — a position Beijing appeared ready to accept when it chose not to side openly with Pakistan during the 1999 Kargil conflict and the 2002 India–Pakistan confrontation.

4.3. *Maritime security in the Indian Ocean*

While proclamations of a new maritime "great game" are premature, there is real potential for a contest of influence between India and China in the Indian Ocean.[66] Concerns in New Delhi and Washington about the stability of this region are based on China's growing power-projection capabilities, commercial maritime facilities and active diplomacy in a region long dominated by the U.S. and Indian navies. Moreover, the PLAN's participation in anti-piracy missions off the Gulf of Aden since January 2009 and the increasing frequency of Chinese port calls in the area have

---

[65] See Malik, M (Spring, 2003). The China factor in the India–Pakistan conflict. *Parameters*, 33, 36.

[66] For a gloomy assessment of China's role in the Indian Ocean and Sino–Indian rivalry, see Kaplan, Center Stage for the 21st Century, pp. 16–32; and Kaplan, RD (2010). The Geography of Chinese power: How far can Beijing reach on land and at sea? *Foreign Affairs*, 89(3), 22–41.

been viewed as indications of Beijing's ambition to eventually develop a permanent naval presence in the Indian Ocean.[67]

Yet, as roughly 80% of Chinese oil imports traverse Indian Ocean sea-lanes, it is no surprise that Beijing does not want to continue outsourcing its maritime security to potential adversaries. Nor should Beijing's stake in a string of regional commercial port facilities designed to link maritime supply chains with mainland China be cause for alarm — given that, at present, there is scant evidence to suggest that the PLAN is involved in these ports.[68] China's energy requirements and its maritime interests as a global trading nation make it a legitimate player in Indian Ocean security.

In this context, India's interests in maritime stability would be well-served by policies seeking to accommodate China's growing regional presence in ways consistent with Indian security. New Delhi would be well advised to begin working closely with other nations to build a multilateral rules-based order in the Indian Ocean region while its own bargaining position is relatively strong. Indeed, India's best bet is to prepare the region for a future Chinese role, rather than to pursue a futile bid to exclude China altogether.[69] It could also be argued that an Indian strategy of asymmetric defense *vis-à-vis* China — which would include a robust nuclear-armed submarine force — might give New Delhi the confidence to adjust to a long-term Chinese presence in regional waters.[70]

Several early steps may help alleviate Indian concerns and place the onus on Beijing to be more transparent about its maritime activities and intentions in the region. New Delhi could, for instance, take the initiative to propose bilateral navy-to-navy talks with Beijing on maritime security and confidence-building. Such discussions would assist both states to build

---

[67] As of February 2011, the PLAN's naval escort flotilla was undertaking its seventh rotation in approximately two years. The rotation began on November 24, 2011.

[68] Chinese corporations have played an important role in establishing port facilities in Pakistan (Gwadar), Sri Lanka (Hambantota), Bangladesh (Chittagong), and Burma (Sittwe and Kyaukpyu), with some indication that the Maldives (Marao) may be next.

[69] Rory Medcalf, India must master the great game (September 2, 2010). *Wall Street Journal — Asia.*

[70] This observation builds on a speech given by a former Indian Chief of Navy, Admiral Suresh Mehta in 2009. See Mehta, S (2009). India's national security challenges: An armed forces overview. Paper presented at the India Habitat Centre, New Delhi (August 10). Online: http://maritimeindia.org/pdfs/CNS_Lec_at_Habitat.pdf

the mechanisms and understandings that are required to prevent the sort of destabilizing incidents at sea that have recently taken place between China and other navies in East Asian waters.[71] Another useful gesture would be for New Delhi to encourage more PLAN refueling stops at Indian ports, rather than elsewhere in the region, and to combine such visits with bilateral exercises — initiatives which might help provide India with a degree of confidence about PLAN activities. Beijing, for its part, could explore the 2010 offer by Indian Minister of State for Defence, Pallam Raju, to allow Indian warships to guard Chinese merchant ships in the Indian Ocean — a move which could help signal China's benign intentions in the region.[72] Finally, both states could do more to bolster inter-navy confidence by establishing even rudimentary levels of operational cooperation and information exchange between the warships they have deployed on anti-piracy duty.[73]

All of this might be augmented by multilateral or, at least, minilateral dialogues on maritime security in the Indian Ocean. Useful multilateral forums might emerge from an expanded IONS involving both China and the United States or, bringing in more East Asian stakeholders, through establishing a maritime security process within the ASEAN Regional Forum (ARF) or ADMM+8. Crucially, any of these moves would, for the first time, bring together the region's three biggest navies to discuss maritime security and crisis management.[74] Alternatively, minilateral arrangements may prove more manageable venues for forging cooperative agreements between the region's major maritime players. To be effective, such processes are likely to require the participation of India, the United States, China, Indonesia, Japan and Australia. To be sure, progress in any of these arenas will be difficult. However, if India and China allow their maritime security diplomacy to drift for even another few years, predictions of Sino–Indian naval rivalry in the Indian Ocean will move closer to reality.

---

[71] See Rory Medcalf, Asia's maritime security is all at sea (September 15, 2010). *The Australian.*

[72] James Lamont and Geoff Dyer, India offers to protect China oil shipments (February 17, 2010). *Financial Times.*

[73] See Sandeep Dikshit, India, China to share anti-piracy information (January 11, 2010). *The Hindu*; and Rory Medcalf, China's gunboat diplomacy (December 28, 2008). *New York Times.*

[74] See Townshend, Sino–Indian maritime relations.

4.4. *The India–China nuclear dynamic*

While their relatively small arsenals and "no first use" policies place India and China at the more responsible end of the spectrum of nuclear-armed states, the bilateral nuclear dynamic remains a potential cause of instability. Above all, Beijing's refusal to acknowledge New Delhi's genuine fears about a nuclear-armed China creates an atmosphere of denial that compounds Indian anxieties. Indeed, Beijing's reluctance to sign a bilateral no first use agreement or to take part in strategic-level nuclear stability talks with New Delhi has deepened mistrust and threat perceptions among Indian officials.[75] This situation could, over time, prompt New Delhi to step-up its efforts to modernize and expand India's nuclear capability. It also creates a significant obstacle to the global nuclear arms control agenda. Indeed, efforts to establish a nuclear stability regime between China and the United States or to create arsenal-capping understandings between India and Pakistan — essential for progress on the stalled Fissile Material Cut-off Treaty — could flounder if India and China were to regard each other as a major reason for expanding their nuclear options.

This highlights the urgent need for nuclear security dialogue between New Delhi and Beijing. For this to occur, China must recognize India's status as a nuclear peer and explicitly declare that it's no first use policy applies toward India, notwithstanding the fact that India remains outside the Nuclear Non-Proliferation Treaty. Given the prevailing asymmetry in the India–China deterrence relationship — China is widely considered to have a second-strike nuclear capability for use against India, whereas India is only beginning to develop its own capability for a second-strike against China — such assurances are all the more important.[76] Although it is difficult to envisage a scenario in which either state would issue nuclear threats against the other, establishing clearly defined nuclear doctrines, red lines and crisis management mechanisms is crucial to preventing nuclear rivalry or escalation.

---

[75]See Jing-dong Yuan, Sino–Indian Relations: A New Beginning (January 19, 2002). *Asia Times Online*.

[76]See, Perkovich, G (2004). The nuclear and security balance. In *The India–China Relationship: What the United States Needs to Know*, FR Frankel and H Harding (eds.), pp. 182–194. Washington: Woodrow Wilson Center Press and Columbia University Press.

5. Facilitating Accommodation: A Role for Smaller Powers?

Despite the risks and challenges underscoring Sino–Indian relations, smaller states in the Indo-Pacific are not entirely helpless in preventing great power rivalry from jeopardizing their national and regional security. But to what extent can small and middle powers help to facilitate better relations among Asia's rising giants?

Regional institutions and middle power diplomacy cannot fundamentally alleviate the strategic mistrust and competitive impulses of the India–China relationship. Of course, it is worthwhile to attempt to enmesh both states within regional institutions, forums and normative practices.[77] Given their broad mandate and Indo-Pacific footprint, the EAS and its security subsidiaries, the ARF and ADMM+8, are logical bodies within which India–China relations might begin to improve. After all, it is worth recalling just how far New Delhi and Beijing have come in their embrace of Asian regionalism. Barely a decade ago, engagement-minded states like Singapore and Australia were merely hoping to involve Asia's giants in dialogues on regional security. In the coming years, these states may well lead the way in setting the agendas for a range of regional institutions.[78] Nevertheless, Asian regionalism is hardly a panacea for Sino–Indian competition. Indeed, if competitive coexistence descends into strategic rivalry, smaller powers and multilateral organizations will become the diplomatic terrain over which India and China flex their muscles.

To prevent a worsening of the India–China relationship, a much greater degree of mutual understanding is required. At present, it remains disturbing how poorly India and China comprehend each other's cultures, concerns and national objectives. Very few of their scholars, officials or analysts spend prolonged periods of time in each other's country. Official bilateral security engagement — such as the annual defense dialogue — is

---

[77]For an excellent account of the role of "omni-enmeshment" in Southeast Asia, see Goh, E (Winter, 2007/2008). Great powers and hierarchical order in Southeast Asia: Analyzing regional security strategies. *International security*, 32(3), 113–157.

[78]For an overview of Asia's regionalism since the 1990s, see Green, MJ and B Gill (eds.) (2009). *Asia's New Multilateralism: Cooperation, Competition and the Search for Community*. New York: Columbia University Press.

dangerously superficial, while nonofficial "second track" initiatives fare little better. Although China has a large number of government funded research institutes, only a small number include specialists on South Asian relations. Meanwhile, many Indian analysts have an exaggerated, one-dimensional notion of China as a threat, while other parts of Indian society still view Beijing through the rose-tinted glasses of an antiquated socialist solidarity.

It is here that small and middle powers may be able to help at the margins. Diplomatically nimble states such as Singapore and Australia not only have an interest in great power stability, but have many opportunities to raise mutual awareness. Through a variety of second track dialogues, collaborative research projects or, in time, joint defense exercises and minilateral forums, such regional stakeholders may be able to provide venues for New Delhi and Beijing to develop mutual understandings and a modicum of cooperation.[79] Such endeavors would not mean that "facilitator" states are shedding their own uncertainties about the strategic implications of a powerful China or, for that matter, a powerful India. Of course, creative diplomacy by small and middle powers might simply be ignored by great powers that lack an inclination to compromise. In this respect, much will depend on the degree to which India and China recognize the scale of their common challenges and shared interest in managing strategic tensions.

6. Conclusion: Unraveling Rivalry

Dire predictions about impending rivalry between China and India serve a didactic purpose for both great powers and the wider Indo-Pacific region. Such assessments warn about what crises might come to pass, providing an added incentive for diplomatic efforts to forestall and manage tensions at an early stage. The danger, however, is that prophecies of doom might involve a self-fulfilling dynamic. In an age when each state's negative messages about the other spreads instantaneously through their media saturated societies, this is a particular concern for maintaining Sino–Indian stability.

---

[79]Rory Medcalf, Squaring the triangle: An Australian perspective on Asian security minilateralism (December, 2008). *NBR Special Report.*

The next decade will be crucial in shaping the long-term trajectory for relations between Asia's two rising giants. There is a limited window of opportunity to build patterns of dialogue and mutual trust before a relationship of competitive coexistence is at risk of becoming something far more dangerous and potentially antagonistic. While smaller powers may be able to help at the margins, stabilizing Sino–Indian relations will require enlightened leadership in New Delhi and Beijing and an improved awareness of each other's imperatives as a great power.

Chapter 2

The Washington and Beijing Consensus in South Asia: How the Colombo Consensus Emerged with New Global Realities

*Patrick Mendis**

1. Introduction

As the 25-year civil war ended with the defeat of the Tamil Tigers nemesis, Sri Lanka entered into another increasingly treacherous conflict — an as yet subtle one between the United States and China to secure the flow of Persian Gulf energy resources and free trade in the Indian Ocean. The new forces of global realities are not purely geopolitics but surely geoeconomics. As such, India's economic progress, security interests and political stability are intertwined with Tamils and Hindu sentiments in India. With India at the epicenter, every capital in the world — from Washington, Beijing and London to Islamabad, Tehran and Tokyo — seeks to play Colombo as the theater of a new "Great Game" for the new century. When Sri Lanka recently drifted towards Beijing as China's "string of pearl" strategy gained momentum, challenges to U.S. hegemony in Asia escalated as if Washington and Beijing were in direct competition with each other. The U.S. Senate Foreign Relations Report of 2009 (also known as the Kerry–Lugar Report) recommended a new "re-charting" strategy to prevent further deterioration

*Former American diplomat and a Military Professor in the NATO and Pacific Commands, is an Affiliate Professor of Public and International Affairs at George Mason University.

29

of American security interests in the island, thus giving birth to the Colombo Consensus: A delicate balancing act for the economic security of the east-west passage in the Indian Ocean. This has subsequently refueled the old political debate on "universal values" in China and the United States.

2. The Current Situation

In the aftermath of the brutal 25-year civil war against the Tamil Tigers nemesis that ended in May 2009, the government of Sri Lanka accumulated huge debts. The war-shattered island nation desperately needed foreign assistance to avoid further crises, support post-conflict reconstruction, and protect the poor and war refugees.[1] To finance rebuilding efforts, Sri Lanka returned to Washington and borrowed U.S. $2.6 billion from the International Monetary Fund (IMF) in July 2009.[2] Sri Lanka has been under the guidance of the World Bank and IMF (both undergirded by the influence of U.S. foreign policy) over the past three decades, including their austerity measures and the conditionality of these two Bretton Woods Institutions' (BWIs) structural adjustment programs. It has been a painful experience for islanders whose social welfare in education, health and agriculture was reduced by structural changes and budget reductions. The conditionality of Washington's policy prescription has primarily been influenced by American-led trade liberalization, economic growth strategy, and democratic system of governance.

With the spectacular rise of Chinese economic success, which had opposed the conditionality of the so-called Washington Consensus, Beijing has begun to challenge the trinity.

In a comparative analysis, the Beijing's offer of U.S. $6.1 billion[3] without conditionality over the Washington loan of U.S. $2.6 billion was

---

[1] See Claire Innes, U.S. rules out IMF loan program for Sri Lanka as humanitarian crisis deepens (May 15, 2009). *Global Insight.*

[2] IMF, Sri Lanka to use IMF loan to reform economy after conflict (July 29, 2009). *IMF Survey Magazine.* See http://imf.org/external/pubs/ft/survey/so/2009/int073009a.htm.

[3] Chinese companies including the China National Aero Technology Import and Export Corporation, China Harbor, China Railway No. 5 Engineering Group, and Synohydro Corporation employ Chinese workers. See Economic Affairs Correspondent, — China gets dragon's share of post-war projects in Lanka (December 6, 2009). *The Sunday Times* (Colombo). See http://sundaytimes.lk/091206/News/nws_02.html.

certainly more attractive for President Mahinda Rajapaksa and his Colombo administration. Since the bloody war ended, his leadership has been under heavy criticism for alleged war crimes, human rights violations, nepotism[4] and corruption by the United Nations, the United States, and other Western donor countries. For Rajapaska, according to the British Broadcasting Corporation (BBC), there were other reasons to break away from the West: When money from the West (i.e., Washington) looked as if it may dry up because of concerns over human rights abuses toward the end of the civil war, the president tried to offset this by making overtures to China.[5]

Indeed, the initial assessment of Sri Lanka's final phase of the war and associated human rights violations was a priority concern for Washington. Since the release of the new American — re-charting strategy for Sri Lanka outlined by the U.S. Senate Foreign Relations Report of December 2009 (also known as the Kerry–Lugar Report), the White House, Pentagon and State Department began to reset the geopolitical priority button — We cannot afford to lose Sri Lanka[6] and the United States needs to use the island to advance its national security interests in the Indian Ocean.

With the Kerry–Lugar Report, the policy orientation in Washington towards Sri Lanka has changed. Secretary of State Hillary Clinton told visiting Sri Lankan External Affairs Minister G. L. Peiris in May 2010 — "I think that the steps that have been taken by the Sri Lankan government are commendable, and we are supporting that effort. The minister and I talked about the continuing role of the United Nations".[7] Secretary Clinton

---

[4]Vikas Bajaj, India worries as China builds ports in South Asia (February 15, 2010). *The New York Times*. See http://www.nytimes.com/2010/02/16/business/global/16port.html?_r=1. Sri Lankan envoy Jaliya Wickramasuriya in Washington is the first cousin of President Mahinda Rajapaksa. See Jeremy Page, Rise of Sri Lankan president's son Namal Rajapaksa sparks concern (February 22, 2010). *The Sunday Times* (London). See http://www. timesonline.co.uk/tol/news/world/asia/article7035564.ece.

[5]See Profile: Mahinda Rajapaksa (September 8, 2010). *BBC South Asia*. See http:// news.bbc.co.uk/2/hi/south_asia/3602101.stm.

[6]The United States Senate Committee on Foreign Relations, *Sri Lanka: Re-charting U.S. Strategy after the War*, December 7, 2009, (Washington, D.C.: U.S. Government Printing Office, 2009), 3.

[7]Remarks by Secretary of State Hillary Rodham Clinton and Sri Lankan Minister of External Affairs GL Peiris on May 28, 2010. See Clinton and Sri Lankan Minister of External Affairs Peiris at the U.S. Department of State: http://www.america.gov/st/texttrans-english/2010/May/20100528153614ptellivremos0.5893976.html?CP.rss=true.

reminded the former Rhodes Scholar that — the United States has long been a friend of Sri Lanka. "Our countries share a history of democratic institutions, and we have an active USAID program that has invested more than U.S. $1.9 billion in Sri Lanka since 1956".[8] Compared to the accumulated amount of less than U.S. $2 billion worth of U.S. foreign assistance over the past 50 years, the current Chinese investment of over U.S. $6 billion speaks louder for the Colombo administration.

In the midst of the Washington and Beijing competition for Colombo, the Indian perception of Chinese threat in South Asia has grown highly sensitive and New Delhi's influence over Sri Lanka has been limited.[9] With the recent U.S.–India civil nuclear pact, the two strongest and largest democracies elevated their bilateral trade relations to a new height with greater military and nuclear cooperation.[10] When the Sri Lankan parliament — led by President Rajapaksa's elder brother and Speaker Chamal — amended the constitution in September 2010 to remove the presidential term limit and gave the executive president extraordinary power and freedom over legislative, judiciary and electoral appointments, democratic partners in Washington and Delhi expressed grave concerns over the power concentration in the presidency. Tisaranee Gunasekara, a respected Sri Lankan journalist, characterized the paradox by noting that — more freedom for the Rajapaksas [to make appointments in every branch of government] means less freedom for the Sri Lankan people.[11] Another commentator described the constitutional amendment as creating — "an imperial President".[12] Despite such criticism, the speaker of the parliament

---

[8] Ibid.

[9] See Sujan Dutta, USA: India engaging with Sri Lanka amid growing China role (March 11, 2009). *BBC News*.

[10] Patrick Mendis and Leah Green. *U.S.-India Civil Nuclear Cooperation Agreement*, A case study prepared for the U.S. Project on National Security Reform (PNSR), July 16, 2008. see http://www.pnsr.org/web/page/700/sectionid/579/pagelevel/3/interior.asp and the Hudson Institute at http://www.hudson.org/index.cfm?fuseaction=hudson_upcoming_events&id=587#.

[11] Tisaranee Gunasekara, More freedom for the Rajapaksas mean less freedom for the Sri Lankan people (October 2, 2010). *Transcurrents*. See http://transcurrents.com/tc/2010/10/more_freedom_for_the_rajapaksa.html.

[12] G. Usvatte-Aratchi, Eighteenth amendment: A rush to elected tyranny (September 6, 2010). *The Island*. See http://www.island.lk/index.php?page_cat=article-details&page=article-details&code_title=6063.

proudly reminded the world via his official webpage that it is the Rajapaksa family — with nine members in parliament alone — that governs the island of 21 million people.[13] Apart from Sri Lankans, the family-led, authoritarian-type political and economic power structure in the island is an especially worrisome development for over 60 million Tamil people in neighboring Tamil Nadu and the large Hindu population in the rest of India.

The gamut of these dynamic relationships and developments is not new to South Asia. For the greater part of the Cold War period, India ironically maintained friendly relations with the former Soviet Union while Sri Lanka aligned more with the United States. These mutually beneficial relations in both economic and military affairs were seemingly contradictory to their (India and Sri Lanka) political pledges to the Non-Aligned Movement, their nominal membership as former British colonies in the Commonwealth of Nations, and as protagonists within the concept of an Indian Ocean Zone of Peace.[14] When the British Empire was eclipsed as a dominant world power, the United States gained global supremacy in the post-World War II era. Sino–American as well as Indo–American relations have reached a critical juncture, particularly after al-Qaeda attacked the United States in 2001. In the meantime, the United States is burdened with the current state of the national debt and the expansive focus of U.S. military involvement in both international maritime security and the global war on terrorism waged within a growing list of countries (Afghanistan, Iraq, Pakistan and Yemen). As a creditor nation to the United States and other countries, China has gained enough economic ascendance to command a new direction in global relations and Indian Ocean affairs.

Within this context, this paper explores strategic developments in the post-9/11 security environment and global terrorism (a shared concern for America, China and India) to advance economic prosperity and human security for all. A case study of Sri Lanka and its experience with terrorism is a prism through which the changing dynamics of global geopolitics and geoeconomics are examined. As a globalizing nation, Sri Lanka is a

---

[13] See the posted biography of Speaker Chamal Jayantha Rajapaksa of the seventh parliament of the Democratic Socialist Republic of Sri Lanka in http://www.parliament.lk/handbook_of_parliament/speaker_bio_data.jsp.

[14] Patrick Mendis, Passage to Indian Ocean (February 16, 1986). *The Minnesota Daily*, p. 9.

geostrategic laboratory within which the international power politics of the island's distinct cultural and predominantly Buddhist heritage, current political developments, and changing global alignment all converge. How might these forces ultimately play out to serve its culturally, linguistically and religiously diverse people peacefully? Over the past 2500 years of recorded history, the island has never been a Robinson Crusoe-like *No Man's Land*. For transiting traders and ancient explorers in the Indian Ocean, the Pearl of the Orient has been the center of globalization since King Asoka of India and Alexander the Great of Macedonia, whose diplomatic relations with the island have been chronicled.

With this backdrop, the emerging confluence of China and the United States in Sri Lanka is examined in Section 2 to provide a conceptual framework — the Washington and Beijing Consensus — as both countries share a different set of philosophies in the marketplace of ideas to advance human progress. It further expands the two separate visions of freedom — political and economic — that emanate respectively from Washington and Beijing. In Section 3, the strategic mission expressed in the Chinese — string of pearls naval strategy is briefly presented to identify emerging flash-points in the Indian Ocean and massive Chinese investment projects in Sri Lanka. In Section 4, evolving Chindian (China and India) and Chimerican (China and America) relations are discussed to illustrate the complexities in international relations as China-centric issues affect bilateral transactions in South Asia.[15] Section 5 illustrates the new American policy in Sri Lanka as the United States has begun to re-chart its approach to a once-neglected but strategic partner of the past. The Colombo Consensus that emerged as a result is described in Section 6. The conclusion puts forward a new debate on the old idea of universal values that has fixed a gulf between the founding conviction of the United States and the Confucian tradition of China.

3. The Washington vs. Beijing Consensus

The neo-liberal economic and trade philosophy advocated by the Bretton Woods Institutions (BWIs) and their structural adjustment programs have

---

[15]For a comparative analysis of China and India, see Green, L and P Mendis (2008). Chindia: Does culture matter in hindu and confucian economies? *Global Economic Review*, 37(4), 429–445.

largely been enveloped within the Washington Consensus since the Ronald Reagan–Margaret Thatcher era of the 1980s. The conditionality of World Bank and IMF loans contains free market theology including:

- Privatizing public sector enterprises
- Removing tariff barriers within import and export regimes
- Eliminating controls on capital flows
- Reducing social expenditures in education and healthcare
- Lowering corporate taxation
- Raising interest rates to contract the money supply and to contain inflation, and
- Advocating a floating and open exchange rate mechanism, among others

These have by default been the mode of policy prescriptions for developing countries by economists and technocrats within these BWIs.[16] John Williamson, an economist at the Washington-based Peterson Institute for International Economics who coined the term Washington Consensus in 1989, described a range of ten specific economic policy prescriptions as the standard reform package.[17] The package promoted by the IMF, the World Bank and the U.S. Department of the Treasury is as popular as their mantra to stabilize, privatize, and liberalize the developing world; however, Professor Dani Rodrik of Harvard University has observed a set of mixed results of the Washington Consensus and noted that other diverse development policy alternatives exist.[18]

Nevertheless, the national development of loan-recipient countries is directly subject to these U.K. and U.S. Treasury-backed, Washington-based institutions often championed by *The Financial Times* and *The Economist*.

---

[16]Williamson, J (1989). Latin American readjustment: How much has happened? In John Williamson (ed.). Washington: Institute for International Economics. See http://www.iie.com/publications/papers/paper.cfm?researchid=486.

[17]See the 10 policy prescription of the Washington Consensus in John Williamson, *What Should the World Bank Think about the Washington Consensus?* A paper prepared as a background to the World Bank's *World Development Report 2000* (Washington, DC: Peterson Institute for International Economics, 1999). See http://www.iie.com/publications/papers/paper.cfm?ResearchID=351.

[18]Rodrik, D (2006). Goodbye Washington consensus, hello Washington confusion? A review of the World Bank's economic growth in the 1990s: Learning from a decade of reform. *Journal of Economic Literature*, XLIV, 973–987.

Domestic development projects — building highways, airports, harbors and dams — launched prior to the 1980s have now become an integral part of the improved Washington Consensus to overcome poverty, enhance growth with care for the environment, and create individual opportunity and hope, according to World Bank President Robert Zoellick.[19] Such evolutionary changes have been widely viewed as a continuation of British–American economic thought and political ideology. Even though the Washington Consensus is a global strategy to reaffirm U.S. power embedded in the free market and political freedom, it works benignly through the BWIs as a national development strategy to alleviate poverty, protect the environment, and fulfill individual human dignity. The primary goal of the Washington Consensus is to integrate the global community of nations, including China, into one world, one dream (as illustrated by the Beijing Olympics slogan of 2008).

Like Reagan and Thatcher, Deng Xiaoping — reform leader of the Chinese Communist Party — launched his own revolution with Chinese characteristics. Reagan adhered to trickle-down economics[20] and Deng liked the slogan, adding a Chinese character to read — let some get rich first, so others can get rich later[21] — as if both were pursuing the neoliberal philosophy of Milton Friedman and his free market economic ideology. But instead of the individual freedom and private property ownership of Western democracy, China's economic reform has long entailed a host of state-owned enterprises (SOEs) that compete with one another alongside foreign corporations and multinational companies. While maintaining its Confucian culture and political philosophy, China has single-handedly embarked on a market-driven, export-led development strategy to address social issues and the economic progress of its 1.3 billion Chinese consumers.

With the establishment of new Export Processing Zones (EPZs) in maritime regions, Deng promoted a mixture of private, semi-private and

---

[19]Robert B. Zoellick, President of the World Bank Group, speaking on An Inclusive and Sustainable Globalization at the National Press Club, Washington, DC on October 10, 2007. See http://digitalmedia.worldbank.org/slideshow/?slideshow_id=201.

[20]Reeves, R (2005). *President Reagan: The Triumph of Imagination*, p. 96. New York: Simon and Schuster.

[21]Joseph, WA (ed.) (2010). *Politics in China: An Introduction*, p. 155. Cambridge: Oxford University Press.

community-owned enterprises with local and most importantly foreign investment by the Chinese diaspora to energize his export-oriented development strategy. For instance, the Pearl River Delta specializes in labor-intensive manufacturing and textile assembly lines; the Yangtze River Delta concentrates on capital-intensive industry like cars, semi-conductors, computers and mobile phones. In collaboration with universities, banks and enterprises, the Communist Party has established a wide range of American-style, Silicon Valley-type, high-tech innovation parks around the country, including *Zhongguancun* in Beijing. The trilaterally diversified economic policy frontiers — based on labor, capital and knowledge — are carefully planned and integrated through China's export promotion formula; thus, China has earned the needed foreign exchange for its own domestic development as a result of their anticipated policy goals.[22]

To promote national development and to increase domestic consumption within its large rural population (estimated at over 600 million), China gainfully exploited the previous agricultural land reform and the educational expansion in the hinterland during the Mao Zedong era.[23] Since the early 1980s, the rural population gained greater freedom of mobility to market their agricultural produce and other crafts in nearby towns. These were then gradually merged as locally-operated Township and Village Enterprises (TVEs) in various locations. Given the unexpected economic success of the TVEs and new-found freedoms of mobility, entrepreneurship and free market activities, local governments were compelled to support (but not regulate) them to address rural unemployment and surplus agricultural production issues. Thus, the TVEs have served as a viable mechanism for decentralized economic development in the rural sector. As a consequence, the growing surplus labor force has even created nonagricultural employment opportunities in the expanding TVEs. In 1993, Deng Xiaoping recognized the importance of these popular TVEs (within his free market vision for China) and Beijing leaders began to formalize them by giving the ownership of these collective enterprises to villagers, and empowering local

---

[22]Yao, S (2005). *Economic Growth, Income Distribution and Poverty Reduction in Contemporary China.* London: Routledge Press.

[23]Bhattasali, D, S Li and W Martin (2004). *China and the WTO: Accession, Policy Reform, and Poverty Reduction Strategies.* Washington: World Bank Publications.

governments to exercise decisions on management issues like the hiring and firing of TVE leaders.

As opposed to the SOEs and EPZs, the explosive growth of TVEs in rural China was able to employ a greater number of workers than the combined employment of all urban-private, jointly-owned, and foreign-managed enterprises.[24] As an economic equalizer and a social stabilizer, the uniquely Chinese defining characteristic within TVEs has emerged as a new taste for freedom in the post-Mao reform era of 1978–96 and beyond. This is the golden age for new China that no other transitional economy has ever experienced, according to Professor Barry Naughton at the University of California at San Diego.[25] The China expert further writes that there is no country where public enterprises play[ed] the pivotal role that TVEs played in China.[26] Over the past decade or so, these TVEs were transformed into privately- and publicly- owned stock companies, and by 2005 contributed over 30% to GDP.[27]

Both planned and emergent strategies have synergized once separate domestic and foreign markets as a conduit to expand the national market and to develop a new social division of labor and a vitally important legion of consumers in China. The labor market has become more mobile and the latter, as a consequence, has mutually reinforced the synergy of consumers and laborers marking the exodus of farm workers from the rural sector to the more prosperous coastal regions. At the same time, rural TVEs were more economically beneficial than the maritime and urban industries as rural China had no need for additional housing, health and social infrastructure for their hinterland workforce. Thus, a large peasant population has benefited from *organic* TVE experiment.

Reformer Deng Xiaoping expressed his overall economic philosophy this way: "Whether a white cat or a black cat, as long as it can catch mice it is a good cat".[28] In pursuing his economic strategy, the Communist Party has

---

[24] *China Statistical Yearbook* (Beijing: China Statistics Press, 2009) and *China Agricultural Yearbook* (Beijing: China Agricultural Press, 2009).

[25] Naughton, B (2007). *The Chinese Economy: Transitions and Growth*, p. 287. Cambridge: The MIT Press.

[26] Ibid.

[27] See a detailed analysis of these changes in Barry Naughton, 280–295.

[28] Stewart, W (2001). *Deng Xiaoping: Leader in a changing China*, p. 64. New York: Twenty-First Century Books.

maintained its centralized political authority by granting greater economic freedom while restricting certain political freedoms — the freedom of expression, the freedom of assembly and the freedom of religious pursuits — from free and open exercise.

In response to wide-spread public corruption reported in the media in 2009, the Party introduced a new intraparty democracy policy of greater transparency and reasonable debate on public issues. Such a policy initiative was not alien to China. Dr. Sun Yat-sen, the father of modern China, envisioned his revolution on the principles of nationalism, democracy and equalization.[29] During the Mao Zedong and the Cultural Revolution period, the idea of democracy disappeared. The returning philosophy of Dr. Sun — a Thomas Jefferson-like founding father of modern China — is a gradual strategy not by Party choice but by the demand of its growing and more educated populace, especially the younger Internet generation.[30]

Unlike the Western idea of individual liberty as the prime denominator of all basic human freedoms, China pursues an Alexander Hamilton-like trade, financial and industrial strategy for their own success in economic freedom.[31] The sheer economic determination of the Chinese people has overshadowed Jefferson-inspired democratic governance to protect minority rights and promote religious freedom. This dichotomy — between Hamiltonian and Jeffersonian visions — is most pronounced between the Beijing and Washington Consensus. The tendency of U.S. foreign policy is to promote democracy and open markets; the former is lacking in the Chinese foreign policy of Peaceful Rising[32] and their low profile approach to world affairs.

In recent years, however, the credibility of the Washington Consensus has been eroding as the economic stability and social equality of the United States was undermined by the collapse of the American housing and financial markets as well as the widening gap between rich and poor. At the same

---

[29]Fung, ESK (2000). *In Search of Chinese Democracy: Civil Opposition in Nationalist China*, 1929–1949, pp. 32–40. New York: Cambridge University Press.

[30]See Mendis, P (2010). *Commercial Providence: The Secret Destiny of the American Empire*. Lanham: Rowman and Littlefield.

[31]Ibid.

[32]Lanteigne, M (2009). *Chinese Foreign Policy: An Introduction*. New York: Taylor & Francis.

time, the Chinese approach of rapid economic growth and political stability has gained greater appreciation and public standing for the Beijing Consensus, where economic freedom matters more than political freedom.

Nevertheless, during a visit to the economically vibrant city of Shenzhen (near Hong Kong) in late August 2010, Chinese Premier Wen Jiabao warned: "Without the safeguard of political freedom, the fruits of economic reform would be lost and the goal of modernization would not materialize".[33] Like Dr. Sun Yat-sen, Wen's underlying democratic philosophy was revealed when the premier told Fareed Zakaria on his CNN program in October 2010 that the wish and will of the people are not stoppable, and disclosed that his two favorite books were *The Theory of Moral Sentiments* by Adam Smith and *The Meditations* by Marcus Aurelius.[34] Similarly, Alexander Hamilton (who reportedly read the same books) also declared that — "Your people, sir — your people is a great beast".[35] For the Confucian leader, the influence of Western and American thought is now quite understandable and reasonable; yet this remarkable revelation by Wen — at a cross-roads in dynamic change — has sent an inevitable tremor-like message to the less flexible, Hamiltonian-like Hu Jintao — Chinese president and Communist Party general secretary — and the unyielding bureaucracy and political apparatus that resist political transformation. The likely Hu successor, Vice President Xi Jingping, is also more associated with economic restructuring and trade promotion than political reform.[36]

With the rapid ascendance of Chinese economy, Beijing has aggressively expanded its global engagements in trade regimes to increase their sphere of influence in the marketplace and to obtain much-needed resources for China's industrial output — especially energy and raw materials. The rise of China has also created an unprecedented demand for natural resources from Africa and Asian countries and expanded market opportunities for

---

[33]Keith B. Richburg, In China, silence greets talk of reform (October 14, 2010). *The Washington Post*, p. A8.

[34]Fareed Zakaria, The new challenge from China (October 18, 2010). *Time Magazine*, pp. 52–55.

[35]Hamilton, A and HC Syret (eds.) (1979). *The Papers of Alexander Hamil*, p. 13. New York: Columbia University Press.

[36]Keith B. Richburg, China promotes likely Hu successor to key position (October 19, 2010). *The Washington Post*, p. A6.

Chinese manufactured goods and investment in Africa and Asia. To facilitate the flow of industrial and commercial goods as well as the passage of Persian Gulf oil through the Indian Ocean, Sri Lanka has become a primary strategic transiting port for China to subsequently achieve its global ambitions and power expansion in both geographic regions. In the meantime, the warming relationship between the United States and India (with its growing middle class of over 200 million having purchasing power parity similar to their American counterparts) is seemingly poised to increase tensions between China and neighbors like India, South Korea and Japan.

4. Sri Lanka: China's Newest "Pearl"

Like the old Silk Road that stretched from the ancient capital of Xi'an all the way to Europe, modern China's strategic and commercial supply line extends over the Indian Ocean to include the focal transit port of Sri Lanka at the southern tip of India, advantageously located within east-west international shipping route. Over 85% of China's energy imports from the Middle East and mineral resources from Africa transit through this and other string of pearl ports, which Beijing seeks to protect as strategic economic arteries anchored all the way from the Persian Gulf and African waters to the South China Sea.[37] Colonel Christopher Pehrson at the U.S. Army War College in Pennsylvania described this elaborate network as the manifestation of China's rising geopolitical influence through efforts to increase access to ports and airfields, develop special diplomatic relationships, and modernize military forces that extend from the South China Sea through the Strait of Malacca, across the Indian Ocean, and on to the Arabian Gulf.[38] To meet increasing demand for oil and other

---

[37] As reported by the United Press International (UPI), Energy resources: China's Sri Lanka port raises concern (February 17, 2010). See http://www.upi.com/Science_News/Resource-Wars/2010/02/17/Chinas-Sri-Lanka-port-raises-concern/UPI-65221266422916// Also see Vishal Arora, Sri Lanka's wartime abuses (June 25, 2010). *Foreign Policy in Focus*. See http://www.fpif.org/articles/sri_lankas_wartime_abuses and Vikas Bajaj, India worries as China builds ports in South Asia (February 15, 2010). *The New York Times*. See http://www.nytimes.com/2010/02/16/business/global/16port.html?_r=1.

[38] Pehrson, C (2006). *String of Pearls: Meeting the Challenge of China's Rising Power across the Asian Littoral*. Carlisle: United States Army War College, See http://www.strategicstudiesinstitute.army.mil/pdffiles/PUB721.pdf.

raw materials as well as to secure their maritime trading routes through the Indian Ocean, China has either built or reportedly planned to construct vital facilities in Bangladesh, Cambodia, Myanmar, Pakistan, Sri Lanka and Thailand.[39] China's comprehensive string of pearls naval strategy includes:

- A planned oil refinery terminal at Chittagong in Bangladesh, the northern Bay of Bengal located just east of India;
- The reported establishment of a naval base and intelligence surveillance station at Sittwe in Myanmar and in nearby islands on the Bay of Bengal;
- The reported building of a surveillance base on Marao Island in the Maldives, just north of the British military base leased to U.S. armed forces on the island of Diego Garcia;
- The construction of a billion dollar deepwater port at Gwadar in Baluchistan province of Pakistan on the Arabian Sea coast close to Iran and the Strait of Hormuz in the Persian Gulf, which will be used as a pipeline terminal to transport crude oil and natural gas from the Persian Gulf to China's western hinterland; and
- The present construction of a billion dollar all-inclusive deepwater seaport at Hambantota in Sri Lanka.[40]

In addition to these projects, China has reportedly been exploring the expansion and establishment of other facilities at eastern and western maritime choking ports of the Indian Ocean — the Gulf of Aden and the Arabian Sea as well as the Strait of Malacca — to address growing piracy issues, especially around Somalia, Indonesia, Malaysia and the Philippines.[41]

---

[39]Michael Richardson, Full steam ahead for naval might (January 15, 2009). *The Straits Times.* See the reprint http://app.mfa.gov.sg/pr/read_content.asp?View,11921. Also see K. Alan Kronstadt and Bruce Vaughn, *Sri Lanka: Background and U.S. Relations,* U.S. Congressional Research Service, Washington, D.C., June 4, 2009 and Peter Lee, Beijing broods over its arc of anxiety (December 4, 2009). *Asia Times.*

[40]China's Export-Import Bank is financing 85% of the cost of the $1 billion project and China Harbor Engineering, part of a state-owned company, is building the port. Other arrangements have been made for an international airport near the port. Also see Chinese billions helping Lanka ward off western peace efforts, fight LTTE (May 2, 2009). *China National News.* See http://story.chinanationalnews.com/index.php/ct/9/cid/9366300fc9319e9b/id/496746/cs/1/.

[41]Gamini Weerakoon, Hambantota in the great game of the Indian Ocean (February 7, 2010). *The Sunday Leader.* See http://www.thesundayleader.lk/?p=7211.

The construction of the massive seaport at Hambantota, a small fishing village of 21,000 people on the southeastern coast of Sri Lanka, is understandably a cause of serious concern in Delhi and Washington. Critics maintain that Sri Lanka has resorted to generous financial, military and diplomatic support from China after India and the United States declined to assist the government of Sri Lanka in defeating the Tamil Tigers, who waged civil war for over 25 years.[42] In exchange, China has now begun to reap the benefits of its strategic investment on the island by using the seaport as a re-fuelling and docking station for the Chinese Navy. Hambantota is also one of President Rajapaksa's constituencies and is represented by his 23-year-old son Namal in parliament — an implicit but solid strategy to continue the political dynasty in Sri Lanka, according to *The Sunday Times* in London.[43]

As a deliberate example of family connections, the Rajapaksa administration is globally portrayed as pursuing a dual-edged covert family enrichment and overtly national development strategy for Sri Lanka. Besides the port at Hambantota, critics have argued that China has financed nearly the entire array of Sri Lanka's other main infrastructure projects including an oil-storage facility, a new airport, a coal-fired power plant, and an expressway. In an internationally-noted article on The Colombo Consensus: Brotherly Love, Massive Aid and No Questions Asked in *The Economist*, the editorial revealed that all of these projects are negotiated and managed by Rajapaksa family members.[44] With cheap commercial credit and imported Chinese labor, Beijing also builds main roads in the war-damaged northern Jaffna and eastern Trincomalee and Batticaloa regions, and constructs a modern performance arts center in Colombo. China has not only sold diesel railway engines and earthmoving equipment in the name of post-conflict

---

[42] Chinese billions helping Lanka ward off western peace efforts, fight LTTE (May 2, 2009). *China National News* (see above).

[43] See Jeremy Page, Rise of Sri Lankan President's son Namal Rajapaksa sparks concern (February 22, 2010). *The Sunday Times* (London), at http://www.timesonline.co. uk/tol/news/world/asia/article7035564.ece. See also Indeewara Thilakarathne, When Mahinda became the youngest MP (November 12, 2006). *The Sunday Observer*. http://www. sundayobserver.lk/2006/11/12/imp04.asp.

[44] Editorial, The Colombo consensus: Brotherly love, massive aid and no questions asked (July 8, 2010). *The Economist*, See http://www.economist.com/node/16542629.

reconstruction, but Chinese companies have also invested in electronic and garment-making industries for which the government of Sri Lanka established a special free-trade zone exclusively for China.[45]

With the sustained flow of Chinese military and economic assistance, Sri Lanka finally crushed the Tamil Tigers in May 2009. The military operation has raised a plethora of concerns over human rights issues from the United States and the European Union. When India and Western governments refused to sell weaponry, Sri Lanka turned increasingly to China[46] — especially after the United States suspended its military aid to Colombo over human rights violations in 2007. Veteran *Atlantic Monthly* journalist Robert Kaplan characterized the situation:

"The international community disapproves of your methods and cuts off military aid because of the human rights violations you've committed? Again, no problem. Get aid from China, whose assistance comes without moral lectures. That is just what the Sri Lankan Government did. In return, the Chinese got the right to help construct a deepwater port in Sri Lanka, close to world shipping lanes"* (italics original).[47]

Given India's previous military debacles in Sri Lanka, New Delhi leaders restrained themselves from direct involvement, especially once Indian premier Rajiv Gandhi was assassinated by a diminutive Tamil Tiger female suicide bomber in May 1991.[48] At the same time, Sri Lankan Buddhist and Sinhalese leaders are sensitive to the fact that the island's northern neighbor Tamil Nadu state, home to more than 60 million Tamils,

---

[45]Ibid.

[46]Chinese arms have been supplied through Lanka Logistics & Technologies, co-led by President Rajapaksa's brother and the defense secretary Gotabhaya Rajapksa. See Jeremy Page, Chinese Billions in Sri Lanka Fund Battle against Tamil Tigers (May 2, 2009). *The Sunday Times* (London), (see above).

[47]Robert D. Kaplan, To Catch a Tiger (July 2009). *The Atlantic Monthly.* See http://www.theatlantic.com/magazine/archive/2009/07/to-catch-a-tiger/7581/.

[48]For an assessment of murderous nature of LTTE, see a background note by Preeti Bhattacharji, Liberation Tigers of Tamil Eelam (aka Tamil Tigers), Council on Foreign Relations, New York, May 20, 2009 at http://www.cfr.org/publication/9242/liberation_tigers_of_tamil_eelam_aka_tamil_tigers_sri_lanka_separatists.html Also see Bruce Fein, American lobbyist for Tamils Against Genocide and former associate deputy attorney general under President Reagan, provides another view of civil war. See Bruce Fein, Genocide in Sri Lanka (February 15, 2009). *The Boston Globe.* See http://www.boston.com/bostonglobe/editorial_opinion/oped/articles/2009/02/15/genocide_in_sri_lanka/.

has a historic kinship with their ethnic and religious counterparts in northern Sri Lanka.[49] More importantly, however, a complex disposition of global geopolitics (e.g., the Nobel Laureate Dalai Lama and his Buddhist followers in the exile Tibetan parliament in Dharmasala, just north of New Delhi) has been a major concern for India as well as for China. Given its military and friendship treaty with the former Soviet Union, for example, India has been preoccupied with balance-of-power politics with the United Kingdom and the United States. India has continued to be vigilant about becoming the traditional nexus between London and Washington, whereas the British Navy used Sri Lanka's natural harbor in Tricomalee as a regional naval base until 1957 and it is still being used by visiting U.S. Navy ships. In addition, their military outpost on the island of Diego Garcia (leased by London to Washington until 2036)[50] is also in close proximity to India and Sri Lanka, and a constant irritant to these Indian Ocean Zone of Peace advocates. As the dominant regional power in South Asia, India is faced with a glut of complex historical issues (like Tibet and Pakistan) and emerging realities (like terrorism and separatism) as China expands its economic and maritime networks in the Indian Ocean.

5. Chindian and Chimerican Relations

As the most powerful and largest democracies in the world, the United States and India seem to be pursuing a mutually-reinforcing and beneficial strategy in advancing their shared political philosophy. Despite India's refusal to sign the Nuclear Non-Proliferation (NPT) Treaty,[51] the United States, for example, agreed anyway to the U.S.–Indian civil nuclear cooperation pact in 2008 and has expanded trade and economic relations between the two

---

[49] See Asoka Bandarage, *The Separatist Conflict in Sri Lanka: Terrorism, Ethnicity, Political Economy* (New York: Taylor & Francis, 2009) and John Richardson, *Paradise poisoned: Learning about Conflict, Terrorism, and Development from Sri Lanka's Civil Wars* (Kandy, Sri Lanka: International Center for Ethnic Studies, 2005).

[50] Richard Beeston, Analysis: Beautiful diego garcia makes forces blush (February 21, 2008). *The Sunday Times.* See http://www.timesonline.co.uk/tol/news/politics/article3412423.ece

[51] China was dismayed by America's double-standard when it comes to China's ally, North Korea, which was treated differently within the NPT framework but overlooked it by approving India, a non-signer to the Treaty. See also Mendis, P and L Green, *U.S.-India Civil Nuclear Cooperation Agreement.*

countries. As American firms begin to invest in India, Japanese companies have also agreed to invest U.S. $10 billion on an industrial corridor that extends 1,500 km between New Delhi and Mumbai, the booming commercial capital on the west coast. With these open economic and trade policies, India has moved away from its historically lethargic Hindu rate of growth and Non-Aligned Movement foreign policy to a more Western-oriented and robust economic, diplomatic and military force on the world stage.

The Chinese leadership in Beijing has perceived these actions as a sign that the United States and its allies (like Japan, South Korea and Taiwan) are deliberately using India not only as a huge consumer market for their products and services but also as a counterweight to China in South Asia. China has simultaneously agreed to build two nuclear power plants for its traditional ally, Pakistan — the Indian arch-rival. Prevailing criticism of the U.S.–India nuclear cooperation agreement has been somewhat muted by the growing nexus of the Sino–Pakistan civilian and military nuclear power programs.[52] With heavy financial investment in both sectors, China has now become Pakistan's second largest economic and trading partner after the United States. There are now over 60 Chinese companies with more than 10,000 Chinese workers employed on 122 major development projects in Pakistan, including the Gwadar port and Saindak copper mine site in Baluchistan as well as the Gomal Zam dam project in Pakistan's federally administered tribal areas.[53] With a range of massive development and deepwater seaports in Pakistan, Bangladesh, Myanmar and Sri Lanka, China has actively put forward counterpoised strategies to discourage or limit the U.S. presence in the region.

The United States has viewed China's string of pearls strategy not only as a balance of power issue but also as a show of force in the Indian Ocean. Perceived threats made India and Sri Lanka equally nervous. With India's leadership, Indian ships and the nuclear-powered *USS Nimitz* and *USS Chicago* participated in a naval exercise with Australian, Japanese and Singaporean ships in the Bay of Bengal in 2007. Moreover, America's

---

[52] Blank, S (2010).The China–Pakistan reactor deal and Asia's nuclear energy race. *China Brief*, 10(12).

[53] Ziad Haider, Pakistan: The China factor in Pakistan (October 2, 2009). *Far Eastern Economic Review*.

involvement in Afghanistan (and increasingly in Pakistan) and the central Asian republics as well as security and military ties to South-East Asian countries (like Indonesia, Singapore and Vietnam) and North-East Asian countries (South Korea, Japan and Taiwan) is more than an emblematic challenge to China's pronounced Peaceful Rising foreign policy. Beijing leaders — especially military leaders — feel that the United States has encircled them geostrategically with U.S. bases and is selling advanced weapons to countries like Taiwan (a renegade republic in the Chinese perspective). The construction of a nuclear-submarine base on the southern Chinese island of Hainan (where an American spy-plane was forced to land in 2002) is another tactical response to project its growing power and protect the South China Sea.

Adhering to the path of Peaceful Rising, China has negotiated a number of settlements of territorial disputes with Russia, Vietnam and India. These unprecedented diplomatic acts by Chinese leadership point to a different vision of power in international negotiation and diplomacy. At the UN Climate Summit in Copenhagen in December 2009, for example, both China and India — the world's largest and fourth-largest emitters of greenhouse gases — joined forces together to oppose American-led demands for supporting strong anti-global warming measures.[54] Such diplomatic triumphs made the evolving scope of international relations more complex and complicated between and among America, China and India.

For Chindian leaders, the common problem is job creation for younger populations, which could easily become a source of internal tension and violence. With the growing importance of geoeconomics as opposed to the traditional mindset of geopolitical calculations, Chindia and Chimerica seem to now share a common sense of economic progress as a primary requirement of political survival in Beijing, Delhi and Washington. This has been more pronounced in the United States since the economic crisis left high unemployment and political frustration (which saw the rise of the tea party movement) with the Obama administration in its wake. Rapid economic growth rates in Chindia are a positive sign for global development as Chimerica has mutually benefited from their symbiotic economic

---

[54]Editorial, India and China: A Himalayan rivalry (August 19, 2010). *The Economist.* See http://www.economist.com/node/16843717?story_id=16843717.

relationship as the two leading world economies. China's advances in manufacturing sectors and India's progress in information technology will soon be equalized as both countries engage in more trading of goods and services, as if working toward Trade for Peace.[55] China's investment in a string of pearls appears to primarily address basic human development concerns and national interests through economic growth followed by human security in the Asian region. The optimism experienced by China, in which more than 250 million people have been lifted out of poverty, is justified not only in Confucian countries like the Asian Tigers (Hong Kong, Singapore, Taiwan and South Korea) but also in South Asian nations whose economies have opened up to Chinese investment and technology.

The leading trio — America, China and India — also shared a common enemy: terrorism both at home and abroad. Having global trade interests and investment opportunities — whether competitive or complementary — each nation continuously searches for greater security and stability in the Indian Ocean region as a prime necessity for their own national progress. President Barack Obama's visit to China, soon followed by Indian Prime Minister Manmohan Singh's trip to Washington in November 2009, clearly signified the importance of the Chindian role in South Asian security.[56] Some commentators viewed the trajectory of political, military and economic interdependence as the new pragmatism of cooperation and competition.[57] As political alliances have changed vividly with evolving post-9/11 global realities, each nation is presented with new opportunities and challenges. The Obama administration — under pressure from the U.S. Congress — has now begun to recalculate and reset its Sri Lanka strategy as a response to Chinese inroads into the Indian Ocean passageway.

---

[55]Mendis, P (2009). *TRADE for PEACE*. Bloomington: iUniverse Press, in which I advocated this hypothesis as an American conviction by its Founding Fathers. Also see how India and China use that concept for greater economic and trade ties in Vikas Bajaj, India worries as China builds ports in South Asia (February 15, 2010). *The New York Times*. See http://www.nytimes.com/2010/02/16/business/global/16port.html?_r=1.

[56]Nirmala Ganapathy, U.S. super cop role for China gets India's Goat (November 19, 2009). *Times of India*.

[57]Chidanand Rajghatta, U.S. more at ease with India's rise than China's ascent (February 3, 2010). *Times of India*, and M. K. Bhardrakumar, China breaks the Himalayan barrier (May 1, 2010). *Asia Times*.

6. Re-charting the U.S. Geostrategic Response

Since the terrorist attacks of 2001, the Bush administration focused more on democratic India and advocated the creation of an Arc of Democracies, all the while justifying and waging two wars in Iraq and Afghanistan.[58] Recognizing China's string of pearls strategy, President Rajapaksa portrayed Sri Lanka's ethnic conflict as part of a global war on terrorism (a similar worldview was conveniently held by President George W. Bush) during this same period. Following victory over the Tamil Tigers facilitated by unconditional military and diplomatic assistance from China, Rajapaksa cheerfully pointed out that Sri Lanka is a model for anti-insurgency military campaigns elsewhere.[59] When the United States criticized the way the Sri Lankan government handled the final military phase of the brutal war, Rajapaksa defended his actions, saying: "They are trying to preach to us about civilians. I tell them to go and see what they are doing in Iraq and Afghanistan".[60] As a result, the United States not only restricted its military assistance to Colombo due to concerns over human rights abuses in the bloody war against the most lethal terrorist group in the world (the U.S. State Department has listed the Tamil Tigers — who invented the suicide vest — as a terrorist group in 1997), but also protested by declining to vote at the IMF on a U.S. $2.6 billion loan to the Rajapaksa government in July 2009.[61]

The Obama administration — with the support of U.N. Secretary General Ban Ki-moon — initially followed a Bush-like foreign policy to isolate Sri Lanka on the grounds of human rights violations and alleged war-crimes committed by both the military and the Tamil Tigers. By overriding America's geopolitical interests in Sri Lanka, the U.S. administration pushed

---

[58]U.S. Secretary of State Condoleezza Rice under President George W. Bush formed a strategic group of Australia, Japan and the United States under the heading Arc of Democracies at a security forum held in March 2006 to counter China as a strategic competitor. Tanja Vestergaard, Man at work: Rudd walks Asian tightrope (April 17, 2008). *Asia Times*. See http://www.atimes.com/atimes/China/JD17Ad01.html.

[59]Lydia Polgreen, U.S. report on Sri Lanka urges new approach (December 6, 2009). *The New York Times*. See http://www.nytimes.com/2009/12/07/world/asia/07lanka.html.

[60]Nicolas Revise, Bitter with west, Sri Lanka turns east for cash and support (May 3, 2009). *Agence France Presse*.

[61]Lydia Polgreen, I.M.F. Approves $2.6 Billion Sri Lanka Loan (July 26, 2009). *The New York Times*. See http://www.nytimes.com/2009/07/27/world/asia/27lanka.html?_r=2.

the U.N. Secretary General to appoint an independent panel to investigate the atrocities committed by each party; Colombo successfully thwarted Ban Ki-moon's initiative (with Indian backing and Chinese support) at the U.N. Human Rights Council. After the vote, Dayan Jayatillaka, Sri Lankan ambassador to the United Nations in Geneva, sarcastically commented:

"This is not a lesson that Sri Lanka taught the West. It is a victory of the developing countries and the global South. It was not a defeat of the Tiger Diaspora alone. It was the defeat of a powerful block of forces. Geneva was a miniature diplomatic Dien Bien Phu or Bay of Pigs for the EU" [European Union].[62]

After continued pressure from the United States, the European Union and the U.N., the government of Sri Lanka established the Lessons Learned and Reconciliation Commission with members appointed by President Rajapaksa himself. As the U.S. media publicized human rights violations alongside horrible images from Afghanistan and Iraq, the Obama administration took a softer view on Sri Lanka and its challenges. Commenting on Sri Lanka's civilian casualties and the humanitarian crises of May 2009, President Barack Obama said:

"I want to emphasize that these photos [of Sri Lanka] that were requested in this case are not particularly sensational, especially when compared to the painful images that we remember from Abu Ghraib, but they do represent conduct that did not conform with the Army Manual. That is precisely why they were investigated — and, I might add, investigated long before I took office — and, where appropriate, sanctions have been applied".[63]

Given the uneasy challenges in war situations and geostrategic interests, the United States subsequently lent implicit legitimacy to the Reconciliation Commission in Colombo. When the Sri Lankan external affairs minister met with Secretary Hillary Clinton by her invitation at the U.S. State Department on May 28, 2010, the secretary said: "I want to thank Minister Peiris for

---

[62]John Stanton, USA fears loss of Sri Lanka: Sri Lanka should become Switzerland of Indian Ocean (August 8, 2010). *The Sunday Leader.* See http://www.thesundayleader.lk/? p=19688.

[63]The White House, *Statement by the president on the situation in Sri Lanka and Detainee Photographs,* see http://www.whitehouse.gov/the_press_office/Statement-by-the-President-on-the-Situation-in-Sri-Lanka-and-Detainee-Photographs/

our productive discussion today and commend him for his commitment to the reconciliation process. The United States pledges our continued support to Sri Lanka".[64] The minister also promised Clinton that detainees would be resettled within three months, but more importantly, he called for a multidimensional relationship with the United States,[65] suggesting movement beyond human rights issues.

The primary rationale for rapid policy change was triggered by a U.S. Senate Foreign Relations Committee Report titled *Re-charting U.S. Strategy on Sri Lanka* released on December 7, 2009.[66] The bipartisan congressional report — endorsed by Senators John Kerry and Richard Lugar, the Democratic chairman and the ranking Republican of the Senate Foreign Relations Committee — bluntly declared:

"As Western countries became increasingly critical of the Sri Lankan Government's handling of the war and human rights record, the Rajapaksa leadership cultivated ties with such countries as Burma, China, Iran, and Libya. The Chinese have invested billions of dollars in Sri Lanka through military loans, infrastructure loans, and port development, with none of the strings attached by Western nations. While the United States shares with the Indians and the Chinese a common interest in securing maritime trade routes through the Indian Ocean, the U.S. Government has invested relatively little in the economy or security sector in Sri Lanka, instead focusing more on IDPs" [Internally Displaced Persons] and civil society. As a result, Sri Lanka has grown politically and economically isolated from the West.[67]

Having a greater awareness of China's strategic and long-term *geoeconomic* foundation in Sri Lanka, the Kerry–Lugar Report made a cautionary note on America's *geopolitical* interest and strategy:

"President Rajapaksa was forced to reach out to other countries because the West refused to help Sri Lanka finish the war against the LTTE.

---

[64]Remarks by Secretary of State Hillary Rodham Clinton and Sri Lankan Minister of External Affairs GL Peiris on May 28, 2010. See Clinton and Sri Lankan Minister of External Affairs Peiris at the U.S. Department of State: http://www.america.gov/st/texttrans-english/2010/May/20100528153614ptellivremos0.5893976.html?CP.rss=true.

[65]Ibid.

[66]The United States Senate Committee on Foreign Relations, *Sri Lanka: Re-charting U.S. Strategy after the War*, December 7, 2009, (Washington, D.C.: U.S. Government Printing Office, 2009).

[67]The United States Senate Committee on Foreign Relations, 2–3.

These calculations — if left unchecked — threaten long-term U.S. strategic interests in the Indian Ocean".[68]

The two senators concluded: "With the end of the war, the United States needs to re-evaluate its relationship with Sri Lanka to reflect new political and economic realities".[69] Then, they added: "While humanitarian concerns remain important, U.S. policy toward Sri Lanka cannot be dominated by a single agenda. It is not effective at delivering real reform, and it shortchanges U.S. geostrategic interests in the region".[70] In the aftermath of the Indian Ocean tsunami in December 2004, it was the American military that quickly reached out to the island and provided the rapidly needed multinational relief, humanitarian assistance, and rebuilding efforts through the Operation United Assistance (OUA) coordinated by the U.S. Department of Defense.[71]

Understanding Sri Lanka's strategic importance to the United States, Sri Lankan Minister G. L. Peiris reinforced a similar vision outlined by the leading two Democrat and Republican senators. Thus, Peiris carefully used the word multidimensional[72] to describe the nature of a new Great Game of larger geopolitical and geoeconomic dynamics in the region involving China and India.[73] While these countries share strategic interests in securing the east-west maritime trade route and air navigation (for refueling and landing rights), the United States has invested relatively fewer economic and military resources in Sri Lanka than China. Instead, the United States has preferred to focus on political freedom and democracy promotion. Consequently, Sri Lanka's geostrategic importance to American security interests — both economic and military — has been undermined. Senators Kerry and Lugar said: "This strategic drift will have consequences

---

[68]The United States Senate Committee on Foreign Relations, 13.

[69]The United States Senate Committee on Foreign Relations, 16.

[70]Ibid.

[71]Alvarado, J and P Mendis (2007). New multilateralism in action for peace: A case study of the U.S.-led operation unified assistance in the Asian tsunami disaster. *Global Economic Review*, 36(2), 83–192.

[72]Remarks by Secretary of State Hillary Rodham Clinton and Sri Lankan Minister of External Affairs GL Peiris on May 28, 2010 (see above).

[73]See a detailed analysis in Sergei DeSilva-Ranasinghe, Sri Lanka: The new great game (October 31, 2009). *The Sunday Observer*. See http://www.thesundayleader.lk/?p=796.

for U.S. interests in the region. Along with our legitimate humanitarian and political concerns, U.S. policymakers have tended to underestimate Sri Lanka's geostrategic importance for American interests".[74] They then pointed out that Sri Lanka is located at the nexus of crucial maritime trading routes in the Indian Ocean connecting Europe and the Middle East to China and the rest of Asia.[75] The two senators reflectively added a shared global interest for greater benefit: The United States, India, and China all share an interest in deterring terrorist activity and curbing piracy that could disrupt maritime trade.[76] American's global and commercial interests trace back to its founding as well as contemporary affairs. The Kerry–Lugar Report acknowledges:

"Sri Lanka has been a friend and democratic partner of the United States since gaining independence in 1948 and has supported U.S. military operations overseas such as during the first Gulf War. Commercial contacts go back to 1787, when New England sailors first anchored in Sri Lanka's harbors to engage in trade. Sri Lanka is strategically located at the nexus of maritime trading routes connecting Europe and the Middle East to China and the rest of Asia. It is directly in the middle of the Old World, where an estimated half of the world's container ships transit the Indian Ocean".

The new realities intersect with America's historical trade relations with Sri Lanka more than ever. As an island nation, its long-term survival is equally dependant on Sri Lanka's continuous connection to the Old World and old friends. The Report highlights that:

"American interests in the region include securing energy resources from the Persian Gulf and maintaining the free flow of trade in the Indian Ocean. These interests are also important to one of America's strategic partners, Japan, who is almost totally dependent on energy supplies transiting the Indian Ocean. The three major threats in the Indian Ocean come from terrorism, interstate conflict, and piracy. There have been some reports of pirate activity in the atoll islands near Sri Lanka".[77]

---

[74]The United States Senate Committee on Foreign Relations, 3.
[75]Ibid.
[76]Ibid.
[77]The United States Senate Committee on Foreign Relations, 12.

The shift in U.S. foreign policy toward Sri Lanka is a clear reflection of the nature of the swinging pendulum between Jeffersonian and Hamiltonian policy orientations. With President Obama, the United States regained its Jeffersonian image of global leadership through democracy and multilateralism as opposed to President Bush's conflicting message in democracy promotion in the Middle East and his unilateral approach to global issues. A realist like Alexander Hamilton, Obama has come to realize that the United States must advocate its time-honored Hamiltonian tradition in protecting American ships (both military and commercial) in the Indian Ocean. More importantly, however, the world recognizes that America's founding conviction of the superiority of democracy over other forms of government[78] has almost always shaped its foreign policy. The Kerry–Lugar Report seems to clarify the delicate yet evolving balancing act of the U.S. role in Sri Lanka.

7. The Making of the Colombo Consensus

As a maritime nation throughout its over 2500-year recorded history (compared to over 250 years of U.S. history), Sri Lanka has enjoyed friendly relations with powerful nations and rulers, and conducted trade relations with colonial America, the middle kingdom of China, the ancient Indian kingdoms, the Japanese emperors and Arab nations. In recent years, Sri Lanka's close allies (i.e., Iran and Iraq in the Middle East) moved away from the United States due in large part to changes in national security interests and dynamics of the geopolitical and geoeconomic environment. During the civil war in Sri Lanka and the recent Wall Street collapse (which restricted American support and engagement), Beijing entered into the vacuum and provided unconditional economic, military and diplomatic assistance to the government of Sri Lanka, winning unprecedented goodwill in Colombo. The last gesture of goodwill from Beijing had come during the Sirimavo Bandaranaike's socialist regime in the 1970s, when China built the Bandaranaike Memorial International Conference Hall (BMICH) in preparation for the Non-Aligned Summit in 1976.

---

[78]Robert Kagan, Obama's phase two: Leadership (October 1, 2010). *The Washington Post*, p. A19.

During his first administration, President Rajapaksa visited China five times (three times before even assuming office), and Sri Lanka recently gained significant progress when both countries signed as many as six major agreements over the renovation of the BMICH, the development of highways, enhanced cooperation in information technology and communication, and the restoration of maritime ports in addition to the second phase of the Hambantota deepwater seaport.[79] The president thanked the 30-member Chinese delegation led by Vice Premier Zhang Dejiang, who was in Colombo for a three-day official visit.[80] The state-owned *Sunday Observer* characterized the visit as emblematic of a silky relationship that reached new heights under the new administration.[81]

In the past, India's foreign policy towards Sri Lanka consisted of military intervention and peace negotiation while engaging constructively with its southern neighbor. With greater focus on trade and commerce, both countries now look to job creation, infrastructure development, and investment in businesses. In January 2010, India funded over U.S. $67 million to upgrade the Southern Railway Line from Colombo to Matara (to double the average operating speed to 80 km per hour, connecting the two cities within two hours). This complemented the previous U.S. $100 million line of credit agreement signed in 2008 by the Export-Import Bank of India. The two countries agreed to institute an annual defense dialogue and promote the use of space technology for a number of societal services. India also offered to extend the bandwidth to build satellite-interactive terminals in Sri Lanka in addition to assist in rebuilding the Palai airport, the Kankesanturai harbor, the Duraippah sport stadium and a cultural center in Jaffna.[82]

---

[79] China and Sri Lanka have a deep bilateral relationship that goes back to the Rubber-Rice Agreement in 1952 and the Maritime Agreements in 1963. See Singh, S (2003). *China–Sri Lanka Limited Access in South Asia: Issues, Equations, Policy.* New Delhi: Lancer Book.

[80] B. Muralidhar Reddy, Committed to Sri Lanka's development: China (Jun 12, 2010). *The Hindu.* See http://beta.thehindu.com/news/international/article454063.ece.

[81] Special Correspondent (Beijing), Bilateral relations at a new high: China Sri Lanka's top lender in 2009 (April 10, 2010). *The Sunday Observer* (Colombo). See http://www.sundayobserver.lk/2010/04/18/fea01.asp.

[82] Special Correspondent (New Delhi), India, Sri Lanka consider energy cooperation (June 10, 2010). *The Hindu.* http://www.thehindu.com/news/national/article451315.ece.

With the American Chamber of Commerce of Sri Lanka (an association of approximately one hundred Sri Lankan and U.S. business companies), the two countries have developed an atmosphere of cordiality and a harmonious trade relationship. Until recently, the main American investors in Sri Lanka were Pfizer Pharmaceutical, Union Carbide and Inter-Continental Hotels. Currently, there are over 85 U.S.-based companies operating in Sri Lanka — including AT&T, NCR, Hewlett Packard, Citibank, American Express, UPS, Motorola, Pepsi, Coca Cola, Pizza Hut and Kentucky Fried Chicken. All of these American companies have liaison offices and franchise operations in Sri Lanka.

The web of these relationships illustrates the complexity of balancing a variety of competing interests among China, India, and the United States, which has always been a challenge for Sri Lanka. As a tear-drop shaped island at the southern edge of the Indian sub-continent, once called Isle of Serendipity for its ever-enriching atmosphere, Sri Lanka is a place where visitors (whether tourists or powerful nations) could hardly imagine a zero-sum game — none would work at the expense of the other. In a globalizing world, every nation strategically balances its national interest in a marketplace of confluences. For example, as Sri Lanka tried to delicately balance the mutual interests of China and the United States, Secretary Clinton simultaneously called the Sino–U.S. relationship the most important bilateral relationship in the world.[83] This emphasizes the mutual interdependence for greater benefit between American and Chinese consumers and producers, as well as debtors and creditors. That description is reflected by the Sri Lankan microcosm and its growing relations with the two most powerful nations.

The American experience demonstrates the dynamic nature of global realities, which is such that nations change their allies, friends, and frenemies (i.e., friends of enemies in countries like the U.S. and Iran, for example). From America's Revolutionary War to the Cold War period, geopolitics and geoeconomics were at the core of almost all human conflicts. With the rise of China, the emerging credibility of the Beijing Consensus based on geoeconomic strategy has led to questioning the validity of the

---

[83]Yan Xuetong, What ails Sino–U.S. relations (August 3, 2010). *The China Daily.* See http://www.chinadaily.com.cn/opinion/2010-08/03/content_11084224.htm.

Washington Consensus and the conditionality imposed by the World Bank and IMF. As a case study, Sri Lanka exemplifies the realist worldview of asymmetric reciprocity, where domestic leadership matters the most in navigating and maximizing national self-interests with the interests of other powerful nations.

In 2008, Palitha Kohona, former foreign secretary (and current Sri Lankan ambassador to the UN), told the *New York Times* that Sri Lanka's traditional donors — namely the United States, Canada and the European Union — had receded into a very distant corner[84] to be replaced by countries in the East. The secretary gave three reasons: "The new donors are neighbors, they are rich, and they conduct themselves differently; then he added that Asians [referring to China] do not go around teaching each other how to behave. There are ways we deal with each other perhaps a quiet chat, but not wagging the finger".[85] Realizing the declining American influence in Sri Lanka, both Senators Kerry and Lugar comment in their U.S. strategy report that sticks do not work with the Sri Lankan Government. They need to hear coordinated, constructive messages that give them time to implement change without losing face.[86] There is a general agreement that Western donors have limited resources for massive infrastructure development projects in Sri Lanka after the economic crises in the United States and European countries. Changes in the global economic power structure naturally prompted China to strengthen its strategic ties with Sri Lanka. With a mighty neighbor to the north (home to over 60 million Tamils), Colombo has always faced a delicate balancing act with Delhi, giving rise to the so-called Colombo Consensus strategically designed to benefit Sri Lanka.[87] In statesman-like style, President Rajapaksa said the following when he visited Indian Prime Minister Manmohan Singh in New Delhi in June 2010:

"We are a non-aligned country. Our neighbors [sic] are Indians. I always say, Indians are our relations. From the time of Emperor Asoka, we have

---

[84] Somini Sengupta, Take aid from China and take a pass on human rights (March 9, 2008). *The New York Times*. See http://www.nytimes.com/2008/03/09/weekinreview/09sengupta. html.

[85] Ibid.

[86] The United States Senate Committee on Foreign Relations, 15.

[87] After the British left in 1948, there existed a long-defunct Colombo Plan within the British Commonwealth of nations.

had that culture. The whole culture, irrigation, architecture has been built up over the last 2500 years. You can't break that. But that doesn't mean we won't get commercial benefits from others. From China, or Japan, or whoever. They will come here, they will build, they will go back. India comes here, they will build and they will stay. This is the difference".[88]

During the same month, Rajapaksa welcomed the Chinese vice-premier in Colombo while sending his foreign minister to Washington (in May 2010) as a symbol of a newly-emerged Colombo Consensus to benefit all. Observing the recent development in Sri Lanka, Barbara Crossette, a prominent journalist who covered South Asia for the *New York Times* for many years, wrote in *The Nation* (in New York) that since its 62 years of independence, "Sri Lanka has never had a better chance than it has now to stamp out the last fires of ethnic hatred, violence and *mindless chauvinisms* that have left more than 80,000 people dead in civil wars across one of the most physically beautiful countries in Asia (Italics added)".[89] She then warned, "Tragically for all Sri Lankans, it looks as if its increasingly autocratic president, reelected in January on a surge of Sinhala triumphalism following the defeat of a Tamil rebel army, is determined to let this hopeful moment pass".[90] In the meantime, the island's new political leadership and nepotism lie at the center of criticism, which intensified with Sri Lanka's constitutional amendment in September 2010 to give the president supreme power over executive, legislative and judiciary matters. On nepotism, *The Economist* editorializes:

"The only urgent compulsions facing Mr. Rajapaksa and his brothers (two have senior jobs in his government and a third is the parliament's speaker) are those of parliamentary arithmetic and personal popularity. Still basking in the glow of military and electoral triumphs, the president has done in haste what he knows he can get away with. That he has preferred to put the consolidation of his family's power ahead of a sorely needed national

---

[88]K. Venkataramanan, India's views matter, don't care about the world: Rajapaksa (Jun 28, 2010). *The Times of India*. See http://timesofindia.indiatimes.com/india/Indias-views-matter-dont-care-about-the-world-Rajapaksa/articleshow/6099633.cms.

[89]Barbara Crossette, Sri Lanka Wins a War and Diminishes Democracy (February 18, 2010). *The Nation*. See http://www.thenation.com/article/sri-lanka-wins-war-and-diminishes-democracy.

[90]Ibid.

reconciliation with an aggrieved Tamil minority is a decision Sri Lanka will repent at leisure".[91]

The family political dynasty or dictatorship is not new to Asia or elsewhere in the world.[92] Referring to the concentration of political and economic power in Rajapaksa's extended family, the London-based *Sunday Times* calculates that with dozens more relatives in prominent positions, the net result is that the Rajapaksas control an estimated 70% of the national budget.[93] It also reports that there has always been corruption, but businessmen in Colombo now complain it has got to the point where you have to know a Rajapaksa to get something done. That is unprecedented when President Mahinda Rajapaksa himself heads four ministries. Gotabaya, his younger brother, is defense secretary. Basil, another younger brother, is an MP and presidential advisor. Chamal, the oldest brother, heads two ministries.[94] This characterization of the island's leadership is now synonymous with the Colombo Consensus and sets off a new international debate associated with the Chinese political debate on universal values, or *pushi jiazhi* (as opposed to American values of freedom, democracy and human rights).

---

[91] Editorial, Sri Lanka's constitutional amendment: Eighteenth time unlucky (September 9, 2010). *The Economist*. See http://www.economist.com/node/16992141?story_id= 16992141.

[92] Some argued that this is no different from the Gandhis in India, the Bhuttos in Pakistan, or the Kennedys and the Bushes in the United States.

[93] Sri Lanka's ruling dynasty, according to *The Sunday Times*, starts with Mahinda Rajapaksa (president), minister of finance, media, religious affairs and moral upliftment, and highways and road development; Gotabaya (younger brother) secretary of ministries of defense, public security, and law and order; Basil (older brother) member of parliament and senior presidential adviser on economic and international affairs; Chamal (older brother) minister of ports and aviation and minister of irrigation and water management; Shashindra (Chamal's son) member of parliament and Chief Minister of Uva province; Jaliya Wickrama-suriya (Mahinda's first cousin) Sri Lankan ambassador to the United States; Udayanga Weer-atunga (Mahinda's first cousin) Sri Lankan ambassador to Russia; and Kapila Dissanayake (Mahinda's cousin) councilor of southern province and president's coordinating secretary in Hambantota. The paper asserts that president's 23-year-old son, who only achieved a third class law degree when he graduated from London's City University in September [2009] is being groomed as the eventual successor. See Jeremy Page, Rise of Sri Lankan President's Son Namal Rajapaksa Sparks Concern (February 22, 2010). *The Sunday Times* (London). See http://www.timesonline.co.uk/tol/news/world/asia/article7035564.ece.

[94] Jeremy Page.

8. Conclusion

After the massive earthquake that killed over 80,000 people in Sichuan province in 2008, *Southern Weekend*, a newspaper magazine in Guangdong province, praised the Chinese government's rapid response (compared to Hurricane Katrina in the United States) and unleashed a new debate on government's responsibility to its people when the editorial concluded that "Beijing had honored its commitments to its own people and to the whole world with respect to universal values".[95] At a press conference at the National People's Congress in early 2007, Premier Wen Jiabao triggered his boldest-ever call for greater liberalization by advocating the adoption of *pushi jiazhi*. Wen said that science, democracy, rule of law, freedom and human rights are not unique to capitalism; he then added, "They are values that all humankind is jointly going after".[96] Beijing — with its Confucius culture that venerates authority and family values — does not seemingly reject American values of democratic governance and freedom. Instead, it redefines them.

With the Colombo Consensus depicted by Rajapaksa Family Inc., Sri Lanka has departed from its long-cherished trademark of Western-style parliamentary democracy onto a unique journey over individual rights, and embarked on a new strategy of a philosophical balancing act between Beijing and Washington. The Rajapaksa administration has equally recognized that Delhi's economic liberalization policy based on an individualistic brand of capitalism might be more robust and effective (though not necessarily efficient) in the long-run than China's state-owned enterprises system for national development (as indicated earlier, China learned that TVEs grew organically with freedom until the government began to regulate their leadership and management). In an interview with *The Asian Age* in September 2010, the president's brother and Defense Secretary Gotabaya Rajapaksa said that China's Hambantota project is

---

[95] Quoting *The Economist*, China: The Debate Over Universal Values (September 30, 2010). See http://www.economist.com/node/17150224.

[96] Lam, W (2010). Premier Wen's southern tour: Ideological rifts in the CCP? *Jamestown Foundation China Brief*, 10(18). See Category: China Brief, Willy's Corner, Elite, Home Page, China and the Asia-Pacific http://www.jamestown.org/programs/chinabrief/single/?tx_ttnews%5Btt_news%5D=36809&cHash=ea62d21370.

purely a business arrangement, and emphasized that with India, "we are not looking at government-to-government relations alone; we are interested in people-to-people ties and trade. I know that Indian investors are interested in infrastructure projects in Sri Lanka. We are studying India's successful PPP [public-private partnership] model".[97] The emerging philosophy was captured when he extended an olive branch to the Tamil diaspora: "They are most welcome. I think they must bring their know-how, knowledge, and invest their wealth here because development is the main requirement".[98] These sentiments are worth noting, but actions speak louder.

As a variant of the Singaporean model of Confucian governance under legendary Premier Lee Kuan Yew, the Rajapaksa family appears to pursue a unique development strategy within a complex environment of global realities and domestic needs. It has the Asian characteristics outlined in the Chinese government's *White Paper on Political Democracy* of 2005, which states that democracy is an outcome of the development of political civilization of mankind. It is also the common desire of people all over the world.[99] Chinese logic seems to resonate more with Alexander Hamilton than Thomas Jefferson, as expressed in America's founding debates on how to create a more perfect union for life, liberty and the pursuit of happiness. As for universal values and democracy, Jefferson has China's Dr. Sun Yat-sen on his side for the ultimate human destiny: freedom at last. For Chinese leaders, however, universal values represent a different meaning, as depicted by the *White Paper*: Democracy of a country is generated internally, not imposed by external forces. Nevertheless, this transformation from the Cultural Revolution to the economic reforms of Deng Xiaoping to the current leadership is part of gradualism for a more democratic China — not by choice or external force but by domestic necessity. The Sri Lankan people, known for championing parliamentary democracy in the developing world, will sooner or later demand the freedom

---

[97]Ramesh Ramachandran, Any country facing terrorism should follow Lankan model (September 15, 2010). *The Asian Age*, as posted in the Sri Lankan Ministry of Defense at http://www.defence.lk/new.asp?fname=20100915_07.
[98]Ibid.
[99]See the full text of the White paper on political democracy (October 10, 2005) published in *The China Daily*. See http://www.chinadaily.com.cn/english/doc/2005-10/19/content_486206.htm

and transparency once punctuated by the dictatorial socialist government of the 1970s. As democratically-transforming China realizes that the wish and will of the people [cannot be stopped],[100] wise leaders in Sri Lanka must resort to the wisdom of past as the triumphalism over the war becomes a distant memory in people's consciousness. Then will come the realization that (as Alexander Hamilton once warned), — Your people, sir — your people is a great beast.[101] Sri Lanka's ancient history has enough examples of violence and suffering, and the dictators and their families who ruled the island were often short lived or disgraced.

As host of the 2008 Olympics, China portrayed its visionary slogan of one world, one dream by reflecting its own Confucian values of social harmony and moral rectitude. Similarly, by emphasizing its deep-rooted values of individual rights and human dignity, America's invisible attraction and commercial providence[102] cannot be denied the world over as every Chinese, Indian, and Sri Lankan aspires to become more like Americans — many of the children of these national leaders (and the leaders themselves) were educated in the United States. For them, the taste of freedom is the sweetest of all; yet their journey at home is a matter of personal choice, cultural tradition and strategic calculation for self-preservation. As they know well, democracy has proven to be a better form of government than dictatorship or authoritarianism. As American history attests, the United States, with its all weaknesses, has been a self-correcting experiment with greater freedom and lower human cost than the dictatorial powers that have caused unimaginable human suffering. After all, human experience suggests that each nation — whether oriented by the Washington or Beijing Consensus — has its own path as guided by history. Yet each individual in every nation aspires for one thing: freedom. In the end, the success of the Colombo Consensus will be defined by the price of freedom for its people — not the freedom of those so-called leaders and their families who govern the nation.

---

[100] See the interview with Wen Jiabao by Fareed Zakaria, The New Challenge from China (October 18, 2010). *Time Magazine*, pp. 52–55.

[101] Alexander Hamilton, 13.

[102] See Mendis, P (2010). *Commercial Providence: The Secret Destiny of the American Empire*. Lanham: Rowman and Littlefield.

Bibliography

Alvarado, J and P Mendis (2007). New multilateralism in action for peace: A case study of the U.S.-led operation unified assistance in the Asian tsunami disaster. *Global Economic Review*, 36(2).

Bandarage, A (2009). *The Separatist Conflict in Sri Lanka: Terrorism, Ethnicity, Political Economy*. New York: Taylor & Francis.

Beeston, R. Analysis: Beautiful Diego Garcia makes forces blush (21 February 2008). *The Sunday Times*.

Bhardrakumar, MK. China breaks the Himalayan barrier (1 May 2010). *Asia Times*.

Bhattasali, D, S Li and W Martin (2004). *China and the WTO: Accession, Policy Reform, and Poverty Reduction Strategies*. Washington: World Bank Publications.

Blank, S (2010). The China–Pakistan reactor deal and Asia's nuclear energy race. *China Brief*, 10(12).

Crossette, B. Sri Lanka wins a war and diminishes democracy (18 February 2010). *The Nation*.

DeSilva-Ranasinghe, S. Sri Lanka: The new great game (31 October 2009). *The Sunday Observer*.

Economist, India and China: A Himalayan rivalry (19 August 2010). *The Economist*.

Economist, Sri Lanka's constitutional amendment: Eighteenth time unlucky (9 September 2010). *The Economist*.

Economist, The Colombo consensus: Brotherly love, massive aid and no questions asked (8 July 2010). *The Economist*.

Fein, B. Genocide in Sri Lanka (15 February 2009). *The Boston Globe*.

Fung, ESK (2000). In *Search of Chinese Democracy: Civil Opposition in Nationalist China*, 1929–1949. New York: Cambridge University Press.

Ganapathy, N. U.S. super cop role for China gets India's goat (19 November 2009). *Times of India*.

Green, L and P Mendis (2008). Chindia: Does culture matter in Hindu and Confucian economies? *Global Economic Review*, 37(4).

Hamilton, A and HC Syret (eds.) (1979). *The Papers of Alexander*. New York: Columbia University Press.

Jeremy Page, Rise of Sri Lankan President's son Namal Rajapaksa sparks concern (22 February 2010). *The Sunday Times* (London).

Kagan, R. Obama's phase two: Leadership (1 October 2010). *The Washington Post*.

Kaplan, RD. To catch a tiger (July 2009). *The Atlantic Monthly*.

Kronstadt, KA and B Vaughn (2009). *Sri Lanka: Background and U.S. Relations* (Washington, D.C., U.S. Congressional Research Service).

Lanteigne, M (2009). *Chinese Foreign Policy: An Introduction*. New York: Taylor & Francis.

Mendis, P and L Green (2008). *U.S.-India Civil Nuclear Cooperation Agreement*, A case study prepared for the U.S. Project on National Security Reform (PNSR).

Mendis, P. Passage to Indian Ocean (16 February 1986). *The Minnesota Daily*.

Mendis, P (2010). *Commercial Providence: The Secret Destiny of the American Empire*. Lanham: Rowman and Littlefield.

Mendis, P (2009). *TRADE for PEACE: How the DNA of America, Freemasonry, and Providence Created a New World Order with Nobody In-charge*. Bloomington: iUniverse Press.

Naughton, B (2007). *The Chinese Economy: Transitions and Growth.* Cambridge: The MIT Press.

Pehrson, C (2006). *String of Pearls: Meeting the Challenge of China's Rising Power across the Asian Littoral.* Carlisle: United States Army War College.

Polgreen, L. I.M.F. approves $2.6 billion Sri Lanka loan (26 July 2009). *The New York Times.*

Polgreen, L. U.S. report on Sri Lanka urges new approach (6 December 2009). *The New York Times.*

Rajghatta, C. U.S. more at ease with India's rise than China's ascent (3 February 2010). *Times of India.*

Reddy, BM. Committed to Sri Lanka's development: China (12 June 2010). *The Hindu.*

Reeves, R (2005). *President Reagan: The Triumph of Imagination.* New York: Simon and Schuster.

Revise, N. Bitter with west, Sri Lanka turns east for cash and support (3 May 2009). *Agence France Presse.*

Richardson, J (2005). *Paradise poisoned: Learning about Conflict, Terrorism, and Development from Sri Lanka's Civil Wars.* Kandy: International Center for Ethnic Studies.

Richardson, M. Full steam ahead for naval might (15 January 2009). *The Straits Times.*

Richburg, KB. China promotes likely Hu successor to key position (19 October 2010). *The Washington Post.*

Richburg, KB. In China, silence greets talk of reform (14 October 2010). *The Washington Post.*

Rodrik, D (2006). Goodbye Washington consensus, hello Washington confusion? A review of the World Bank's economic growth in the 1990s: Learning from a decade of reform. *Journal of Economic Literature*, XLIV, 973–987.

Sengupta, S. Take aid from China and take a pass on human rights (9 March 2008). *The New York Times.*

Singh, S (2003). *China–Sri Lanka Limited Access in South Asia: Issues, Equations, Policy.* New Delhi: Lancer Book.

Stanton, J. USA fears loss of Sri Lanka: Sri Lanka should become Switzerland of Indian Ocean (8 August 2010). *The Sunday Leader.*

Tisaranee Gunasekara. More freedom for the Rajapaksas mean less freedom for the Sri Lankan people (2 October 2010). *Transcurrents.*

United States Senate Committee on Foreign Relations, *Sri Lanka: Re-charting U.S. Strategy after the War* (Washington, D.C.: U.S. Government Printing Office, 2009).

Usvatte-Aratchi, G. Eighteenth amendment: A rush to elected tyranny (6 September 2010). *The Island.*

Venkataramanan, K. India's views matter, don't care about the world: Rajapaksa (28 June 2010). *The Times of India.*

Vestergaard, T. Man at work: Rudd walks Asian tightrope (17 April 2008). *Asia Times* .

Vikas Bajaj, India Worries as China Builds Ports in South Asia. *The New York Times*, February 15, 2010.

Weerakoon, G. Hambantota in the great game of the Indian Ocean (7 February 2010). *The Sunday Leader.*

Whitney Stewart (2001). *Deng Xiaoping: Leader in a changing China.* New York: Twenty-First Century Books.

William A Joseph (ed.) (2010). *Politics in China: An Introduction.*Cambridge: Oxford University Press. Williamson, J (1989). Latin American readjustment: How much has happened? In *What Washington Means by Policy Reform*, J Williamson (ed.). Washington: Institute for International Economics.

Williamson, J (1999). *What Should the World Bank Think about the Washington Consensus?* Washington: Peterson Institute for International Economics.

Yan Xuetong. What ails Sino–U.S. relations (3 August 2010). *The China Daily.*

Yao, S (2005). *Economic Growth, Income Distribution and Poverty Reduction in Contemporary China.* London: Routledge Press.

Zakaria, F. The new challenge from China (18 October 2010). *Time Magazine*, pp. 52–55.

Ziad Haider. Pakistan: The China factor in Pakistan (2 October 2009). *Far Eastern Economic Review.*

Chapter 3

Riots, Elections and Society: Discerning Social and Political Trends in India and Pakistan in Coming Decades

*Peter Mayer**

1. Introduction

Just as lightning flashes can momentarily illuminate a landscape at night, so extreme events in nations can sometimes permit us to glimpse the changing structure in society. In this paper, I will examine a series of such extreme events — communal riots — in India and consider their relationship to the timing of elections. This study is related to broader debates about the relationship between political competition and communal violence. And, to the extent that it adds to the evidence that there is a connection, it is interesting and relevant in its own right. What I want to suggest later in the paper is that the changing nature of the patterns of that violence may also throw light on our understanding of how politics is changing, and not just in India. I will suggest that we may now be seeing similar changes emerging in Pakistan.

2. Does Political Competition Play a Significant Part in Instigating Communal Riots?[1]

In 1968, as a rather naïve postgraduate student conducting his first fieldwork in India, I asked a veteran Communist trade unionist — I will refer to

---

*Associate Professor of Politics and Visiting Research Fellow at the School of History and Politics, University of Adelaide.

[1]The material in this section is adapted from my paper "Are There Political Patterns in Communal Violence in India?" presented to the 18th Biennial Conference of the Asian Studies Association of Australia in Adelaide, 5–8 July 2010.

him simply as S. M. — in Jabalpur to explain to me the origins of the Hindu–Muslim riots which had convulsed that central Indian city in 1956 and 1961. He responded — somewhat impatient at my obtuseness — that communal riots had nothing to do with religion.

> "Both of the riots were just before the elections. The rest of the time no one cared. But in elections everyone is interested. Each party tried their own methods and that ended up in a riot.[2]
>
> All these riots are political — otherwise there is no point ... [in 1956]. The Congress and the Jan Sangh organized this offensive to wrest the Muslims from the P.S.P.'s [Praja Socialist Party] hold [and influence the votes of the Hindu community]. Muslim corporators supported the P.S.P.; without them the P.S.P. would have lost. The Congress wanted to teach the Muslims a lesson: When they came to the Congressmen for help, they were told "Don't come to us for help; you vote for the P.S.P., let them protect you".[3]

I recall his observations not to assert the accuracy of his characterization of the actions of politicians in a long-forgotten communal disturbance but because they express one shrewd local observer's view of the relationship between politics and incidents of communal violence. S. M. was hardly alone in attributing a political cause to post-Independence communal violence. Asghar Ali Engineer, for example, has argued that "communalism is fundamentally a political and socio-economic phenomenon, and not a religious one".[4] Elsewhere, Engineer has stated that

> "Most riots today are pre-planned ... More often than not, communal riots are planned to serve a political purpose, and hence a political party is inevitably involved".[5]

In a thoughtful recent article comparing a riot in Bareilly in 1871 and a second in Bhiwandi in 1970, Ian Copland has observed:

> "Riots are not isolated events; they are embedded in, and mirror, to some extent, the socio-political life of their times ... What drives groups to get

---

[2]Mayer, 1970, p. 351.

[3]Mayer, 1970, p. 340.

[4]Engineer, 1989, pp. 2–3.

[5]Engineer, 1996, p. 128.

involved [in a communal riot]? In modern times, it almost always has to do with the business of winning elections".[6]

Many others[7] over the years have also asserted that communal violence is essentially linked to electoral politics.

In a remarkable study, Steven Wilkinson has used detailed data to demonstrate that political competition at the state-level best explains where communal violence will occur. Where there is strong multi-party competition — which forces parties to compete for Muslim votes — riots are suppressed. Where there is weak multi-party competition and — critically — the governing party is not dependent on Muslim votes, then communal violence is allowed to proceed.[8] Wilkinson also found a positive correlation with the level of communal riots and a state election within the following six months.[9] There was a negative correlation if a national election was held within six months. He did not, apparently, look at more distant periods from the election date.

In this paper, I use a different method and different data to explore the relationship between elections and when incidents of communal violence, measured here by homicides attributed to communal motives.

3. Methods and Data

India is a federal democracy with local, state and national levels of government. In principle, since there are elections to public office at each level, an ideal test for an association with communal violence should look at each level. We lack, however, centralized reporting of municipal elections. Equally, except for the very largest cities, we do not have data on individual towns and cities. In principle, though, a study of individual municipal elections would offer the most sensitive test of the political relationship

---

[6]Copland, 2010, pp. 139 and 141.

[7]Among those who have commented on the connection between politics and communalism in India are (Ahmad, 1996; Arslan and Rajan, 1994; Bidwai, Mukhia and Vanaik, 1996; Brass, 1997; Brass, 2002; Chandra, 1999; Damle, 1982; Dixit, 1974; Kothari, 1998; Malik, 1996; Mehta, 1998; Vanaik, 1997; Varshney, 2002).

[8]Wilkinson, 2004, passim esp. Chapter 5.

[9]Wilkinson, 2004, p. 151.

since there is a one-to-one relationship between event and location.[10] We do, however, have data on both elections and communal homicides at the state level, and it is these which are utilized in this paper which uses state-elections between 1989 and 2006. Let me begin with the pivotal elections which occurred between 1989 and 1990. This period of state elections is the first for which relevant data on communal homicides are available from The National Crime Records Bureau.[11]

3.1. *Temporal agglomeration*

In this study, I used a variation on the "temporal agglomeration" method employed by Garfinkel and Glazer to look at political signals in the U.S. electoral cycle.[12] Their study involved looking for a periodic "signal" in the average proportion of events experienced during the period in question. In their study of the timing of wage contract negotiations in the U.S., they looked at the number of contracts settled in each quarter between 1961 and 1992. They found that in years when there were both presidential and congressional elections, 50% of contracts were signed after the election. In the other years, 39% of contracts were signed after November.[13] The differences were significant at the 0.5 level.

3.2. *The 1989–1991 elections*

In this initial analysis, the following elections were analyzed: Andhra Pradesh 1989, Bihar 1990, Gujarat 1990, Karnataka 1989, Kerala 1991, Madhya Pradesh 1990, Maharashtra 1990, Rajasthan 1990 and

---

[10]Wilkinson has undertaken such a study for the north Indian state of Uttar Pradesh. Although he reports a significant positive correlation between communal deaths and a state or national election within the following six months, he did not report on the impact of municipal elections (Wilkinson, 2004, p. 45).

[11]All the data on homicides attributed to communal causes are derived from successive annual issues of *Crime in India*, published by the National Crime Records Bureau in New Delhi.

[12]Garfinkel, MR and A Glazer (1994). Does electoral uncertainty cause economic fluctuations? *American Economic Review*, 84(2), 169–173. Stable URL: http://www.jstor.org/stable/2117823.

[13]Garfinkel and Glazer 2004, p. 170.

Table 1. Number of communal homicides by election cycle year, 1989–1991.

	Election − 1	Election Year	Election + 1	Election + 2	Election + 3	Total
Andhra Pr. 89	3	1	178	113	8	303
Bihar 90	33	23	10	8	14	88
Gujarat 90	12	99	38	119	63	331
Karnataka 89	1	4	54	0	40	99
MP 90	31	46	9	93	12	191
Maharashtra 90	6	7	14	64	242	333
UP 89	39	11	151	28	41	270
Kerala 91	5	0	17	7	0	29
Rajasthan 90	18	11	0	11	0	40
Total	148	202	471	443	420	1684

Uttar Pradesh 1989.[14] For each state, the number of homicides attributed to communal motives in the year before an election, in the election year and in each of the three years after a state election were recorded. Deviations from the average for each state were then computed and the overall results for each "electoral year" summed.

When we inspect Table 1 we can see that, unlike the result reported by Wilkinson, the number of homicides attributed to communal motives rose from a relative low the year before a state held its election to an apparent peak in the year after the election. The number of murders then fell away but at a relatively slow rate.

Only 8% of the total communal murders in this five year electoral period occurred in the year before the election. 12% occurred in the year of the election. There is a big jump to 28% in the year following the election. The percentage falls slightly to 26% in the second year out from the election and by just 1% to 25% in the third year following the election.

A chi-square test of the distribution between years for the states shows that it is highly statistically significant ($p < 0000$), that is, it is very unlikely to have arisen by chance.

---

[14]The elections in this period were the first for which data on homicides attributed to communal causes were available.

3.3. *Regression analysis*

Is there more that we can say about the years in which violence occurred?

Figure 1 presents the overall summary of the differences from the mean for each state, over the five year electoral period 1989–1992. Starting from a low point in the year preceding the election, they rise to relatively high levels in the years immediately after the election. This pattern of rising communal homicides for the elections which clustered around 1990 is striking and suggests the hypothesis that, in the Indian parliamentary system where electoral terms are not fixed, there may be a tendency for violence to rise after an election, presumably in anticipation of a subsequent election of uncertain date.[15] The linear trend is reasonably strong and the coefficient of determination R^2 indicates that nearly 70% of the variance in communal homicides is described by the regression line. The largest difference between the regression line and the actual data (the "residual") occurred in the year following the election when there were 134 more deaths than estimated.

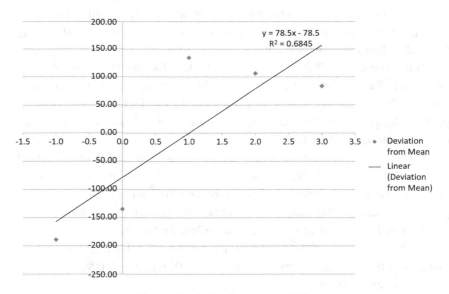

Fig. 1.   Deviation from mean, 1998.

---

[15]There were, for example, state elections in Uttar Pradesh in 1998, 1991, 1993 and 1996.

3.4. *A tactical political pattern?*

The pattern which emerges from regression analysis suggests that there may be a tactical dimension to electoral violence, at least around the elections of the early 1990s. It suggests that for what Paul Brass has called communal riot "specialists"[16] there is preferred point in the electoral cycle for riots to occur. Ideally, riots should not immediately precede the next election, whenever it may be called. A moment one-to-two years or so after an election appears to be the preferred time if the consequences of a riot are to achieve their effect.[17]

3.5. *Patterns in elections 1989–2006*

Do we find the same apparent relationship between election timing and communal homicides in subsequent elections? The figures for elections held in the larger Indian states between 1993 and 2006, which I have not included in this paper, indicate that, broadly speaking, we do. The one exception is for the elections held in the 1997–1999 period (Gujarat, Madhya Pradesh, Rajasthan, Andhra Pradesh, Karnataka and Maharashtra) when communal homicides fell in the years *after* the election.

If we aggregate the results for the 133 elections which occurred in the major Indian states between 1989 and 2006, two slightly divergent results emerge. Because of the varying number of communal homicides which have occurred in different years, an Analysis of Variance (ANOVA) test of the differences between successive electoral years is not statistically significant ($p = 0.17$), indicating that it not possible to reject the null hypothesis of that electoral years come from a single sample.

When we aggregate the long term results, on the other hand, the differences between means for electoral years is clearly apparent. As can be seen in Fig. 2, the regression line for the means closely fits the data points ($p = 0.001$). The Coefficient of Determination (R^2) indicates that 98% of the variance in the long-term data is explained by the regression equation. For each year after an election, the long-term deviation of the mean of homicides increases by 10.

---

[16]Brass, 1996; Brass, 2002.
[17]See (Wilkinson 2004, pp. 23–4 and Chapter 5) for a discussion of the incentives which may lead a party to use ethnic wedge issues to mobilize its potential supporters.

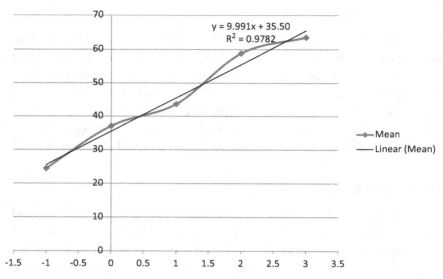

Fig. 2.   Mean of communal homicides by electoral year, 1998–2005.

3.6. *Political competition and communal homicide*

Though this repeated pattern to communal homicides is striking, there is one further aspect which requires investigation. As can be seen in Fig. 3, which presents the annual communal homicide totals between 1989 and 2008 (the bars in this chart indicate the years in which national elections were held), there were very few communal homicides between 1994 and 2001. Is there also a political variable which may explain the apparent peaks and troughs in the long-term data on communal homicides?

One possible explanation is the hypothesis with which I began: Riots are engineered to affect political outcomes. This observation is almost a commonplace amongst both commentators on the secular-Left of Indian politics and scholars. It relates to the role which those affiliated to the BJP and the "Sangh Parivar" [the "family" of organizations affiliated with the Rashtriya Swayamsevak Sangh (RSS)] in attempting to utilize communal violence to promote their political objectives.

I observed earlier that Wilkinson has found that intense two-party competition at the state level is a pre-condition of higher levels of communal violence. Is it possible that a similar argument about political competition

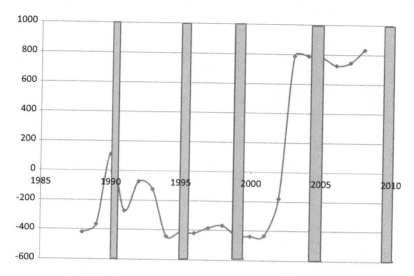

Fig. 3.   Annual communal homicide totals, 1989–2008.

can help explain the longer term patterns which we observe when we aggregate state-level data to the national level?

Because there is no obvious way to test the second part of Wilkinson's hypothesis, the degree of dependence or not on minority votes, I have sought to investigate a variant: I hypothesize that when the BJP is increasing its share of seats in the lower house of the national parliament (the Lok Sabha), especially *vis-à-vis* its major national rival the Indian National Congress, and therefore feels less urgency to use ethnic wedge issues, then there may be less perceived need to attempt to resort to communal violence. The converse of the hypothesis would suggest that when the BJP-to-Congress share of seats in parliament is declining, there may be a heightened perception of the need to manipulate social factors influencing voting intentions via communalism.

To test this hypothesis, we may start by comparing the trend of BJP vote percentage to total communal homicides in the year of an election, bearing in mind that these totals may actually be lower than those in a following year. To make the test tractable, I have used the ratio of seats won by the Congress divided by those of the BJP in the lower house of the national parliament, the Lok Sabha, (the fraction is then multiplied by 1000 to produce a number comparable in magnitude to that for communal homicides).

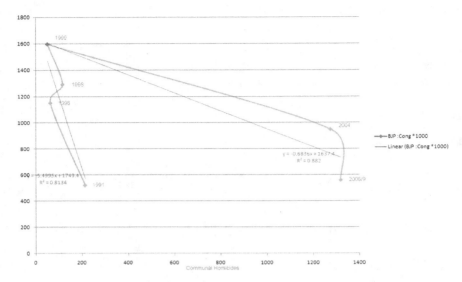

Fig. 4.   BJP, Congress ratio ∗ 1000.

Inspection of Fig. 4 indicates that there are two phases to the relationship between the changing BJP vote and communal homicides. On the left side of the graph, it is evident that between 1991 and 1999, the number of seats secured by the BJP rose rapidly, surpassing those of the Congress in the national elections of 1996. In this phase, the number of communal homicides fell rapidly. In the second phase, from 1999 to 2009, the BJP's seat share fell sharply; there was at the same time a large increase in the deaths attributed to communal motives. A piecewise regression on the number of communal deaths, using a dummy variable for the changing fortunes of the BJP, results in an R^2 value of 0.79. The overall regression is significant at the 0.09 level and the dummy variable for the increase and decrease in BJP seats is significant at the 0.07 level.

The limited number of national elections places restrictions on how confident we can be about the statistical significance of this result, but it is entirely consistent with the hypothesis that changing dynamics of electoral competition at the national level can explain changes in the amplitude of communal homicide over the period of several decades. This is a theme to which I will return in my conclusion.

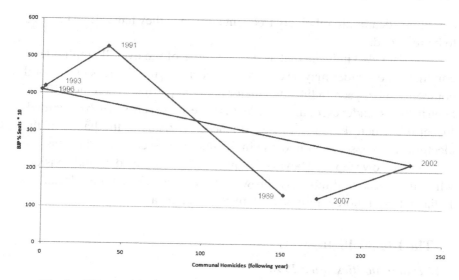

Fig. 5. UP assembly elections (BJP % seats % ∗ 10 v communal homicides).
Source: Election Commission of India (http://eci.nic.in/eci_main/StatisticalReports/ElectionStatistics.asp).

A similar pattern is evident when we undertake a comparable analysis for U.P. using the homicide figures for the year following the election (Fig. 5). Once again, from a relatively high figure in the year after the 1989 election, we observe a precipitate drop in the number of communal homicides as the BJP became the largest party in the U.P. Vidhan Sabha in 1991. In 1996, there were actually no homicides attributed to communal motives. In 2002, the BJP secured fewer seats than did either the Samajwadi Party (SP) or the Bahujan Samaj Party (BSP). In the following year, there was a huge increase in communal murders. While communal murders remained relatively high, they fell somewhat following the 2007 election in which the BJP had its poorest showing in two decades.

4. Voting and Violence

The investigation presented thus far has confirmed that there is a pattern of communal violence associated with state-level elections, though the periodicity appears to differ from that reported by Wilkinson. This pattern is repeated in most electoral periods and is evident in both periods when communal deaths are relatively frequent and when they have almost ceased to be recorded.

The data also indicate that as much as 80% of the overall amplitude of communal homicides may be causally connected to the changes in electoral competition between India's two major national parties. When the BJP has been in the ascendency, communal deaths have almost ceased to be recorded. In periods when the party has experienced reversals at the hands of the electorate, we observe a rapid rise in the numbers of communal deaths.

Let me now step well beyond the narrow focus of my data and consider what light these findings may throw on trends over the coming decade in India and even more wildly speculatively, in Pakistan.

5. The Bigger Picture

5.1. *Indian politics since 1996*

To do that, let me summarize in outline form the sweep of political developments over the past decade and a half.

6. Era of Coalition Governments in New Delhi

6.1. *The united front government — 1996*

It is a contemporary convention to point to 1991 as a turning point in Indian economic history. That is, of course, because the foreign exchange crisis of that year triggered the process of economic reforms which laid the foundations for the current period of sustained economic growth at unprecedented levels in India.

It is less common to identify the events of 1996 as of equal significance. That year marked, in my view, the final end of Congress one-party dominance of national government in India. In that year, the Congress suffered a heavy defeat in the national elections. The elevation of H. D. Deve Gowda as Prime Minister and the formation of the United Front government — an unprepossessing, ramshackle and relatively short-lived minority coalition — can nevertheless be seen in retrospect as the beginning of the contemporary era of coalition governments in New Delhi.

Deve Gowda's United Front coalition was composed of 14 parties of the centre-left who subscribed to a Common Minimum Programme. Its parliamentary majority was sustained for nearly 2 years with support from the Congress Party which was outside the coalition. Perhaps, the most important policy binding the coalition together was the joint opposition of its members and supporters to the BJP.

In 1998, the Congress Party grew dissatisfied with the lack of direction of the UF government and forced the replacement of Gowda by I. K. Gujral. The coalition limped on until late 1997 when political crises forced it to an early general election.

6.2. *The first NDA government — 1998*

The BJP and its ally the Shiv Sena secured the largest block of seats in the election held in 1998, but they did not win enough seats to govern in their own right. To form government, they too, were forced to create a coalition, this one named the National Democratic Alliance (NDA), with a major regional party from Tamilnadu which had won 30 seats, the All India Anna Dravida Munnetra Kazhagam (AIADMK) led by film-star-turned-politician, Jayalalitha.

Although she drove a hard bargain for seats in Cabinet in 1998, Jayalalitha brought the coalition down a year later by withdrawing her followers after Prime Minister Vajpayee refused her demands to dismiss her political rivals from office and to drop corruption charges against her.

6.3. *The second NDA government — 1999*

When the elections were held, the BJP campaigned at the head of a 23-party alliance, an updated NDA. The patriotic fervor aroused during the conflict with Pakistan in Kargil and subsequent military successes there seem to have redounded to the benefit of the BJP and its allies which increased their tally of seats in the new Lok Sabha. Prominent among the parties in the winning coalition were Jayalalitha's regional Tamilnadu rivals, the DMK, led by M. Karunanidhi and the Telugu Desam party of Chandrababu Naidu. Though the coalition as a whole achieved a substantial majority (299 out of 543), the BJP's own tally of seats remained almost unchanged. As we shall see, this confirmed the emerging trend of large ruling coalitions in which major national parties play a coordinating, but not a dominating role.

For the Congress Party, the election delivered a humiliating defeat — the third in a row since the 1996 elections. Major party leaders, including current Prime Minister Manmohan Singh, were defeated. The losses in states where the Congress had done well a year earlier were attributed to the inexperience of newly-installed Party President, Sonia Gandhi.

6.4. *The general election of 2004*

For the BJP, this was the "India Shining" and "Feeling Good" election. The results of the election surprised both the pollsters and electoral commentators who read the emerging evidence of voter intentions as foreshadowing a comfortable win for the NDA with increased representation for the BJP. In the event, of course, the Congress alliance won an unexpected but convincing victory. The Congress secured twice the seats it was projected to and the BJP only half those indicated by polling. The results for the two main parties were significant. The BJP slumped from 182 seats in the old house to 138 in the new. The Congress increased its representation from 114 to 145 seats.

It was confidently expected that Congress Party leader Sonia Gandhi would become the new Prime Minister. Gandhi surprised almost everyone by "renouncing" the Prime Ministership, nominating instead Dr. Manmohan Singh, while retaining the leadership of the Congress for herself. The Singh–Gandhi team worked surprisingly well during the NDA's first term in office.

Even though it was the largest single party in the new house, the Congress held fewer seats than the BJP had in the old house. Neither party was close to a majority in its own right in a Lok Sabha of 543 seats; the Congress held 29.6% of the total, the BJP 28.2%. Even with its direct allies, the Congress block held only 219 seats, 53 short of a majority. Hence, it would be dependent on support from the Communist Parties if it were to form a government. That posed problems for the Congress and the NDA coalition when contentious issues such as the United States–India Civil Nuclear Cooperation came before the Lok Sabha in 2008.

6.5. *2009 — Congress alliance returned to office*

In May 2009, India again went to the polls. The Congress-led UPA alliance was returned to office with a solid majority. Renewed organizational efforts in the party's former heartland of Uttar Pradesh paid dividends in increased seats. That pattern was repeated in other states especially Andhra Pradesh and Tamil Nadu. Growing concern over issues of corruption in the country must make it doubtful that the NDA coalition can hope to extend its term to an unprecedented third term.

7. Peering into the Future

7.1. *Trend 1: Future Indian governments will be coalitions*

There are a number of mid-to-long term trends which seem likely to continue to give shape to Indian politics in the future. The first of these is the continuing growth in the importance and political dominance of state-based parties. The rise of the DMK in Tamilnadu in the 1960s was the first wave in what has proved to be an irresistible tide. One can see the impact of this trend clearly in a graph of the proportion of seats in the Lok Sabha held by the five largest national parties since 1952.

There are a number of things to remark on here. First, the cumulative percentage of seats held by the top 5 parties has remained roughly constant at around 80%. Second, since the "sympathy wave" following the assassination of Indira Gandhi in 1984, the Congress Party's share of

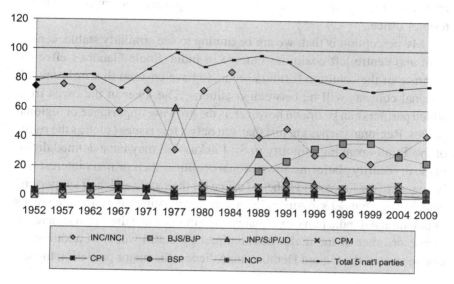

Fig. 6.   Lok Sabha seats (%).

seats has fallen from a peak of over 80% to under 30% of total seats. In part, this reflects the rise in the late 80s and early 1990s of the BJP so that the two major parties divide roughly 60% of the seats between them. That has meant that, all national governments have had to be, and as far as one can project into the future will continue to be, coalition governments.

The bifurcation of Uttar Pradesh, Bihar and Madhya Pradesh in 2001 is likely to be only the first such rearrangement of India's political geography, especially in the Hindi belt. Uttar Pradesh, for example, is arguably far too large in its present form and there is a growing body of evidence which appears to demonstrate that smaller administrative units are better governed and achieve better human development outcomes.

7.2. *Trend 2: Coalitions will become increasingly coherent and stable*

There is here, perhaps, a parallel with the experience of the traditional Liberal Party/National Party coalition in Australia.[18] There are, of course, always moments of tension in the coalition. In many seats, the partners are electoral rivals and there are always major issues which put the bonds of the alliance to the test. But equally, each of the partners has so much to lose from the breakup of the coalition that every government runs its allotted term of office.

My perception is that, we are beginning to see similarly stable, centre-right and centre-left coalitions emerge in India. Sonia Gandhi's effective embrace of the coalition formula seems to have ensured that in future, all national contests will be between coalitions. The joker in the cards from which partners can be drawn however, is the growing importance of regional parties. Regional parties are just that. On only a few issues (such as the rights of the Tamil-speaking minority in Sri Lanka) will they have defined diplomatic or security platforms. In a national coalition, their primary interest will be to secure the loaves and fishes of office for their state and their supporters. And, just as it happens in Australia, in state-level politics, they are often rivals of potential All India party candidates. That implies that their firm adherence to one or other of the major national parties is still weak. In addition, as can be seen in the United Democratic Alliance, the major parties on the left

---

[18]The new Labor/Green/Independent alliance is too recent to warrant discussion here.

are likely to continue to offer only tactical support from outside to future centre-left coalitions based around the Congress Party. But, increasingly we are seeing the emergence of similar sorts of coalitions at the state level, which suffer from similar stresses. If they become the norm as well, then the coalitions which form may reinforce the emerging pattern of stability.

7.3. Trend 3: The South is the Social and Political Fugelman of India [and perhaps of Pakistan, too?]

As a student of the comparative politics of the Indian states, it has been my view that the broad pattern of politics which became evident in Tamilnadu in the 1960s has come to apply to more and more states in India over succeeding decades. There are a number of different ways of characterizing what this South Indian pattern is, but at heart, it is a reflection of the growing assertion of a stake in the political process by those further down the social order. If the first claimants in Tamilnadu were "forward non-Brahmins" like the Mudaliars, they have been followed by "backward non-Brahmins" and by Dalits. The emergence of the Dalit-based Bahujan Samaj Party in U.P. appears to be part of this broad process of social and political mobilization.

7.4. Mayawati and the Bahujan Samaj Party — A rival to both Congress and BJP?

In April, 2007 India's giant Uttar Pradesh state held elections to its provincial assembly. It was widely expected on the basis of opinion polls that the BJP and its allies would replace the Samajwadi Party (SP) of Mulayam Singh Yadhav. In the event, it was the Bahujan Samaj Party (BSP $\sim$ Majority People's Party) led by Mayawati Naina Kumari, an ex-untouchable woman, which secured enough votes to form a government in its own right. Mayawati herself is a seasoned politician having served three times previously as Chief Minister of U.P. What was novel in Mayawati's campaign in 2007 was both her relative "neglect" of the cities and her forging of a completely new electoral alliance, enlarging her core untouchable constituency to include both Brahmins — at the opposite end of the traditional caste hierarchical scale — and Muslims.[19] The additional groups in what was dubbed the

---

[19] Strictly speaking, the alliance strategy itself was not new; it used to be part of the Congress strategy before the 1990s.

"BMW [Brahmin–Muslim–Weaker Sections] alliance" have tended to be ignored by the other major parties in recent elections'. The sweeping success of the BSP emboldened Mayawati and others in her party to think of replicating the BMW strategy in other north India states such as Madhya Pradesh, Rajasthan and even the Punjab. In the event, Mayawati's dreams of being a future Prime Minister suffered a bruising reality check in the 2009 General Elections. Her love of statues of herself, jewels and garlands made of 1000 rupee notes have certainly affected her popularity.

Note: Hindu article March 17, 2010. "Furore over Mayawathi's currency garland."

Nevertheless, the emergence of north Indian parties based on the mobilization of backward castes and untouchable marks a significant social change with lasting political implications: It may be a clear sign that the patterns of politics pioneered in south India is now becoming entrenched in the north as well.

8. The Pattern of South Asian Politics in Coming Decades?

There appear to be at least two broad political effects which arise from this broad pattern of social and political awakening. The first is that, the pattern of indirect political engagement through the intermediation of political patrons which until recently was characteristic of north Indian politics ceases to work. Let me cite as illustration a single anecdote which will have to serve in place of the many others which could be used. James Manor related an incident witnessed by Hugh Gray during the 1980 general elections.

"A group of poor peasants [in a south Indian village] came to the house of their village headman who belonged to the locally dominant caste. After offering the usual obeisances, they explained that once again they humbly asked his guidance on how they should vote since he alone possessed the wisdom to enlighten them. The headman laughed heartily but with more than a hint of irony. He told them that he knew as well as they did that this was a sham and that they would vote as they pleased no matter what he said. They replied with more earnest appeals for advice and with protests that he should think them capable of ignoring his wishes. Again he laughed, this time with genuine bitterness. The old times and old ways had gone for good, he said, and he would not allow them to mock him. He shouted at them to clear off and they hastened away, still protesting. Subsequent inquiries confirmed that their requests were mere formality."[20]

Ashutosh Varshney has argued that one possible impact of the southern style of politics is that ending social discrimination based on caste becomes a major focus of politics. Having broken free from the older clientelist system, these new elites find that they cannot secure the political power they seek solely on their own. Hence, as the recent election of Mayawati in U.P. in 2007 exemplifies, they have to forge cross-caste and cross-religious alliances.[21]

If this analysis is correct, the failure of the upsurge in communal incidents in the middle of this past decade to turn around the fortunes of the BJP in either 2004 or 2009 which was outlined in Figs. 4 and 5 may signal the growing ascendancy of the "southern pattern" in much of north India. If this interpretation is correct, one result would be the fading away and eventual disappearance of communal violence in the country. It is certainly one indicator which I will be watching in the coming decade.

Although the search for social justice has been a driving force of the entry of the subaltern classes into politics, I see significance in the ideological form in which the drive for political power has been formulated in different cases. In Tamilnadu, for example, the assertion of non-Brahmin solidarity took the form of a very powerful articulation of Tamil identity, a

---

[20]Manor 1981; see also my paper Mayer 1990.
[21]Varshney, 2000.

message which was spread with creative brilliance through the Tamil film industry by leading members of the DMK.

But, the ideology of lower-class assertion need not always be so inclusive. I think that it is possible to argue that the violent, and violently suppressed, demand for Khalistan — a separate Sikh nation in Indian Punjab — which was articulated by Sant Bhindranwale in the 1980s and which led to the bloody siege of the Golden Temple and ultimately the assassination of Indira Gandhi, was a similar subaltern mobilization for political power. If I am correct in this, then the form of the subaltern mobilization is as important as the fact of its existence.

Let me now crawl out even further on a limb and consider the northern Indian subcontinent — specifically India and Pakistan — more broadly. I have argued elsewhere that, one can discern a broad zone of poor governance which stretches from Iran to Burma.[22] Figure 7 presents a map taken from that paper which indicates the zone of poor performance on one crucial dimension of development: The achievement of female literacy around the turn of the new millennium.[23] The question I wish to touch on here is: Do the changing social dynamics which seem to characterize India apply across the border?

The broad process of subaltern mobilization which has characterized India leads me to speculate even more broadly whether the growing influence of Islamist movements in Pakistan may have more in common with the social forces which have transformed Indian politics for the past 40 years than may be apparent on the surface. The two great family-led political concerns in Pakistan, the Bhutto family party, The Pakistan People's Party, and the Sharif family concern, the Pakistan Muslim League (Nawaz) are, in terms of the analysis of India which I have just canvassed, classical elite-dominated, clientalist parties. Yet they competed reasonably

---

[22]Mayer, 2010.

[23]By 2011, the palpable changes which had occurred in the first decade of the 21st century were evident in India. In Mayawati's Uttar Pradesh, the female literacy rate had risen sharply from 34.1% in 2001 to 59% in 2011 (Census of India 2011, various years and tables). The new Nitish Kumar-led government in Bihar also achieved significantly higher levels of performance. Preliminary results from the 2011 Census of India showed that female literacy rates in Bihar jumped from only 33.12% in 2001 to 53.33%, another remarkable increase (Banerjee, 2011). The changes which have occurred in the last decade are clearly evident in the two GIS maps of female literacy included in the Appendix to this paper.

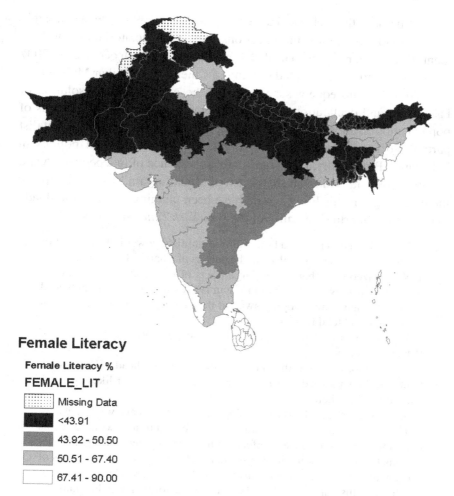

Female Literacy

Female Literacy %
FEMALE_LIT

▨	Missing Data
■	<43.91
▨	43.92 - 50.50
▨	50.51 - 67.40
□	67.41 - 90.00

Fig. 7.   Female literacy in the Indian subcontinent, c. 2000.

vigorously, at least in the 1990s until they were overthrown by General Zia.[24] Husnain offers persuasive evidence that the conventional description of the parties as "feudal" is reductionist and fails to capture the complexity of distributive politics.[25]

---

[24] Keefer and Khemani, 2005, p. 13.

[25] Hasnain, 2008, p. 139.

But perhaps things have changed slightly since 1999. It seems possible that, the evidence of mass mobilizations against the dictatorial rule of President/ General Pervez Musharraf, the mass protests which occurred in 2007 against Musharraf's attempted sacking of Chief Justice Iftikar Muhammad Chaudhry, his subsequent suspension of the constitution, dissolution of Parliament and declaration of a state of emergency, are possible signs of popular mobilizations occurring outside the sphere of the two clientalist parties. So too, I think, is the emergence of populist jihadi politics in Pakistan.[26] But equally, I see signs in the emergence of independent "ward heeling" politicians like Jamshed Dasti of Muzaffargarh, who — except for the threats against his life — could have been winning votes in Tamilnadu in the 1960s. Sabrina Tavernise of the *New York Times* says this:

> "Mr. Dasti's rise is part of a broad shift in political power in Pakistan. For generations, politics took place in the parlors of a handful of rich families, a Westernized elite that owned large tracts of land and sometimes even the people who worked it. But Pakistan is urbanizing fast, and powerful forces of change are chipping away at the landed aristocracy, known in Pakistan as the feudal class.
>
> The result is a changing political landscape more representative of Pakistani society .... .
>
> "I have more enemies than numbers of hairs in my head," [Dasti] said, bouncing down a road in a borrowed truck. "They don't like my style, and I don't like theirs."
>
> Whatever the case, he is deeply appealing to Pakistanis, who have chosen him over feudal lords for political seats several times. Local residents call him Rescue One-Five, a reference to an emergency hot line number and his feverish work habits. Constituents clutching dirty plastic bags of documents flock to his small office for help, and he scribbles out notes for them on his Parliament letterhead like a doctor in a field hospital .... .
>
> He wields his lower-class background like a weapon, exhorting local residents to oppose the rich elite and the mafias of landlords, bureaucrats and other petty power brokers who support them.[27]

There will almost certainly be a major backlash against the inadequate and incompetent response by government to the terrible Indus River floods in 2010. What we cannot foresee is what form it will take.

---

[26]For a pessimistic reference see (Hoodbhoy, 2010).
[27]Tavernise, 2010.

Social change occurs slowly in South Asia, but it is also as unstoppable as continental drift. If we try to foresee what the coming decades hold in store, the emergence of vigorous but unpredictable populist politics based on assertive lower castes and classes is as near to a certainty as there is in the social sciences.

9. Appendix

9.1. *India — Political divisions*

Source: Census of India [http://www.censusindia.net/results/2001maps/index.html] accessed 29/8/2007.

9.2. *Female literacy in India, 2001*

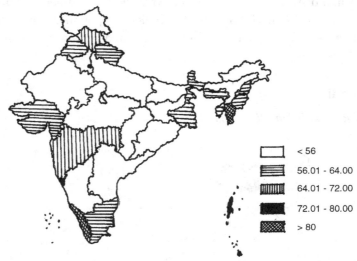

Source: Based on Census of India. 2011. *Census of India* Government of India, Ministry of Home Affairs, 2011 [cited 2011]. Available from www.censusindia.gov.in.

9.3. *Female literacy 2011*

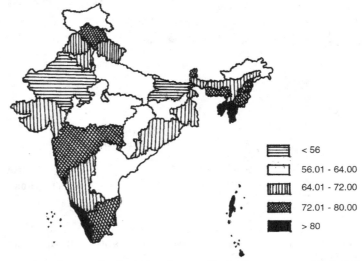

Source: Based on Census of India. 2011. *Census of India* Government of India, Ministry of Home Affairs, 2011 [cited 2011]. Available from www.censusindia.gov.in.

Bibliography

Ahmad, A (1996). Radicalism of the right and logics of secularism. In *Religion, Religiosity and Communalism*, P Bidwai, H Mukhia and A Vanaik (eds.). New Delhi: Manohar.

Arslan, Medi and J Rajan (eds.) (1994). *Communalism in India*. New Delhi: Manohar.

Banerjee, S. Massive jump in Bihar female literacy rate: Census (13 April 2001). *The Hindu on-line edition*.<http://www.hindu.com/2011/04/13/stories/2011041357801400.htm viewed 13/4/2011>.

Bidwai, Praful, H Mukhia and A Vanaik (eds.) (1996). *Religion, Religiosity and Communalism*. New Delhi: Manohar.

Brass, PR (ed.) (1996). *Riots and Pogroms*. Washington Square: New York University Press.

Brass, PR (1997). *Theft of an Idol: Text and Context in the Representation of Collective Violence*. Princeton: Princeton University Press.

Brass, PR (2002). *The Production of Hindu–Muslim Violence in Contemporary India*. New Delhi: Oxford University Press.

Census of India (2011). *Census of India* Government of India, Ministry of Home Affairs, 2011 [cited 2011]. Available from www.censusindia.gov.in.

Chandra, P (1999). *Changing Dimensions of the Communal Politics in India*. Delhi: Dominant Publishers and Distributers.

Copland, I (2010). The Production and Containment of Communal Violence: Scenarios from Modern India. *South Asia*, XXXIII(1), 122–150.

Damle, YB (1982). *Caste, Religion and Politics in India*. New Delhi: Oxford and IBH Publishing Co.

Dixit, P (1974). *Communalism: A Struggle for Power*. New Delhi: Orient Longman Limited.

Engineer, AA (1989). *Communalism and Communal Violence in India: an Analytical Approach to Hindu-Muslim conflict*. Delhi: Ajanta Publications.

Engineer, AA (1996). Communal violence and the role of law enforcement agencies. In *Religion, Religiosity and Communalism*, P Bidwai, H Mukhia and A Vanaik (eds.). New Delhi: Manohar.

Garfinkel, MR and A Glazer (2004). Does electoral uncertainty cause economic fluctuations? *The American Economic Review*, 84(2), 169–173. <JSTOR Stable URL: http://www.jstor.org/stable/2117823 accessed 27/6/2010>.

Hasnain, Z (2008). The politics of service delivery in Pakistan: Political parties and the incentives for patronage, 1988–1999. *The Pakistan Development Review*, 47(2), 129–151.

Hoodbhoy, P (2010). Why Pakistan is not a nation (June). *Himal Southasian*. <http://www.himalmag.com/tbc.php?bid=187 accessed 1/6/2010>.

Keefer, P and S Khemani (2005). Democracy, public expenditures and the poor. *The World Bank Research Observer*, 20(1), 1–27.

Kothari, R (1998). *Communalism in Indian Politics*. Ahmedabad: Rainbow Publishers.

Malik, D (1996). Three riots in Varanasi 1989–1990. In *Religion, Religiosity and Communalism*, P Bidwai, H Mukhia and A Vanaik (eds.). New Delhi: Manohar.

Manor, J (1981). Party decay and political crisis in India. *The Washington Quarterly*, 4(3), 25–39.

Mayer, Peter (1970). Mofussil: Political Change and Community Politics in Two Indian Provincial Cities, Political Science, University of Wisconsin, Madison.

Mayer, P (1990). The year the vote-banks failed: The 1967 general elections and the end of congress party dominance. In *India: Creating a Modern Nation*, J Masselos (ed.). New Delhi: Sterling Publishers Pvt. Ltd.

Mayer, P (2010). Old regions, new states: Why is governance weak in the Indus–Ganges plain? *Asian Journal of Political Science*, 18(1), 20–47.

Mehta, DV (1998). *Sociology of Communal Violence*. New Delhi: Anmol Publications Pvt Ltd.

Tavernise, S (2010). Upstarts chip away at power of feudal Pakistani landlords (August 28). *New York Times*.

Vanaik, A (1997). *Communalism Contested: Religion, Modernity and Secularization*. New Delhi: Vistaar Publications.

Varshney, A (2000). Is India becoming more democratic? *The Journal of Asian Studies*, 59(1), 3–25.

Varshney, A (2002). *Ethnic Conflict and Violence: Hindus and Muslims in India*. New Haven & London: Yale University Press.

Wilkinson, SI (2004). *Votes and Violence: Electoral Competition and Communal Riots in India*. Cambridge: Cambridge University Press.

Chapter 4

Reducing Poverty in South Asia through Regional Cooperation

Sadiq Ahmed[*]

1. Introduction

South Asia continues to grow rapidly led by its largest economy, India. This is a remarkable transformation of a region where countries have been infamously dubbed as a "basket case". Well up to the late 1970s South Asia, which includes eight countries — Afghanistan, Bangladesh, Bhutan, India, Maldives, Nepal, Pakistan and Sri Lanka — was known for conflict, violence and widespread and extreme poverty. Since the initial years after independence, the South Asian countries adopted import substitution growth strategies with heavy trade protection, curbed the growth of private firms, and introduced restrictive labor laws to protect workers. After some 30 years, the outcome of these policies turned out to be very different from what the leadership had in mind. South Asia delivered sluggish growth, continued dependence on low-productivity agriculture, low levels of industrialization, weak export performance and inadequate creation of good jobs. Between 1960 and 1980 South Asia grew at only 3.7% per year. Much of the labor force was engaged in low income activities in agriculture and informal services and some 60% of the population lived below the poverty line.

---

[*]Sadiq Ahmed is the Vice Chairman at Policy Research Institute of Bangladesh. Parts of the analysis of this paper draw from an earlier research by Ahmed and Ghani, 2010.

South Asia's prospects changed in the 1980s as it adopted pro-growth policies. It opened up markets to international competition, replaced the public sector with the private sector as the engine of growth, and improved macroeconomic management (Ahmed, 2006). The results were impressive. South Asia's annual GDP growth rate climbed to around 6% during 1980–2000, which further accelerated to 7% plus during 2000–2009. It is now the second fastest growing region in the world, after East Asia. During 2006–2008, India's GDP growth exceeded 9% per annum. Other South Asian countries like Bangladesh, Pakistan and Sri Lanka experienced average growth rates of 6%–7% over the same period. Private investment has boomed, supported by rising national saving rates in South Asia. It now attracts global attention because of rapid growth, global outsourcing, and skill intensive service exports. South Asian economies also demonstrate resilience to external shocks. For example, South Asia has weathered the global financial crisis much better than most other regions. As a result, the downturn in the average growth rate was much less severe and the recovery has been faster than in other regions.

Rapid growth has been instrumental in reducing poverty in South Asia. Poverty has come down sharply in all countries (Fig. 1). Progress has also been made in improving human development and the social indicators compare favorably with countries in other regions with similar income levels (Ahmed 2006).

2. Poverty and Regional Disparities

2.1. *South Asia's poverty challenge*

While there is much to celebrate the achievements in South Asia, there are a number of major concerns. First, notwithstanding the progress with poverty reduction, poverty remains a major challenge in South Asia. For example, using a PPP adjusted U.S. $1.25 a day measure of poverty the World Bank estimates South Asia's headcount poverty rate at 40.3% for 2005 (Fig. 2). This is the second highest rate after Sub-Saharan Africa (50.3%). In terms of number of people, this amounts to some 641 million people in 2009 as compared with 425 million poor in Sub-Saharan Africa. The sheer magnitude of poor people located in South Asia makes large scale global poverty reduction impossible unless poverty is tackled head-on in South Asia.

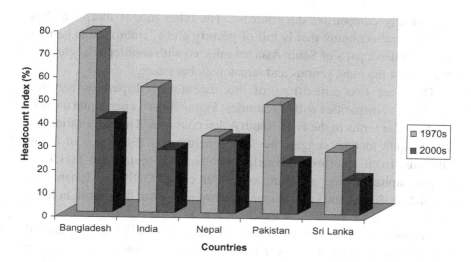

Fig. 1.   Poverty Reduction in South Asia 1970s–2000s.
Source: World Bank Regional Database.
Note: (i) Poverty estimates use national poverty lines. The respective dates are: Bangladesh (1975 and 2005); India (1974 and 2005); Nepal (1977 and 2004); Pakistan (1970 and 2005); and Sri Lanka (1976 and 2005).

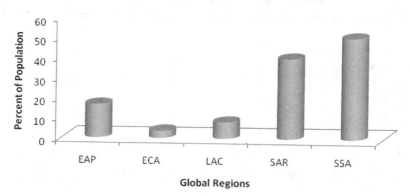

Fig. 2.   Poverty Head Count Ratio (U.S. $1.25/day PPP).
Source: World Bank 2008a.

2.2. *Regional disparities: The lagging regions problem*

The other problem is the large disparity in living standards in South Asia. As a result of this disparity, there are two faces of South Asia. One face is that of a thriving urban economy with high standards of living and functioning in a globally competitive environment. The other face is that of a slow growing rural economy that is full of poverty and is embroiled in serious conflict. Indeed, parts of South Asia are infected with conflicts that globally are amongst the most serious and threaten global peace.

There are two dimensions of this dichotomy: disparities between countries and disparities within countries. Figure 3 shows per capita income in U.S. dollar terms in the eight South Asian countries. The large variations in per capita income suggest the large intercountry disparities in living standards. Even ignoring the small economies of Bhutan and Maldives, the per capita income gaps are large. Per capita GDP in Afghanistan, Bangladesh, Nepal and Pakistan are substantially lower than those in India and Sri Lanka.

The income gaps at the national level carry through at the sub-national level (Fig. 4). During the period 1993–2004, GDP growth in the leading states in India grew at twice the rate compared to the lagging states. The average annual growth rate for the leading states (Andhra Pradesh, Gujarat, Haryana, Karnataka, Kerala, Maharashtra, Punjab, Tamil Nadu, and West Bengal) was 5.9%. The average growth rate for the lagging states (Bihar, Madhya Pradesh, Orissa, Rajasthan, and Uttar Pradesh) was 3% per annum.[1] In Sri Lanka, the leading regions grew at an annual average rate of 6.5%

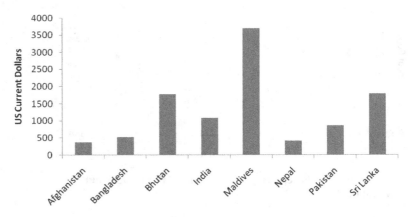

Fig. 3.   Per capita GDP in South Asia 2008.
Source: World Bank 2010.

---

[1]More recently, the lagging states of Bihar and Orissa have shown signs of economic recovery. Its long-term sustainability remains an issue.

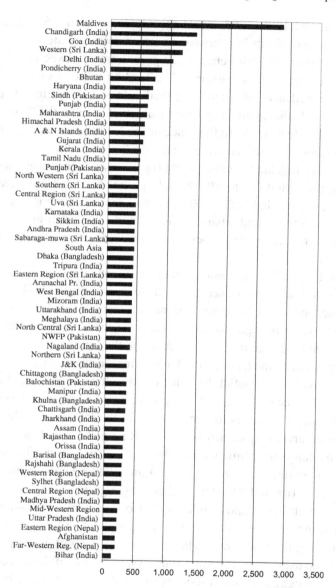

Fig. 4.   Per capita income in South Asia (2004 Constant US$).

Source: India — Directorate of Economics & Statistics of respective State Government; Sri Lanka — Central Bank of Sri Lanka; Bangladesh- Statistical Yearbook of Bangladesh; Nepal (household income per capita) — CBS and World Bank staff calculations using NLSS I and II; Pakistan — World Bank Staff; Bhutan, Afghanistan and Maldives — World Development Indicators.

during the period 1996–2005, while the lagging regions (Sabaragamua, Central, Uva, and North Western) grew at an average rate of 1.5% per annum. In Pakistan, the difference in the growth rates between the leading and lagging regions is less striking. The leading regions of Punjab and Sindh experienced an average annual growth rate of 2.3% during the period 1991–2000, while the lagging regions of Baluchistan and NWFP grew at an average annual rate of 1.8%. In Bangladesh, the leading regions (Dhaka and Chittagong) grew at an annual average rate of 5.2% annum while the lagging regions (Barisal, Rajshahi, Khulna, Sylhet) grew at an average annual rate of 4.7% during the period 1990–1999. Nepal's growth since 2000 has averaged a paltry 3%, around half of the South Asian regional average. Conflict, poor road connectivity, and urban bias associated with earlier growth spurts have resulted in a clear divide between Nepal's lagging regions and the Kathmandu valley.

Regional disparities are not uncommon in other parts of the world. Yet, the development experience of South Asia, where rapid GDP growth has been accompanied by high regional disparities, contrasts with the regional experience of high income market economies. There is evidence of convergence among regions in U.S., Japan, and the European Union.[2,3] The income gap between the leading and lagging regions in South Asia is much larger compared to the spatial disparities in developed countries. In India, GDP per head in the state where it is highest (Haryana) is five times greater than in the state where it is lowest (Bihar). In the USA, the difference is only 2.5 times, and in Japan only two times. Regional disparities are indeed expected to change over time with the level of development. The big issue is whether future developments in South Asia will bring about convergence or divergence between the leading and lagging regions.

Given the strong negative relationship between income and poverty globally and in South Asia, it is hardly surprising that with few exceptions, most lagging regions also show higher than average rates of poverty (Fig. 5). As of 2005 and using national sample surveys, some 400 million people live in the lagging regions of South Asia. Nearly 60% of the poor in India live in the lagging states. Every seventh poor Indian lives in Bihar, a lagging

---

[2] See Barro and Sala-I-Martin, 1995, Chapter 11.

[3] See European Union 2007, which provides evidence on convergence occurring both at the national and regional levels within European Union.

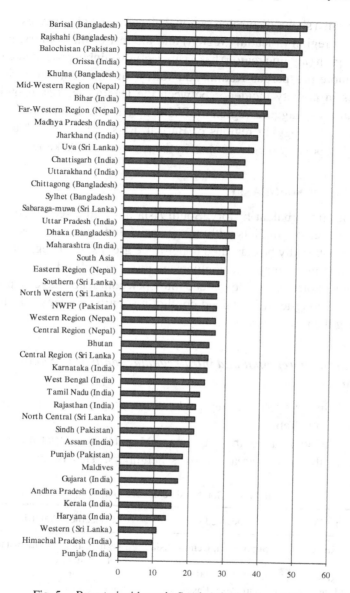

Fig. 5.   Poverty incidence in South Asia (headcount %).
Source: Pakistan — World Bank Staff; Sri Lanka — HIES 2002; Nepal — NLLS 2003-04;
Bangladesh — HIES 2005; Bhutan — IMF; Maldives —ADB.
Note: For India, data for poverty headcount rate based on 2004/2005; For Sri Lanka data
for poverty are based on 2002; Pakistan — 2005/2006; Bangladesh — 2005; Nepal —
2003/2004; Bhutan — 2000; Maldives — 2004.

state. Sri Lanka shows disturbing regional disparity in poverty rates between the Western region (a leading region) and the rest of the country. Nepal's Western region (lagging region) has a substantially higher poverty incidence than the more prosperous Kathmandu valley. In Pakistan, interprovincial disparities in poverty incidence between the leading regions (Sindh and Punjab) and the lagging regions (NWFP and Balochistan) are huge. In Bangladesh, the lagging regions of Barisal, Rajshahi and Khulna have a much higher poverty incidence than in the prosperous Dhaka Division.

3. Conflict in South Asia

Throughout its turbulent history, South Asia has witnessed a serious and recurring series of conflicts with heavy social and economic costs. These conflicts can broadly be classified under three groups: inter-regional; intra-regional; and in-country. The conflicts are inter-related and the root causes are socio-economic in nature, fanned into open conflict by adverse political pressures. A long-term, sustained conflict resolution strategy will require addressing the root causes.

3.1. *Major inter-regional and intra-regional conflicts in South Asia*

A broad listing of open inter-regional and intra-regional conflicts in South Asia is shown in Table 1.

A careful look at South Asia's map (Map 1) shows that much of the conflicts in the border areas involves neighbors. This is not accidental.

Table 1.   South Asia conflict typology.

Conflict Type	Concerned Regions	Concerned Countries
Inter-Regional	South Asia; Central Asia	Afghanistan, Turkmenistan, Tajikistan, Uzbekistan
Inter-Regional	South Asia; Middle East	Afghanistan, Iran
Inter-Regional	South Asia; East Asia	India, China
Inter-Regional	South Asia; East Asia	Bangladesh, Myanmar
Intra-Regional	South Asia: North-West Sub Region	Afghanistan, Pakistan; India, Pakistan
Intra-Regional	South Asia: North East Sub Region	Bangladesh, India; Nepal, India; Sri Lanka, India; Bhutan, Nepal

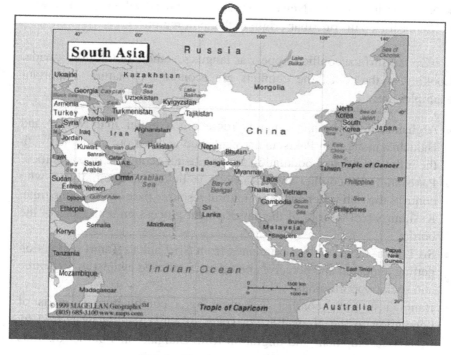

Map 1. South Asia and neighbors.

Conflicts involve long-standing territorial disputes, sharing of common natural resources (water), and religious, language or ethnic disputes. Another dimension is cross-border mobility of people seeking better economic opportunities on the other side of the border. While the conflicts have varying elements of religious, ethnic and other social dimensions, irrespective of the source, internal and external conflicts are inter-linked. Important examples are:

- Afghanistan–Pakistan conflict (Pashtun ethnicity spillover in internal Pakistan conflict);
- India–Pakistan conflict (religious divide spilling over in internal conflicts in both countries)
- India–Sri Lanka conflict (Tamil ethnicity spillover in Sri Lanka internal conflict)
- Bangladesh–India conflict (religious divide at least on the surface contributing to internal political divide)

- Nepal–India conflict (Nepali Pahadi (hilly areas) ethnic conflict with Madhesi Nepalis of Bihar origin in the terai region)

On the surface conflicts appear as language, ethnic or religious divide. Looking at the roots, the conflicts are economic in nature. Important examples are:

- Afghanistan–Pakistan conflict is rooted in a belief that NWFP and Baluchistan areas in Pakistan are neglected and left out combined with the inflow of Afghan population seeking better economic opportunities.
- Pakistan–India conflict over Kashmir is linked substantially to who controls the rich water and other natural resource base. At the same time, Kashmiris feel left out of the development process on both sides of the border.
- Sri Lanka–India conflict originates from Sri Lanka's Tamil population getting alienated and perceives being discriminated against in economic and social opportunities.
- Bangladesh–India conflict is fanned by a combination of parts of population in the North-Eastern states of India feeling by-passed by India's development and migration from Bangladesh's border districts into India seeking better economic opportunities.
- Nepal–India conflict is rooted in deep-seated perception that Nepal is not getting a good deal from its various cooperation agreements with India and restrictions on Nepal's access to other neighboring countries.
- Bhutan–Nepal conflict is linked to the ouster of Bhutanese inhabitants of Nepali origin from Bhutan and Nepal's refusal to take them back, causing these people being restricted to refugee camps in Nepal.

3.2. *Conflict, lagging regions and poverty*

At the macroeconomic level, these economic conflicts are broadly correlated with South Asia's lagging regions problem. These lagging regions, most of which are also beset with serious conflict, are either landlocked countries (Afghanistan and Nepal) or are border districts/states/provinces of Bangladesh, India, Pakistan and Sri Lanka. This is obvious from Fig. 4, Map 2 and Table 1 that show the following results.

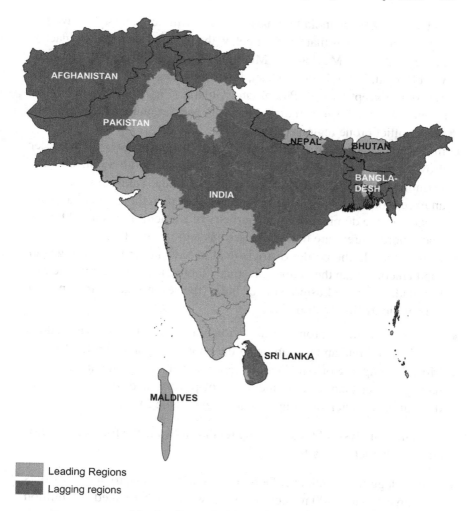

Leading Regions
Lagging regions

Map 2.   Per capita income in South Asia.

Source: Figure 4.

Note: (i) Leading/lagging regions are defined at the national level based on per capita incomes above or below the national average. (ii) Afghanistan, Bhutan and Maldives show national averages as subnational data are not available.

- The landlocked countries of both Afghanistan and Nepal are among the lowest per capita income group in the region (Fig. 4). Both are afflicted with serious conflict.

- Out of 14 states of India that have borders with neighbors, 12 have per capita income levels that are at or below the national average (Arunachal Pradesh, Assam, Meghalaya, Mizoram, Nagaland, Tripura, Manipur, West Bengal, Bihar, Uttar Pradesh, Jammu and Kashmir, and Rajasthan). The only exceptions are Punjab and Gujarat (Fig. 4 and Map 2). The seven sisters of Eastern India, Bihar, UP, and Jammu and Kashmir are also conflict prone regions of India.

- In Pakistan, per capita income is lower than average in the border provinces of North-West Frontier, Balochistan, rural Sindh and the Kashmir part of Pakistan. As in the case of India, Pakistan's Punjab is an exception. Similarly, urban Sindh is richer than the national average because of the dominance of the port city of Karachi (Fig. 4 and Map 2). These border areas are hotbeds of serious regional conflicts.

- In Bangladesh, the border districts tend to have lower than average per capita income than the national average (Table 2). The border districts of Bangladesh on the Eastern side of India (the seven sisters) are a part of the conflict region with India.

- Sri Lanka's conflict-prone Jaffna region is also a border area with India's Tamil Nadu State and it is amongst the poorest region in Sri Lanka.

- Most lagging regions in income terms are also lagging in terms of having higher than average incidence of poverty and/or poorer human development indicators (Fig. 5, Map 3, and Table 2)

Detailed analysis of these lagging regions indicate the following socio-economic characteristics.[4]

- These lagging landlocked/border countries/states/provinces/districts have an estimated 400 million people of which an estimated 200 million people are poor (reference year of 2005). This is about 50% of South Asia's estimated total number of poor for the year 2005.[5]

---

[4]Massum, 2008; Government of India, 2008; World Bank, 2005a; World Bank, 2005b; World Bank, 2005c; World Bank, 2007a; World Bank, 2008b; and World Bank, 2008c.

[5]These are based on poverty estimates from National Sample Surveys of respective countries and provinces/districts. The poverty incidence estimates are therefore different from the estimates emerging from $1.25/day PPP adjusted poverty line.

Table 2.   Population mass, economic mass and poverty mass: Bangladesh districts bordering India's North East and West Bengal (2000).

Districts	Population	Per Capita Income US$	Economic Mass US$	Human Poverty Index	Poverty Mass	Literacy rate (age 7 +) Both Sexes	Female
Bordering North East							
Bandarban	298120	339	101062680	39.77	118562	31.66	23.67
Brahmanbaria	2398254	304	729069216	37.65	902943	39.45	36.68
Comilla	4595557	266	1222418162	26.72	1227933	45.98	42.63
Feni	1240384	262	324980608	28.15	349168	54.26	51.18
Habiganj	1757665	299	525541835	34.45	605516	37.72	33.62
Jamalpur	2107209	277	583696893	41.87	882288	31.80	28.02
Khagrachari	525664	239	125633696	37.58	197545	41.80	32.65
Kurigram	1792073	282	505364586	39.42	706435	33.45	27.55
Lalmonirhat	1109343	265	293975895	35.63	395259	42.33	36.25
Maulvibazar	1612374	280	451464720	32.69	527085	42.06	38.45
Mymensingh	4489726	305	1369366430	34.70	1557935	39.11	36.26
Netrokona	1988188	303	602420964	37.06	736822	34.94	31.88
Nilphamari	1571690	261	410211090	38.50	605101	38.84	32.58
Panchagarh	836196	277	231626292	35.03	292919	43.89	37.33
Rangamati	508182	365	185486430	35.74	181624	43.59	34.21
Sherpur	1279542	277	354433134	42.98	549947	31.89	28.55
Sunamganj	2013738	262	527599356	39.44	794218	34.37	30.47
Sylhet	2555566	315	805003290	35.06	895981	45.59	41.51

(*Continued*)

Table 2. (*Continued*)

Districts	Population	Per Capita Income US$	Economic Mass US$	Human Poverty Index	Poverty Mass	Literacy rate (age 7 +) Both Sexes	Female
Bordering North East							
Thakurgaon	1214376	329	399529704	35.87	435597	40.32	35.87
Dinajpur	2642850	311	821926350	33.31	880333	36.24	33.31
Joypurhar	846696	323	273482808	35.70	302270	37.23	35.70
Naogaon	2391355	305	729363275	32.32	772886	36.91	32.32
Nawabganj	1425322	255	363457110	39.66	565283	41.68	39.66
Rajshahi	2286874	339	775250286	33.57	767704	35.98	33.57
Kushtia	1740155	320	556849600	35.78	622627	36.79	35.78
Meherpur	591436	318	188076648	36.01	212976	36.91	36.01
Chuadanga	1007130	305	307174650	32.11	323389	34.02	32.11
Jhenaidah	1579490	317	500698330	32.37	511281	35.74	32.37
Jessore	2471554	357	882344778	28.20	696978	30.77	28.20
Satkhira	1864704	309	576193536	31.74	591857	35.53	31.74
Dhaka	**8511228**	**758**	**6451510824**	**26.51**	**2256327**		
Bangladesh	**124355263**	**355**					

Note: Population data refer to 2001, per capita income data refer to 1999/2000, and human poverty index refers to 2000.
Source: Massum 2008.

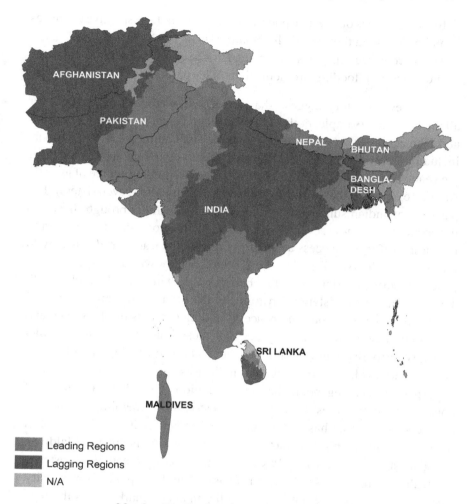

Map 3.   Distribution of poverty in South Asia.

Source: Figure 5.

Note: Afghanistan, Bhutan, and Maldives show national poverty rates.

- Much of the population is rural (90%) and most are engaged in low-productivity agriculture.
- The human development indicators tend to be below the comparable national average and many indicators are lower than the average in South Asia.

- Infrastructure is on average poorer than the rest of the respective countries and poorer than the average for South Asia.
- The border regions on average tend to be more vulnerable to water shortages and flooding problems than other parts.

A review of history suggests that not all areas were lagging and poor for all the time. For example, both Afghanistan and Nepal prospered in the 18th and 19th centuries on the basis of free trade and commerce with neighbors including Central Asia, Middle East, Indian sub-continent and China. Over the years, conflict and border restrictions removed this key source of growth. Another example is that of North-East India (the so-called seven sisters). The partition of Indian subcontinent into Pakistan and India brought havoc to the economies of these seven sisters, especially the booming state of Assam, by cutting off its sea-access and sharply raising the transport distance with the rest of India (see Box 1). The Kashmir valley was a prosperous and peaceful tourist resort until conflict between Pakistan and India took its toll. The Federally Administered Territories of Pakistan (FATA) and the NWFP were similarly prosperous and peaceful trading outposts until regional and global conflicts converted many parts of these border areas into conflict prone, security risk regions with low per capita incomes, high incidence of poverty and low human development indicators.

Apart from being poor, the lagging regions also share a number of common vulnerabilities. First and foremost is the vulnerability to natural disasters. South Asia has lost a significant amount of its GDP because of natural disasters. This loss has been especially significant for Maldives, Bangladesh, Sri Lanka and Pakistan. The impact of natural disaster is particularly strong in South Asia because of its high population density. The losses are typically not insured in the financial market. It is the poor who are adversely affected by disasters.

A second and related vulnerability is the access to water for irrigation and transport. An estimated 500 million people, many of whom are poor, directly or indirectly depend on the water flows of the three mighty rivers of Indus–Ganges–Brahmaputra for their livelihood. Frequent water shortages (and floods) create serious challenges to maintaining the income level of this large number of poor people.

Box 1. Bangladesh and India: A Tale of two border regions

India's North East and West Bengal lag behind the rest of India in per capita gross state domestic product (GSDP). So do the Bangladesh districts adjoining West Bengal and India's North East. These districts have considerable similarities such as predominantly agricultural base (agriculture accounting for the largest share of employment); narrow manufacturing base; and low levels of consumption of electricity which significantly constrain their growth prospects. The three hill districts of Bangladesh have large shares of tribal population, so do three states of India's North East, and people of both subregions have been practicing the same low productive agricultural technology featuring shifting cultivation called *Jhum* for generations. The two regions formed a single economic entity under the British rule, shared common infrastructure and developed close linkages which contributed to economic growth of both regions. Partition of British India in 1947 into two separate states, India and Pakistan, and the two regions falling in two countries which did not maintain friendly relations, caused havoc to the economy of India's North East, as sudden snapping of all economic linkages made its economy extremely vulnerable besides converting it into a virtually land locked region. The adjoining Bangladesh (then East Pakistan) districts also suffered by losing their traditional sources of supplies and markets for their products, but as they retained most of the common infrastructure including access to the sea, and thereby to the outside world, their situation was not as bad. Their growth performance, however, indicate that they performed relatively poorly compared to most other Bangladesh districts. So did Bangladesh districts bordering West Bengal. With the emergence of Bangladesh as an independent country in 1971, it was expected that the linkages earlier lost would be restored, but little progress has been made so far in this direction. It is, however, believed that improved economic linkages between India's North East and West Bengal, and the adjoining Bangladesh districts, would promote development of all these regions.

Source: Massum (2008)

A third vulnerability is exposure to climate change. The adverse effects of climate change on weather pattern, natural disasters such as flooding, and rising sea level have serious implications for the poor who are much more exposed and less well equipped to cope with climate change effects.

3.3. *Politics and conflict: Who gains from conflict*

It is clear that conflict and poverty are correlated. There is also a vicious reinforcing mechanism: Poverty fans conflict and conflict worsens poverty and human deprivation. Conflict has a tendency to be self-sustaining, especially if this conflict is low-intensity and provides a political forum to acquire and retain a strong political base. Conflict hurts poverty, yet it prevails over a long period of time. So, somebody must gain from conflicts. Who gains? There are indeed several special interest groups who benefit from conflict.

- Military: Higher defense budget and strong voice in civil administration
- Politicians: Anti-neighbor stance often helps drum political support at home
- Business: Trade and investment barriers help protect inefficient enterprises
- Rent seekers: Trade barriers support a flourishing illegal trade with huge financial gains

Collectively, they can be a powerful lobby for status quo. Some specific examples will illustrate these points.

- Kashmir conflict underpins large defense budgets in Pakistan, an estimated 5% of GDP per annum that is almost twice that of public expenditure on health and education. Additionally, owing to conflict with India, the Pakistan military has an exceptionally strong voice in national administration.
- Kashmir conflict is also a rallying point for major political parties in both Pakistan and India.
- Anti-India sentiments have drummed up support for major political parties in Bangladesh and Nepal.

- Reduction of trade and investment barriers with India is opposed by a large segment of local enterprises in Bangladesh and Pakistan owing to the fear that Indian enterprises might out-compete local enterprises.
- Illegal trade flourishes in Afghanistan, Bangladesh, India and Pakistan with huge losses for the Treasury but large gains for the smugglers.
- Large number of studies has shown that illegal trade between Pakistan and India far exceeds legal trade.

Status quo will not be easy to break. What is the way out? At the national level, strong leadership from the top can break this cycle. Public opinion based on informed analysis, debate and discussions can also help. At the multilateral level support from regional organizations such as the SAARC can play a positive role. The UN organizations and OEDC country leaderships may also be able to help out in breaking this vicious cycle.

4. Regional Cooperation for Poverty Reduction

Why some areas grow faster than others is determined by three key drivers: movement of productive factors, transportation costs, and scale economies. This is derived from spatial economics — the study of where economic activity takes place and why.[6]

There are two types of geography — first and second nature geography. First nature geography favors some regions by virtue of endowments of proximity to rivers, coasts, ports, and borders. Economic activity may concentrate in coastal urban areas because of proximity to the domestic and external markets, and better logistical link between foreign suppliers and customers, than can interior based industry. First level geography explains why some leading regions are located in coastal areas (Maharashtra, Gujarat, and Tamil Nadu in India; Karachi in Pakistan; Chittagong in Bangladesh; and Colombo in Sri Lanka). Real GDP per capita growth rates for the coastal states in India grew at 4.5% per annum during the 1990s compared to 2.5% for the land locked states. Second nature geography is determined by human made infrastructure. Physical infrastructure influences the interactions

---

[6]Fujita, Krugman and Veneables, 1999; World Bank, 2008f.

between economic agents. Improved infrastructure lowers transportation costs, encourages mobility of labor, goods, capital, and ideas, and increases the size of the market. These interactions give rise to scale economies. As agricultural productivity increases, it releases labor and capital from rural areas, which migrate to urban areas, to take advantage of agglomeration forces. Regions with a higher urbanization rate tend to have higher productivity. These forces can generate virtuous circles of self-reinforcing development. Empirical studies identify the second nature geography — physical infrastructure — as a *key* causal factor in explaining level and trend in regional disparities (see Kanbur and Veneables, 2005).

Geographic, institutional, and trade differences are larger in South Asia compared to Japan, Europe and USA. In Japan, nearly 97% of people live within 100 km of the coast. In Europe, more than half the population lives within 100 km of the coast or an ocean navigable waterway. USA is more like India with a large proportion of the land area away from coast. But because of high labor mobility and an efficient agriculture in USA, a high proportion of the population lives close to the coast. In India, factor mobility has not been able to arbitrage geographical disparities. Lagging regions in South Asia suffer from poor connectivity due to poor infrastructure and policy-induced barriers to regional trade, transport connections and mobility of people.

In addition to enabling national policies, regional cooperation can be instrumental for raising growth in the border lagging regions, thereby reducing the gap between leading and lagging regions. Better regional cooperation can help accelerate growth and reduce poverty by supporting market integration and by strengthening infrastructure, drawing on the geography and density aspects of South Asia. Better cooperation can also sharply reduce vulnerabilities for South Asia's poor through sustainable solutions to water management and climate change. Benefits of cooperation in terms of income gains and lower poverty rates can be a powerful and sustainable instrument for breaking political gridlocks and reducing conflict.

Specifically, it can be argued that South Asia has the potential to accelerate growth and reduce poverty by exploiting four underutilized spatial features of the region: geography, transportation, factor mobility, and scale economies. Regional cooperation can facilitate this process.

- First, South Asia is densely populated, with a significant proportion of the population living close to the borders between countries. After Europe, South Asia has the largest concentration of people living close to the border. It has the maximum "city pairs" within 50 km with a population of more than 25,000 people. Almost all the South Asian countries share a common border with the largest regional partner (India). Regional integration initiatives will unlock the growth benefit of geography and support income convergence across regions and countries. Regional trade is more sensitive to transport costs, scale economies and factor mobility than global trade.
- Second, South Asia suffers from high trade and transportation costs compared to other regions because of border restrictions and poor transport. The cost of trading across borders is nearly double for India and Bangladesh compared to China. It is more than three times higher for Afghanistan, Bhutan and Nepal. The quality of transport infrastructure, especially the highway networks, in South Asia is poor. Truck operating speeds are low, delays at state/provincial check posts are frequent and can be long, and delivery times are consequently subject to significant variation. The regions away from the main trade corridors have the poorest infrastructure and face the greatest constraints. Raising the level of the infrastructure and reducing regulatory barriers to trade, whether international or national, will help integrate the lagging regions into both the national and global economies, reducing the relative advantages of the coastal states.
- Third, factor mobility, and in particular migration rate, is low in South Asia. Only two million people migrate every year in India from rural to urban areas, compared to nearly 20 million people in China. Increased agricultural productivity will help to reallocate labor and capital from low value activities (agriculture) to high value activities (manufacturing and services sectors) and support growth.
- Fourth, South Asian firms are disproportionately small. They are unable to reap the benefits of scale economies because of labor and regulatory restrictions which prevent them from growing. The policy changes aimed at taking advantage of the interactions between geography, transportation, factor mobility, and scale economies will lift growth not only in the lagging regions but also support higher growth economy wide.

4.1. *Regional cooperation for supporting growth in the lagging regions*

In terms of policy focus, the two main ways by which regional cooperation can foster higher growth in South Asia and especially in the lagging regions is by promoting market integration and by improving infrastructure.

4.1.1. *Market integration*

Market integration allows economic agents to interact across spatial scales: local, regional, and international. The extent to which economic agents take advantage of market integration is impacted positively by density, but negatively by both distance and division.[7] A high level of economic density implies "thick markets" in the exchange of goods and services, as well as in the informal exchange of ideas. This creates productivity advantages for firms and welfare advantages for workers. By contrast, a high level of distance to density denies economic agents the opportunity to access these markets with consequent negative impacts on poverty and well-being.[8] Likewise, divisions, created by conflict, transport costs and both formal and informal barriers to trade, separate economic agents in one country from the advantages of density in other countries. By reducing distance and division, market integration, both within and between countries, brings economic agents in lagging regions closer to the density of leading regions, promoting positive spillover effects which enhance spatial multipliers.[9] Given that South Asia is the most densely populated region in the world, it is well placed to bring areas close to the market and bolster the value of the spatial multiplier. Market integration (global, regional, and within country) can ignite growth, as countries benefit from increased demand, agglomeration and scale economies, improved factor mobility, and the free

---

[7] See Fujita, M, P Krugman and A J Veneables (1999).

[8] Distance here is to be interpreted as an economic and social concept, rather than a purely physical concept. As such, a location which is physically close to a region of high density can, in principle, still be economically distant. This will be the case, for example, if the quality of spatially connective infrastructure linking the two areas is poor or there are economic, social and institutional barriers to commuting and the free flow of labor between the areas.

[9] A spatial multiplier is a concept which captures the additional beneficial effects which result from a policy change as a result of the feedback from spillovers between neighboring regions.

flow of ideas and technology. Market integration can pull weak countries towards income levels that they would be unable to achieve in isolation. Land locked countries, in particular, (Afghanistan, Nepal) can benefit from cross-country growth spillovers and neighborhood effects. Neighboring countries can provide mutually beneficial economic linkages, spillovers, and complementarities that allow groups of countries to increase their incomes.

The region has significantly more room to benefit from market integration globally, across countries within South Asia, and within country. Globally, South Asia's rapid GDP growth benefited from rapid expansion in trade. Yet, the region has more room to benefit from trade. Despite recent reforms, South Asia continues to have the most restrictive tariff policies compared to other regions (Fig. 6). Among developing countries, South Asia has the most protective trade policies.

Within South Asia, market integration is the lowest in the world as reflected by official intraregional trade between countries being less than 2% of GDP for South Asia compared to 40% for East Asia. Border barriers to trade and services have mostly disappeared in the rest of the world but not in South Asia. Divisions across countries in South Asia have increased dramatically over the last four decades.[10] In 1948, South Asia's share of intra-regional trade as a share of total trade was 18%. In 2000–2007, it fell

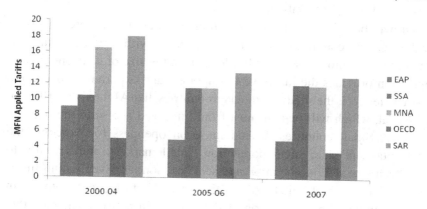

Fig. 6.   Trade tariff restriction index.
Source: World Bank World Trade Indicators 2008d.

---

[10]Borders and divisions are not the same thing. Borders define a nation state whereas divisions influence the flow of people, goods, services, capital, ideas and technology across borders.

to 5% of total trade. Cost of trading across borders in South Asia is high. At the Petrapole–Benapole, one of the main borders between Bangladesh and India, trucks wait for more than 100 hours to cross the border. It takes 200 signatures in Nepal to trade goods with India, and some 140 signatures in India to trade goods with Nepal. It is estimated that trade between India and Pakistan, currently at U.S. $1 billion,[11] could jump to U.S. $6 to 10 billion, if divisions were removed. Divisions in South Asia have been aggravated by conflict.

The geographical configurations of South Asia contain huge agglomeration potential to propel growth.[12] East Asia is an example of a region with a high level of intra-regional trade and intra-industry trade that enabled firms to internalize externalities arising from agglomeration (Gill and Kharas, 2007). Firms exporting to the regional markets in South Asia are more constrained by the quality of connectivity and productivity enhancing infrastructure. It is the seamless interaction of improved trade, better connectivity, and converging institutions that can accelerate growth in the lagging regions, and benefit the slower growing and smaller land locked regions and countries. In Latin America, Brazil's growth creates export opportunities for Bolivia. In Africa, resource landlocked countries piggy-backed on the growth of Kenya. In East Asia, Thailand is an important market for Laos and Cambodia.

Growth benefits of market integration are likely to be more important for the smaller economies. India, a large country, with a big home market, can get by with more restrictive borders, since the size of its economy and population provides the incentive to importers and exporters to overcome these barriers. It is the small, landlocked countries, like Afghanistan, Bhutan, and Nepal, which will benefit most from improved access to the markets of others. Small countries depend more on openness to overcome the disadvantage of size: small population, small markets, and inability to take advantage of agglomeration and scale economies. Even within India, the peculiar geography that isolates the seven North-Eastern states from mainland India with the location of Bangladesh in-between suggests that

---

[11] Includes both formal and informal trade.

[12] For example, given the large economies of scale in services industries (e.g., telecoms), incentives to invest are greater if the markets are not segmented from other the neighboring countries.

market integration requires trade and transit arrangements with neighbors to benefit all regions that are lagging and isolated from the growth centers. Tradable economic activities are inherently scalable in the sense that small economies can expand output without running into diminishing returns (unlike domestic services).

Rapid economic growth, associated with modern sector export growth, can be "lumpy" (Venables, 2006). Spatially, it can be uneven, with production being concentrated in some countries, regions or cities. In product space, specialization is likely to increase, with regions specializing in a few tasks rather than production of integrated products. Examples of specialization from South Asia include information and communications technology (ICT) service export from Bangalore in India; shirts, trousers and hats exported from Bangladesh; and exports of bed linen and soccer balls from Pakistan. Temporally, rapid growth will happen only once some threshold level of capabilities has been reached. Some countries may experience growth before others, resulting in sequential rather than parallel growth. The benefits of market integration, however, cannot be achieved without improving the infrastructure.

4.1.2. *Infrastructure*

Improved infrastructure that enhances connectivity and contributes to market integration is the best solution to promoting growth as well as addressing rising inequality between regions. The Ganga Bridge in Bihar in India is a good example of second-nature geography. The bridge has reduced the time and monetary costs of farmers in the rural areas in north Bihar to reach markets in Patna, the largest city in Bihar. The Jamuna Bridge in Bangladesh is another good example of spatially connective infrastructure. The bridge has opened market access for producers in the lagging Northwest areas around the Rajshahi division. Better market access has helped farmers diversify into high value crops and reduced input prices.

So far, South Asia has achieved impressive growth rates despite poor infrastructure. This may be difficult to sustain in the future. Poor infrastructure is a key factor that has restrained the growth of manufacturing sector and prevented firms from growing.[13] The service sector in South

---

[13] See Fernandez and Pakes (2008).

Asia, led by India, has done well because it relies less on transportation and is less energy intensive than manufacturing. South Asia has the highest share of services in its exports at 31%, which is higher than OECD high income countries. Information and Communications technology exports and global outsourcing have benefited from the use of the internet which has reduced information transmission costs dramatically. While other countries can emulate India's successful efforts to boost services export, sustained high growth will require a substantial effort to raise manufacturing growth in all South Asian countries.

South Asia suffers from three infrastructure deficits. First, there is a *service deficit*, as the region's infrastructure has not been able to keep pace with a growing economy and population. Power outages and water shortages are a regular occurrence in India and Bangladesh. Rural roads are impassable in lagging regions in India (e.g., Bihar, Uttar Pradesh) and Sri Lanka. India has 6000 km of four lane highways and China in the last 10 years has built 35,000 km of four to six lane highways. Every month, China adds power capacity equivalent to what exists in Bangladesh. Second, South Asia suffers from a *policy deficit*, given highly distorted pricing, poor sector governance and accountability, and weak cost recovery. It is estimated that eliminating the financial losses from the power and water sectors alone would provide a substantial chunk of the incremental funds for infrastructure investment that India needs. Third, South Asia suffers from a *cooperation deficit*. India, one of the energy thirstiest nations sits next to an immensely energy rich neighbor, Nepal. Yet there is very little exploitation of Nepal's hydropower potential because of inadequate cooperation with India. Similarly, India, which has attracted global attention in ICT, contrasts with other South Asian countries that are lagging in ICT. In South Asia, only 7% of the international calls are regional compared to 71% in East Asia.

South Asia needs to overcome a huge gap in infrastructure. It has invested only 3%–4% of GDP per year in infrastructure over the period 2000–05. This is lower than what the East Asian countries have invested: Vietnam and China invested around 8%–10% of GDP. In 1980, India actually had higher infrastructure stocks — in power, roads and telecommunications — but China invested massively in infrastructure, overtaking India by 1990 and the gap is currently widening. It is estimated that for the South Asia region to sustain a growth target of 8%, it will require an investment in infrastructure amounting to 8% of GDP per year (Harris,

2008). Higher growth rate in the 10% range will require an even more rapid pace of investment to modernize the infrastructure.

Much of the infrastructure investment gap has to be financed at the national level along with necessary improvements in sector policies and institutions. Yet, regional cooperation can be of great help to meet a significant part of this need. The three priority areas for regional cooperation include telecoms and internet, energy, and transport. A regional telecom network and a high-bandwidth, high-speed internet-based network could help improve education, innovation, and health by facilitating better flow of ideas, technology, investments, goods and services. It would enable greater interactions between knowledge workers in areas such as high-energy physics, nanotechnology and medical research. There are untapped positive synergies at the regional level that would come from information sharing and competition in ideas among universities, nonuniversity research and teaching entities, libraries, hospitals, and other knowledge institutions. It also could help in the building and sharing of regional databases, and in addressing regional problems, including multi-country initiatives such as flood control, disaster management, climate change, and infectious disease control. Importantly, such an effort could help spark higher and more sustainable regional growth.

Regional cooperation in telecoms and the internet could strengthen the competitiveness of South Asia in the services-export sector. India has established itself as a global player in ICT and outsourcing. Other countries in South Asia could potentially benefit from neighborhood and spillover effects. The expansion of services exports would contribute to growth, create jobs, and other sectors would benefit from improved technology and management.[14] The service-export sector, although less infrastructure intensive than manufacturing, needs different types of infrastructure than the traditional export sectors. For these exports, there would be a need to invest in fiber optic highways, broadband connectivity, and international gateways and uplink facilities. Investments in tertiary education and in technical and English proficiency would need to be increased. South Asia would need to remove barriers to trade in ICT services, eliminate restrictions on the flow of intraregional FDI, and remove visa restrictions on the flow of people.

---

[14]Hamid, 2007.

The potential gains from regional trade in energy are substantial (World Bank, 2008e). This is best seen by looking at Map 4 that shows South Asia's potential sources of hydro-power (black) and its demand (gray). The Map tells a powerful story. Afghanistan and Nepal are sitting on water resources that could potentially generate some 24,000 MW of electricity from Afghanistan and an estimated 83,000 MW from Nepal. These together account for 40% of South Asia's presently installed capacity. Bangladesh, India, and Pakistan are all power deficit countries, especially India. The growing electricity constraint is threatening the ability to sustain rapid growth. Yet, less than 1% of this potential has been used so far. The reason is lack of cooperation and absence of energy trade among South Asian countries. Indeed, if one were to imagine South Asia without borders, perhaps the highest priority investment would have gone to develop the hydro-power resources. While all countries would benefit from the development of South Asia's hydro-power resources, Afghanistan and Nepal, the two poorest South Asian countries, would benefit most.

After decades of insignificant cross-country electricity trade and the absence of any trade in natural gas through pipelines, regional political leaders and businessmen have recently evinced a great deal of interest and enthusiasm in cross-border electricity and gas trade, not only within South Asia but also with its neighbors in the west (Central Asia and Iran) and in the east (Myanmar). There are two regional energy clusters in South Asia. The Eastern market includes India, Bangladesh, Bhutan, Nepal, and Sri Lanka, extending to Myanmar, and the Western market includes Pakistan, Afghanistan and India, extending to Central Asia and Iran. India bridges the two clusters. A number of activities are underway in the Eastern market including a very successful hydro-power trade between Bhutan and India, electricity trade between India and Nepal, and electricity grid connection between India and Bangladesh. Activities in the Western market are less developed, although an ongoing project if successfully implemented will bring electricity from Tajikistan and Kyrgyzstan to Afghanistan and Pakistan.[15]

---

[15]This is the Central Asia-South Asia (CASA) energy project that seeks to sell 1000 MW of surplus power from Tajikistan and Kyrgyzstan to Afghanistan and Pakistan. The project is being developed in cooperation with a number of multi-lateral financial institutions including the World Bank.

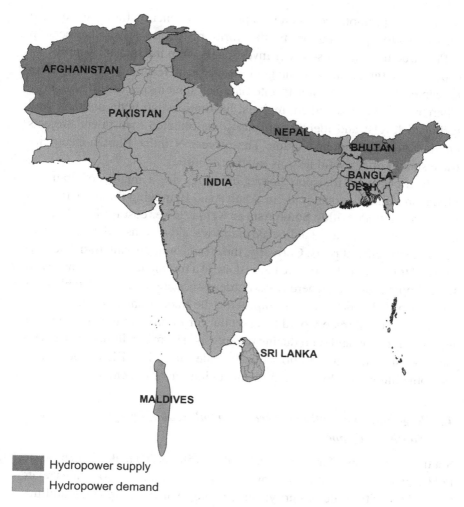

Map 4.   Distribution of hydro power potential.
Source: World Bank 2008e.

What can governments do to promote energy trade? They need to continue reducing political and security tensions; consider energy trade as enhancement of energy security and political and economic cooperation; continue energy sector reforms; improve commercial performance of the utilities; improve the credibility, competence, and accountability of regulation; adopt sustainable (cost-reflective) tariffs and a social protection framework; promote commercial approach to energy trade; encourage private sector participation in the form of public–private-partnership (PPP) structures in cross-border investments; help the transit countries — especially Afghanistan — integrate; engage in reaching water sharing agreements; seek accession to international agreements (such as Energy Charter Treaty); strengthen regional institutions at both political and technical levels; and identify priority trade-oriented investment projects and pursue their implementation. The success of India–Bhutan electricity trade should offer useful lessons to other countries.

Restrictions in transport border crossings are a major constraint to global and intra-regional trade in South Asia. Removing these restrictions would boost trade within South Asia as well as lower cost for international trade in general as many landlocked countries and regions will benefit from access to the closest ports. Currently, the efforts at improving trade facilitation and transport networks are being done in a fragmented manner and with little cooperation even where cross-border issues are involved. Establishing corridor-based approaches for improving the trade–transport arrangement for intra-regional trade would be essential for improving the efficiency of regional transport and for reducing trade costs. The recent initiative between Bangladesh and India to allow transit trade via rail and land routes is a welcome initiative. However, implementation remains a challenge.

4.2. *Regional cooperation for reducing vulnerabilities of South Asia's poor*

South Asia's poor suffer from several vulnerabilities that make them prone to fall frequently in and out of the poverty trap. The major vulnerabilities relate to: food security; water security; and climate change. These vulnerabilities are interlinked primarily through the management of South Asia's water resources.

5. Regional Cooperation For Food Security

The magnitude of the extent of trade shock along with the acceleration of food prices, especially staple food grains of wheat and rice, during 2006–2008 clearly imposed a tremendous burden on South Asian countries, especially on the low income economies of Afghanistan, Bangladesh and

Nepal. Governments responded in varying degrees to contain the rise in prices as well as to mitigate the adverse effects on the poor. Yet, the negative impact was substantial. While the subsequent decline in food and fuel prices are a welcome development for South Asia, this gain has been clouded by the onslaught of the global financial crisis that has lowered exports, investment and economic growth. Furthermore, food prices have been climbing in 2010.

Policies taken by the government in the first round were aimed at stabilizing food prices. Some of the policies like trade bans, price controls and subsidies may have been justifiable as short-term response on political economy grounds, but they have adverse implications for efficiency and resource allocation over the longer term. As well, the fiscal space is scarce and the magnitudes of the subsidies entailed are not likely to be sustainable. Finally, the longer term agenda of addressing the supply side aspects of the food security challenge remains to be fully tackled. At the heart of South Asia's inadequate supply response is the challenge of farm productivity. Policy attention now needs to shift toward efforts to increase farm productivity, improve rural infrastructure, and lower the vulnerability of the poor. In this regard, the increase in food crop prices provides a golden opportunity to policy makers to re-examine the complex system of input–output pricing interventions, reduce spending on input subsidies and instead refocus public spending on areas that will raise farm productivity (irrigation, rural roads, and rural electricity). Public policy also needs to move toward reducing the vulnerabilities resulting from climate change and inadequate attention to cross-boundary water management.

5.1. *Agriculture productivity*

Despite rapid growth since 1980, South Asia's dependence on agriculture remains substantial. While agriculture's contribution to value added has declined rapidly, it still remains higher than most regions (Fig. 7). More importantly, between 35%–50% of the labor force remains reliant on agriculture for livelihood, suggesting very low average productivity (Fig. 8).[16] Since world commodity prices of energy and fertilizer are likely

---

[16]Employment shares range from a low of 35% in Sri Lanka to a high of 50% for Bangladesh (World Bank 2007b).

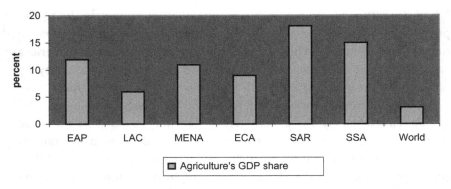

Fig. 7.   Agricultures share in GDP.
Source: World Bank 2007b.

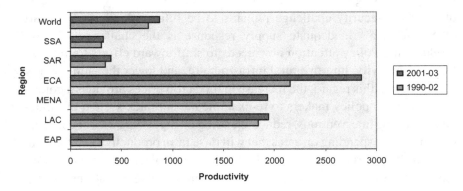

Fig. 8.   Agricultural productivity (2000$/worker).
Source: World Bank 2007b.

to remain substantially higher than the levels in 2006, the only sustainable way of reconciling higher input costs with low and stable prices of wheat and rice for citizen's is to pay attention to farm productivity. This is among the most urgent policy focus for South Asian governments.[17]

The scope for productivity improvements is clear from Fig. 8, but this can be seen more specifically from the productivity comparisons of the two major food crops, wheat and rice. The trend in productivity improvements

---

[17]See Joachim von Braun (2008) on the role of productivity improvements and R&D to attack the food crisis at the global level.

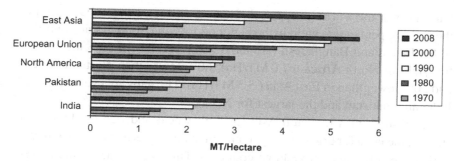

Fig. 9. Wheat productivity trends.

Source: USDA database.

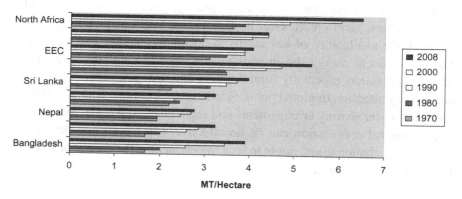

Fig. 10. Rice productivity trends.

Source: USDA database.

in South Asia and global comparators for wheat and rice per hectare of land cultivated is shown in Figs. 9 and 10.

Focusing on land productivity is particularly important in South Asia where land endowment is likely to emerge as a binding constraint. Regarding wheat, the two major South Asian wheat producing countries (India and Pakistan) achieved substantial gains in wheat productivity between 1970 and 2000, but faced stagnation since then. Productivity improvements and yield per hectare compare positively with North America but yield remains way behind EEC countries and East Asia. For example, the present productivity gap in wheat per hectare is 50% with East Asia and 70% with EEC. Concerning rice, South Asian countries show significant gains since 1970, especially in Bangladesh and Sri Lanka. Yet the productivity gap with most of the world (except Sub-Saharan Africa) is large. For example the average per hectare yield in the better performing South Asian countries of Sri Lanka and Bangladesh (around 3.7 MT/Ha) is still 80% lower than the yield in North Africa (7.0 MT/Ha), 60% lower than North America, and 30% lower than in East Asia (5.5 MT/Ha). The gaps are even larger for India and Pakistan and the largest for Nepal.

The yield gaps in South Asia for both wheat and rice are huge and suggest the need for urgent policy attention to find ways to catch up with the performance in the high-yielding countries. This entails addressing issues relating to technology, inputs (especially water, fertilizer and energy), pest control and farmer incentives. The range of policies that impact productivity include incentive policies for farmers (pricing policies, ownership and tenancy issues, farm credit, crop insurance and public expenditure) and ensuring the availability of key inputs in adequate quantity and on time. The rising cost of energy, the emerging water shortages, and the frequency of natural disasters especially from flooding and drought, suggest also the need to pay attention to global public goods such as climate change, cross-boundary water sharing arrangements and regional energy trade. More and better regional cooperation can be an effective way to manage the farm productivity challenge and ought to be a key element in the design of future food policy strategies in South Asia.

5.2. *Regional cooperation for supporting farm productivity*

A major factor underlying South Asia's low farm productivity is the relatively poor rural infrastructure. While South Asia has made progress to improving irrigation facilities for agriculture, the coverage of irrigated agriculture still remains relatively low (39%).[18] More importantly, the availability of water is a serious issue (Table 3), except for Nepal which has surplus water resources. Similarly, the rural population's access to roads and electricity is a serious handicap to farm productivity and incomes. Evidence from international experiences as well as from South Asia demonstrates the high rate of return from investments in rural infrastructure.

---

[18]World Bank 2007b.

Table 3.   Access to water and rural infrastructure.

Countries	Renewable internal freshwater resources per capita cu. m. 2005	Rural population access to an all-season road % 1993–2004	Rural household access to electricity % 1995–2006
Bangladesh	96	37	19
India	1152	61	48
Nepal	7305	17	17
Pakistan	336	61	69
Sri Lanka	95	n.a.	n.a
China	2156	97	n.a
Indonesia	12867	94	90
Vietnam	4410	84	72

Source: World Bank 2007b.

Regional cooperation can help raise farm productivity by easing energy and water constraints. Better energy cooperation along the lines discussed above can be instrumental in ensuring assured supply of power to agriculture for water as well as for availability of fertilizers. Furthermore, this can ease the power access constraint in rural areas.

Water availability and flooding are a huge challenge for farm productivity and incomes. Given the geography of South Asia, where all waters originate from up on the mountains along the Himalayan range, better water cooperation with the upstream countries of Afghanistan, China, Nepal, Bhutan and India is essential to support the long-term availability of water and for flood control in the downstream countries and regions of India. Water cooperation issues are discussed in some more detail below.

5.3. *Regional cooperation for water security*

The quantity and quality of available water are of critical importance for the welfare of South Asia's population. As we saw in Table 3 above, the availability of water is a serious challenge for South Asia. Access to clean drinking water is a major problem; access to irrigation water is also a challenge for all South Asian countries. Countries that are most seriously threatened by water crisis and are already in conflict over water sharing include Afghanistan, Bangladesh, India and Pakistan.

5.3.1. *Water issues on the north western borders of South Asia*

The water conflict issues here relate to: Afghanistan and its Central Asian neighbors; Afghanistan and Pakistan; and India and Pakistan. In Afghanistan, which is the poorest and most conflict ridden South Asian country, the livelihoods of some 80% of the population are based on agriculture and related occupations. Despite being the upper riparian for five water basins, Afghanistan suffers from a major water crisis. The Amu Darya basin accounts for about 40% of Afghanistan's irrigated lands. A combination of conflict and poor management has further damaged the outdated and poorly constructed irrigation canals. In the south and eastern parts of Afghanistan, droughts and dry years have substantially reduced cultivated areas. The four nations sharing the Amu Darya, Afghanistan, Tajikistan, Turkmenistan and Uzbekistan appear to have conflicting interests in terms of water sharing. As a result, the proper development of the river basin that could benefit all parties has not happened. Afghanistan has a similar problem on the east in regards to sharing of the Kabul river water with Pakistan.

In Pakistan and India, extensive irrigation has put the Indus river water resources under heavy stress, with about 90% of the available flow utilized. Ground water levels are under pressure from extensive pumping. There are serious concerns that Pakistan and parts of India will likely face severe water shortages unless adequate mitigating measures are taken. Rising water demand in these countries is adding to trans-border conflicts as well as internal conflicts.

5.3.2. *Water issues on the north eastern borders of South Asia*

The water issues in this subregion involve the South Asian countries of India, Bangladesh and Nepal and the East Asian country of China. Two river basins are involved: the Ganges river basin (India, Bangladesh and Nepal) and the Brahmaputra river basin (China, India and Bangladesh). China and Nepal are the upper riparian; India is in the middle; and Bangladesh is at lowest end where these two mighty rivers meet and merge with the Bay of Bengal. Not surprisingly, Bangladesh is the most disadvantaged and has much at stake. Issues concern both water shortages in winter and also severe flooding risks during monsoon. These problems are increasingly exacerbated by the adverse effects of climate change. Parts of India are also at serious risk from both factors. The flooding problems in Bihar and the adverse effects on poverty are an example of these concerns.

5.3.3. *How cooperation can help*

South Asia's poor would probably gain most from regional cooperation in water. Cross-border cooperation on water between and among India, Bangladesh and Nepal offers the only long-term solution to flood mitigation. The benefits of cooperation are clear. For example, watershed management and storage on Ganges tributaries in Nepal could generate hydropower and irrigation benefits in Nepal and flood mitigation benefits in Nepal, India (U.P., Bihar) and Bangladesh; water storage in Northeast India could provide hydropower and flood benefits in India and Bangladesh; and both would also provide increased and reliable dry season flows. There is an emerging and promising opportunity on the specific cooperation between India, Nepal and Bangladesh on the Ganges. The other specific river basin idea concerns water cooperation between China, India and Bangladesh on the Brahmaputra River. This can similarly be multi-purpose with benefits in terms of water storage for better sharing in lean periods; reduced incidence of flooding, and sharing of hydro-electricity. Both the Ganges and Brahmaputra Water Basin Management Projects are of critical importance for South Asia with immense long-term benefits for the poor. Only a cooperative solution will work.

There are similar benefits of water cooperation between India and Pakistan; between Pakistan and Afghanistan; and between Afghanistan and Central Asian neighbors. The success of the Indus Water Treaty between Pakistan and India has already demonstrated that cooperation that benefits people can withstand all political obstacles. The Treaty also provides a model for how future cooperation might proceed. Building on this success, other water disputes and potential water markets could be developed through a cooperative solution. As noted, Afghanistan sits on the upper riparian of some five water basins that have huge potential for irrigation and hydro-power benefits which could well transform Afghanistan's economy. Yet, very little of the critical investments required to transform this natural resource into a productive asset for the benefit of the people of

Afghanistan have happened so far. As a result, Afghanistan is a severely water constrained economy with also a serious power shortage. A key constraint is the lack of a framework for water sharing agreements with neighbors. A specific project that appears of very high priority is the Kabul River Water Basin Project that will yield substantial hydro-power and irrigation benefits for both Afghanistan and Pakistan. A key requirement for this project to move forward is riparian agreement between Afghanistan and Pakistan. Similarly a proper water sharing framework on the Amu River Basin between Afghanistan and its Central Asian neighbors would provide a basis for water cooperation with multiple benefits. Clearly a cooperative solution will be a win-win for all.

5.4. *Regional cooperation for climate change*

Arguably, few regions globally are more at risk from the climate change issue in terms of adverse impact on the poor than South Asia. The reasons are easy to see when one pays attention to the possible adverse effects of climate change identified by the panel of world experts working on the 4th IPCC report last updated in September 2007. In summary, the possible consequences could include:

- Melting glaciers on the Himalayan-Hindu Kush mountain range. According to Oxford University climatologist Mark New, over the past 30 years snow cover and ice cover may have been reduced by 30% in the eastern Himalayas. There is now a real risk that these glaciers might disappear altogether in the coming decades.
- The rapid melting of glaciers is initially expected to contribute to excessive water flow and flooding in the region. Eventually, the full loss of glaciers, if it happens, would have a severe affect on the availability of fresh water to the three mighty rivers of Indus, Ganges and Brahmaputra (and other smaller tributaries); these rivers are the life line for an estimated 500 million people in India, Pakistan and Bangladesh who are dependent on water from these rivers. Much of this population is very poor.
- The associated loss of farm production, water for human needs, fisheries, river transport, and livelihood will be devastating.
- Water loss would also reduce the availability of power, which is already a serious development constraint in South Asia.

- Changing climate patterns are lowering rainfall in arid and semi-arid zones and intensifying floods in other areas.
- The coastal population in South Asia is already facing a serious flooding problem from rising sea level due to climate change. Even under conservative assumptions, the sea level could rise to 40 cm higher than the present level by the end of the 21st century and submerge a huge area of the South Asian coastal belt. Over 70 million people living along the coastal belt will be forced to relocate causing tremendous human miseries. The threat is particularly serious for Maldives and Bangladesh.
- Human health is also at risk from growing incidence of diseases linked to rising temperatures and rainfall variability. Effects may range from diarrheal diseases to increase malnutrition.

Clearly, climate change poses a serious risk to poverty reduction in South Asia and ought to be a central issue underlying country level poverty reduction strategies. Given the regional/global nature of the issue, actions at the country level alone will not do. Only sustained collective actions at the regional level coordinated with global efforts and combined with country specific interventions will help bring about the required changes. Climate change management will require actions on several fronts.

- South Asia is still a small player in global carbon emission on aggregate and especially in per capita terms. As such, it has a justifiable claim in its favor to a fair distribution of the cost of mitigation and adaptation to climate change. Yet, rapid economic growth in the region, especially India, and growing demand for energy is contributing to a rising incidence of carbon emission that needs to be managed.
- In general, concerted efforts are needed to reduce the emission of carbon dioxide and other greenhouse gases through more sustainable use of energy, improved forestry management and better urbanization. Fortunately, South Asia's largest carbon emitter India is taking steps to achieve a low carbon-growth trajectory. It could play a lead role in continuing to pursue this.
- Using tax, pricing and regulatory policies to discourage use of technologies and activities that generate greenhouse gases.
- A major factor contributing to India's carbon emission is the rapid growth in energy use based on coal and oil as primary fuel. Other countries like

Bangladesh, Bhutan and Nepal have very good gas-based or hydro-power supply potential. More energy trade at the regional level based on use of hydro-power and natural gas along with lower reliance on coal and oil will be a win-win for all.

- Regional cooperation to improve water management and allocation aimed at reducing the incidence of floods while ensuring a more equitable distribution of water in each of the concerned countries for irrigation and other uses.

- Regional cooperation for knowledge generation and sharing on climate change, water and energy resources to improve disaster management and promote private investments in sustainable energy and water resources.

- Greater regional voice and activism in global fora to influence international action on climate change including equitable cost sharing arrangements, seek better international funding for climate change agenda in South Asia, and stronger participation in carbon trading and other related global facilities.

Given the ongoing adverse effects of climate change reflected in frequent natural disasters in the form of floods and drought, and the growing opportunity cost of inaction, the urgency of taking action cannot be overemphasized. South Asian governments ought to seize this opportunity as a common agenda and come together to develop a long-term regional strategy for effective management of climate change with a view to securing poverty reduction on a sustainable basis.

5.5. *Managing the politics of cooperation in South Asia: The way forward*

The potential benefits of economic cooperation are obvious. Global examples of successful cooperation agreements reinforce the point that possible gains for South Asia from effective cooperation and partnerships can be substantial. In particular, the experience of East Asia is illustrative of the potential gains from more and better cooperation.[19] Cross-border physical connectivity has improved tremendously through land, sea and air-based transport network, private sector-led vertical integration of production

---

[19]Gill and Kharas, 2007.

networks has spurred industrial productivity and growth, and e-commerce is flourishing.

Yet, the actual experience with cooperation in South Asia so far has been rather dismal. What are the key constraining factors?

- First and foremost is the prevalence of a number of regional disputes. These include the long-standing conflict between India and Pakistan over Kashmir, which has continued to strain relations between these two large neighbors. The Afghan–Pakistan relations are constrained by allegations of support for Talibans from sources in Pakistan. Similarly, securing the immigration and security issues in the India–Bangladesh border areas is a source of concern.
- Second is the lack of good analysis and information in the public domain about the benefits of regional cooperation. On the contrary, there are unfounded populist negative perceptions in the smaller countries about how more cooperation will simply result in greater domination of India in political and economic matters of these countries.
- A third factor has been internal political interests in countries that are divided along nationalistic, religious and ethnic lines which substantially complicate policy making that involve cross-border dialogue and cooperation.
- Finally, and perhaps most importantly, the approach to international cooperation has been seriously flawed in that this has been largely seen as a bilateral politically-driven agenda rather than a cross-boundary commercial investment. The bilateral political approach has partly contributed to suspicions in smaller countries of India's dominance.

International experience suggests that political constraints and historical conflicts need not be permanent barriers to development cooperation. Neither is the presence of a dominant member country a necessary threat to cooperation and shared gains. For example, the members of the European Union have fought numerous wars in the past, many of them far more intense, long drawn and expensive in terms of loss of human lives and material resources than South Asia. Similarly, member countries diverge considerably in economic strength. Yet, they have found it mutually advantageous to come together and formulate a formidable economic union.

In East Asia, the economic dominance of China has not prevented very effective regional cooperation with the much smaller East Asian countries.

Fortunately, the political environment for cooperation in South Asia is now changing. Historically, the regional cooperation efforts in South Asia culminated in the formation of the South Asian Regional Cooperation (SAARC) in 1985. Until very recently, SAARC has basically functioned as an annual event for meeting of heads of governments with declarations of cooperation intentions, but with very limited implementation due to conflict and political difficulties. Armed with recent economic successes, the political space for better regional cooperation is now growing in South Asia. The last two SAARC meetings have succeeded in bringing the countries much closer than ever before in recognizing the merits of regional cooperation and taking significant actions to realize these benefits.

A wide variety of small steps have been taken in all aspects of cooperation under the SAARC ambit. Much of these steps involve establishment of committees and task forces and multiple meetings. These dialogues are important and should continue. However, to operationalize some of the most important resolutions and decisions, a somewhat different institutional architecture might be required. Here SAARC might want to carefully review the experiences of other more successful regional organizations like the European Union and the ASEAN. Even Africa has better cooperation experiences than South Asia and there may be important lessons that could be learnt and implemented.

Institutional change at the SAARC level however desirable will likely take a long time. In the meanwhile, from a pragmatic point of view, the next step is to identify concrete areas of cooperation where multi-country efforts would yield tangible benefits for citizens. The immediate priority areas are well known: promote trade facilitation by removal of all trade barriers; improving regional transport by removing transit restrictions and opening up port facilities for international trade; promoting trade in energy in all possible ways including hydro-power, gas pipelines and regional grid facilities; and water cooperation to resolve flooding and irrigation problems. These need not involve all member countries in all projects. Specific projects will need to be realistically based on geography and location and will likely involve only the immediate neighbors and become subregional type initiatives.

Very Importantly, cross-border transactions must be de-politicized and pursued on a commercial basis. Enabling national and international private investors to participate in these transactions hold the most promise of success than bilateral political deals. International financial institutions can also play a useful role. Where legal agreements are needed, these can be best pursued multilaterally to avoid any perceptions of dominance.

It is not realistic or necessary to expect that all political and social conflicts will have to be resolved first before meaningful cooperation can happen. Indeed, economic cooperation is also a powerful means for resolving political and social conflicts. Trust and goodwill at the citizens' level can be a credible way for resolving conflicts. Economic cooperation by raising citizen's welfare can be instrumental in building this trust. Political forces can provide impetus to this by reducing policy barriers to regional integration.

Bibliography

Ahmed, S (2006). *Explaining South Asia's Development Success: The Role of Good Policies*. Washington: World Bank.

Ahmed, S and E Ghani (2010). Making regional cooperation work for South Asia's poor. In *Promoting Economic Cooperation in South Asia: Beyond SAFTA*, S Ahmed, S Kelegama and E Ghani (eds.). New Delhi: SAGE Publications.

Barro, RJ and X Sala-i-Martin (1995). *Economic Growth*. New York: Macgraw Hill.

European Union. 2007. *Growing Regions, Growing Europe*. Fourth Report on Economic and Social Cohesion, Brussels.

Fernandes, AM and A Pakes (2008). Evidence of underemployment of labour and capital in Indian manufacturing. In *Accelerating Growth and Job Creation in South Asia*, S Ahmed and E Ghani (eds.). New Delhi: Oxford University Press.

Fujita, M, P Krugman and AJ Venables (1999). *The Spatial Economy: Cities, Regions, and International Trade*. Cambridge: MIT Press.

Gill, I and H Kharas (2007). East Asian Miracle. Washington: World Bank.

Government of India (2008). *North Eastern Region Vision 2020, volumes 1 and 2*. Ministry of Development of North Eastern Region and North Eastern Council, New Delhi.

Hamid, N (2007). South Asia: A development strategy for the information age. In *Report on the South Asia Department Economists' Annual Conference 2006*. Manila: Asian Development Bank.

Harris, C (2008). Is South Asia closing the deficit in its infrastructure? *Mimeo*. Washington: World Bank.

Joachim von Braun (2008). *Agriculture for Sustainable Economic Development: A Global R&D Initiative to Avoid a Deep and Complex Crisis*. Charles Viley Memorial Lecture. Washington: International Food Policy Research Institute.

Kanbur, R and AJ Venables (2005). Spatial inequality and development. In *Spatial Inequality and Development*, R Kanbur and AJ Venables (eds.). Oxford: Oxford University Press.

Massum, M (2008). *Bangladesh and the North East Exploring Development Possibilities through Economic Linkages*. Draft Paper, South Asia Region. Washington: World Bank.

Venables, AJ (2006). *Shifts in Economic Geography and their Causes*. Federal Reserve Bank of Kansas City Economic Review, Fourth Quarter.

World Bank (2005a). *India: Rajasthan: Closing the Development Gap*. Report Number 32585-IN. Washington: World Bank.

World Bank (2005b). *Bihar: Towards a Development Strategy*. New Delhi: World Bank.

World Bank (2005c). *Pakistan: North West Frontier Province Economic Report*. Report Number 32764-PK. Washington: World Bank.

World Bank (2007a). Jharkand: *Addressing the Challenges of Inclusive Development*. New Delhi: World Bank.

World Bank (2007b). *Agriculture for Development: World Development Report 2008*. Washington: World Bank.

World Bank (2008a). *World Development Indicators 2008*. Washington: World Bank.

World Bank (2008b). *Accelerating Growth and Development in the Lagging Regions of India*. Report No. 41101-IN. Washington: World Bank.

World Bank (2008c). *Balochistan Economic Report: From Periphery to Core*. Joint World Bank, ADB and Government of Balochistan Study, Draft, Washington.

World Bank (2008d). *World Trade Indicators*. Washington: World Bank.

World Bank (2008e). *World Development Report 2009: Reshaping Economic Geography*. Washington: World Bank.

World Bank (2008f). *Potential and Prospects for Regional Energy Trade in the South Asia Region*. ESMAP and South Asia Regional Programs. Washington: World Bank.

World Bank (2010). *World Development Indicators 2010*. Washington: World Bank.

Chapter 5

Satellites, Politics and India's TV News Revolution: Challenges and Prospects*

Nalin Mehta[†]

"Other countries have think-tanks, India makes do with prime-time chat shows"

1. Introduction

In September 2009, India's Prime Minister, Army Chief and National Security Advisor launched a coordinated attempt to douse intense television news speculation about alleged Chinese military incursions on the disputed eastern border. All three leaders issued denials after days of intense focus by India's private TV news networks who had effectively accused the government of hushing up Chinese aggression. Such reports were not restricted to television alone — in fact matters came to a head when the *Times of India* reported that two border guards had allegedly been injured in a skirmish. Many analysts, however, noted that the general tone of the aggressive media discourse overall was set by what one newspaper editor called "war-mongering TV channels".[1] Both governments denied

*Indian television is a highly fluid medium with regular flow of staff between different networks. All designations of interviewees in mentioned below are accurate as of time of interview.

[†]Nalin Mehta is Visiting Senior Research Fellow at the Institute of South Asian Studies and Asia Research Institute, National University of Singapore and Joint Editor, South Asia History and Culture (Routledge).

[1]Gupta, 2009.

the incidents,[2] but the story had created such heat that the then National Security Advisor M. K. Narayanan appeared on a television interview on CNN-IBN (2009) with a dire warning:

> "I don't know what the reason is why there is so much reporting . . . but I think this is a national security issue . . . the more you raise people's concerns, the tensions could rise and we would then be facing a situation of the kind that we wish to avoid [sic]. . . It could create a problem of a kind and I have been through [in] [the] 1962 [war]. . . then of course we didn't [then] have the media of this kind. . .
>
> What we need to be careful of is that we don't have an unwarranted incident or an accident of some kind, that's what we are trying to avoid. But there's always concern that *if this thing goes on like this someone somewhere might lose his cool and something might go wrong.*"

That this statement came on a television interview was no accident. The government was effectively asking India's TV networks to tone down. This, at least, was the majority view in Delhi's news rooms. Television was seen to have largely led the debate; print was seen to have followed. Anecdotal evidence certainly supported this view. Among others, B. V. Rao (2009), a former TV news editor and media columnist, noted that the government was asking the media to "back off" because "this time the frenzy seemed to have spread even to print [from television]".

Whether the allegations about border incursions were true or not is outside the scope of this presentation. Such shadowboxing between the media and the government on tricky issues is part of every democracy and India is no exception. It is pertinent for our purposes though that this was the second time in the year that India's TV news networks, were accused of side-tracking bilateral relations with another country.

When some Indian students were injured in a racist attack in Melbourne in May 2009, the story was initially virtually ignored in the national print press. It was first given prominence on Times Now, the Times Group's 24-hour English news channel, which ran an emotional campaign around it. The network made the story its first headline and ran a hard campaign about injured Indian pride. Though only six years old, Times Now is now the most watched English news network in India and its commercial success

---

[2]China Foreign Ministry, 2009.

has been built on an aggressive policy of pursuing stories with a nationalist angle — especially those involving non-resident Indians; a hard line on security, especially on Pakistan and China; and the notion of a powerful India, an India that is no more a pushover. Television ratings show that its audiences, or at least the miniscule few who make up the rating panels, like that tone and this in turn reflects back on its choice and treatment of stories.

The Australian racism story fit its template very well. Once it got traction and the Ministry of External Affairs was forced to react, every other media group, television and print, followed suit. This is the nature of the media — the story had become too big.[3] The intense focus meant that every attack on an Indian thereafter — even ones that were part of general crime patterns and not racist — were framed through the same lens. Once such reports would have been relegated to the inside pages of newspapers or, at best, would have made it to a box item on the front page. Now, they became part of an ongoing media discourse about a resurgent India that would not take things lying down.

At a time when Indo–Australian relations had just been on the upswing after years of historical mistrust, the story completely upset the trajectory of bilateral relations, with the Indian Foreign Minister, facing middle class anger in television studios, issuing warnings to Australia. The central role of television in this discourse was best summed up in a tongue-in-cheek account published in the *Hindustan Times*:

> Other countries have think-tanks, India makes do with prime-time chat shows. . .
>
> To media consumers who got initiated into Australian society this past week, that country must seem formidably scary, almost the fastness of Ming of Mongo. There was discussion on a "white Australia" policy that went out of business 30 years ago. Clips of Australian cricketers sledging or arguing with Indian, West Indian and Sri Lankan cricketers were juxtaposed with reportage of attacks on Indian students, as if one were dealing with a nation of all-purpose bigots.
>
> On one television show, an anchor said Australia had been preceded by attacks on Indians in Germany, the United States and Idi Amin's Uganda and wondered why the world hated Indians. This is a happy universe of nuance-free non-sequiturs.

---

[3]Wade, 2009a; Wade, 2009b.

Even so, India's television-propelled middle class opinion is a clear and present reality. It will shape discourse that will hassle and harangue governments, demand instant action and colorful rhetoric. In some senses, the drama outside the Delhi airport during the IC-814 hijack was a teaser trailer. This is the new India. Now even Kevin Rudd [then Australian PM] knows that.[4]

For our purposes, it is immaterial whether the television coverage was right or wrong, nuanced or simplistic, sensationalist or measured. The point is that both the examples cited above, clearly underlined the centrality of 24-hour private satellite news as a new factor in the Indian political and social matrix. In both cases, the discourse of Indian television had serious consequences for domestic policy imperatives and an impact beyond India's borders. A detailed study of Indian news television's impact on foreign policy is still to be written but it is important to reiterate how recent the phenomenon of private TV news is.

This is a country where as late as 1994, a Prime Minister cancelled the launch of a new state TV channel because it promised to show live current affairs programmes. Narasimha Rao's reasoning could not have been clearer: "We cannot have live broadcasts. It is too dangerous," he said, while cancelling the launch of DD 3 in October 1994.[5] The fear was that there would be no way of controlling anybody from saying anything against the ruling Congress on live programming. Historically in India, control over television has been central to and constitutive of the state's self-image — broadcasting's principal objective was to "display and enact government control"[6] — and live television threatened to break down the very edifice on which Indian television had been built. This was seen most starkly in the case of news programming.

By 1998, however, the first of India's private 24-hour news channels was on the airwaves and by 2009 more than 400 satellite channels were officially broadcasting into Indian homes. Of these, more than a hundred broadcast news in 15 languages and more than 70 are 24-hour news channels in 11

---

[4]Malik, 2009.
[5]Ghose, 2005, pp. 189–190.
[6]Rajagopal: 78.

languages.[7] I have detailed the reasons behind the remarkable rise of private Indian satellite television elsewhere.[8] But the numbers are a stark illustration of the massive changes in Indian broadcasting. These upheavals in the nature of Indian television have been accompanied by a simultaneous expansion in its reach and penetration. In 1992, if you divided India's population of 846,388,000.[9] By the total number of television sets in the country,[10] the number of people clustering around a set would have been a little over 26. By 2006, that ratio had come down substantially to just over ten people per television set, despite a substantial increase in the population.[11] In a little over a decade, the total number of Indian television households tripled to reach an estimated 112 million.[12] It made India the world's third largest television market, just behind China and the United States.[13]

Much like India's "newspaper revolution"[14] that started in the 1970s, and the "cassette culture"[15] of the 1980s, the availability of privately produced satellite television has meant that "people discovered new ways to think about themselves and to participate in politics that would have been unthinkable a generation before".[16] Operating at the junction of public culture, capitalism and globalization, satellite news networks have had profound implications for the state, politics, democracy and identity formation. These are the linkages this presentation sets out to explore.

It focuses, in particular, on the meaning of 24-hour television in the vernacular languages and it argues that the emergence of local television news networks has greatly enhanced and strengthened deliberative Indian democracy. There is no evidence to show that satellite television has benefited Indian democracy if we understand it in the narrow procedural

---

[7] MIB, 2009.

[8] Mehta, 2008.

[9] Registrar General of India, 2001.

[10] India had 34,858,000 TV sets in 1992. Joshi & Trivedi, p. 16.

[11] The National Readership Studies Council 2006 survey estimated a total of 112 million television sets in India. *NRS 2006*, p. 4. The Indian population in 2006 had gone up to 1.12 billion. Population Reference Bureau, p. 1.

[12] NRS, 2006, p. 4.

[13] PricewaterhouseCooopers, 2005, p. 36.

[14] Jeffrey, 2003, p. xi.

[15] Manuel, 1993.

[16] Jeffrey, 2003, p. 1

terms defined by the voting process alone.[17] My claim refers to a broader understanding of democracy as a deliberative process involving larger collaborative processes of decision making, identity and interest formation with the media acting as a crucial hinge. Democracy is intimately connected with mechanisms of public discussion and interactive reasoning. Indeed, the new disciplines of social choice theory and public choice theory are connected to ideas of individual values and their impact on decision-making.[18] In this context, Amartya Sen has famously shown that no substantial famine has ever occurred in a country with a democratic form of government and a relatively free press.[19] When the audience for news expands, the shape of politics changes.

The first part of this essay uses separate case studies of regional language news television from the states of West Bengal, Maharashtra, Chhattisgarh and Punjab to illustrate what happen to politics and society when television emerges as an independent factor. It focuses on the specific ways in which the new medium affected the daily spectacle of Indian politics and how political leaders and parties adapted the daily practices of politics to the 24-hour publicity it provided. We will then move to a brief discussion on the meaning of Indian television in the wider South Asian region before concluding with an outline of some of the key challenges that Indian television engenders.

2. "More Impact than in Delhi": The Meaning of Local News TV

There is much that is wrong with Indian news television. Critics have called it too loud, too sensationalist, too focused on urban middle class audiences and overtly obsessed with the holy grail of weekly ratings. All that is true but a great deal of its problems are linked to a structural problem inherent in the business models of satellite TV networks. In economic terms, the Indian satellite networks are inordinately dependent on weekly ratings, more so than their western counterparts. I have shown elsewhere

---

[17]Procedural models of democracy focus on the systems and institutions of democracy as symbolized predominantly by the act of voting.

[18]Sen, 2002.

[19]Sen, Dreze, 1989.

that this is partly a direct derivative of the peculiar "illegal" origins of satellite broadcasting in India which meant that channels never had full control of their own distribution and therefore lost out on a large chunk of subscription revenues. In most developed TV markets, roughly about 70% of television earnings on average come from subscription and about 30% from advertising. In India, it is the exact reverse. In most cases, the business models of TV networks and channels are entirely dependent on advertising revenues. In a market where more than 70 news channels are competing for advertising, the structural economy of television forces many channels to focus on content with the lowest common denominator that will register on television rating panels.[20] Given the extremely narrow base of these ratings, cricket and Bollywood have emerged as an easy option to register on them. Both have a pan-Indian appeal cutting across socio-economic and regional categories. News of a farmer suicide in Vidarbha may not interest anybody in Kerala, a news producer may reason, but news of the Indian cricket team interests people in every region of India. This is why when national news editors want to lift the ratings of any show they look towards cricket and Bollywood and these genres increasingly dominate news space.[21] News, as such, is a commercial product packaged to suit commercial targets.

However, the economic imperatives of creating a market and sustaining it simultaneously drive news channels to create a public sphere, however imperfect. The meaning of the message is not static and takes different forms for different people.[22] The crucial point is that politics, unlike before, has to unfold in an open arena and in the glare of a new visibility that has a life of its own and is often difficult to control. The media's importance lies not in whether anybody is watching or is getting influenced, but in the assumption of it by political leaders and decision-makers.[23] It is in this context that television assumes an important role and — regardless of its actual impact on the voting public — becomes central to the political process.

---

[20] Mehta, 2008, pp. 140–193.

[21] Interview with Uday Shankar, CEO and Editor STAR News, 2003–2007. Shanghai: August 22, 2005.

[22] Thompson, 1994, pp. 34–41.

[23] Schudson, 1995, pp. 22–25.

When Network Eighteen launched its Marathi language 24-hour news channel, Channel IBN Lokmat in April 2008, it began by setting up 13 bureaus across the west Indian state of Maharashtra and hiring more than a hundred stringers. The channel began its coverage by devoting a half hour daily special to the farmer suicides in Maharashtra's Vidarbha region. This is a chronic issue that since 2005 has only been covered sporadically by the national press which, with few honorable exceptions, failed to build sustained coverage around the crisis.[24] Within hours of the first telecast, Lokmat's Managing Editor received an angry phone call from an angry Member of the Legislative Assembly (MLA) on whose constituency the first part of the series had been based on. He wanted the story to be pulled off air and threatened to use his clout with the local cable operators to blank off the new channel from the airwaves. The incident revealed both the potential and the limitations of satellite television. On the positive side of the ledger, the MLA's phone call was proof that he was worried about viewers in his constituency watching the story and drawing conclusions about his performance. As Lokmat's Managing Editor explained:

> "We have done many similar stories on farmer suicides on our English [CNN-IBN] and Hindi [IBN-7] channels but never have I received a phone call from any minister or elected representative. It is like they did not care. But in this case, in the Marathi channel, for the first time, I got a call. The MLA was angry because he knew the people who would vote for him would be watching.
>
> I realized that this was the real impact. If you show something to people in the language that they speak then it percolates down to the grassroots and that is why the MLA was worried. It had much more impact there than in Delhi".[25]

This contention about the power of language ties in with my own observations while covering Parliament proceedings in Delhi. In the late 1990s when private satellite news networks were still a novelty members of Parliament would happily give interviews to national networks like NDTV

---

[24] Sainath, 2005.

[25] Conversation with Rajdeep Sardesai, Managing Editor, CNN-IBN, IBN-7 & IBN-Lokmat. New Delhi: 1 May, 2008.

and Zee. This was partly due to the glamour of the new media, but as India's politicians became more savvy with television a new pecking order emerged.

Reporters for national networks found that they were no longer the first choice to give interviews to. MPs discovered that it made more political sense to speak in their own language on their own regional language channel. All through 2004–07 for instance, the Teleugu Desam's Parliamentary Party Leader Yerran Naidu who began by being the most accessible of politicians for reporters in Delhi gradually became more difficult to get hold of for national channels. Yet, he would make it a special point to step out of Parliament virtually on a daily basis when it was in session to give long interviews on the Telugu ETV network because he knew that his constituents would be watching. He had decided who was important for him. This was about space as well as strategy. According to the Tamil Jaya TV's Vice President K. P. Sunil:

> "For a public figure in a state, the most important platform now is the most local cable channel. Earlier, they used to come on Jaya TV easily. Now if a murder happens in a district, the District Magistrate knows that if he speaks to a national channel he will get 15 seconds of a sound byte, on a regional channel he will get maybe a minute but on a local cable channel he will get half an hour. Localization translates into power and they have understood this". [26]

Coming back to the Marathi farmer suicides, Network Eighteen also runs two other national news channels — CNN-IBN in English and IBN 7 in Hindi — but its Managing Editor felt that market dynamics made it difficult for his network to run such campaigns on social issues on these "national" language platforms.[27] As he put it, in a local language channel important stories that are cut out of national networks — due to commercial constraints — do find space. This is not because of any special altruistic reason but because on this platform, local stories make imminent commercial sense. Ratings are as important in Marathi television

---

[26]Interview with KP Sunil, Vice President, Jaya TV. Chennai: 15 Oct, 2005. Designations are accurate as of time of interview.
[27]Conversation with Rajdeep Sardesai, Managing Editor, CNN-IBN, IBN-7 & IBN-Lokmat. New Delhi: 1 May, 2008.

as in the so-called national languages of Hindi and English: IBN Lokmat is competing with Zee and Star's 24-hour news channels in the language, but here in-depth local coverage is a sure way of registering on the ratings.

To cite another example from a different state, when the Bengali news channel STAR Ananda started operations in June 2005, it announced its launch by instituting daily live public debates between candidates contesting the Kolkata municipal election. These debates marked an important signpost in the political campaigning culture of the city. They were conducted in the city's open public spaces and took the form of public meetings where sometimes as many as some of 10,000 people turned up as live audiences in addition to regular television viewers. The tapes of that programming make for riveting viewing. They show large public rallies of the kind that are familiar to observers of Indian politics but differ in one crucial aspect: These were joint political events, organized by a television channel and moderated by a STAR Ananda newsman as rival candidates debated their political views while their followers raised lusty slogans.[28]

This was happening in a city which had been ruled by the same political conglomerate, the Left Front, since 1977. The debates unleashed political passions and for the first two weeks, mini-riots broke out during virtually every one of the daily events. Rival political groups attacked each other with swords and sticks. In one instance, petrol bombs were also used. The news anchors were roughed up for daring to ask tough questions and all this happened on live television. The debates created such a problem that the police commissioner of Kolkata called up the channel and asked it to stop, citing the fear of public rioting. As the founding editor of STAR Ananda, who also anchored these debates, explains:

"It created such a furore and became such an instant hit . . . I didn't even know . . . that these two warring groups would come with daggers and bombs, and there was one shoot-out incident . . . The police commissioner personally requested me 25 times . . . He said to please withdraw this programme . . . This is creating hell of a lot of *jhamela* [problem]".[29]

---

[28]STAR Ananda, n.d.

[29]Interview with Suman Chattopadhyay, Founding Editor, STAR Ananda. Kolkata: 22 Dec, 2005.

STAR Ananda responded to the commissioner's suggestion with a public campaign for the strengthening of democratic traditions and debate. The editor went on air with news that the police commissioner wanted the public debates to stop and argued that this was a dangerous precedent for Bengali democracy. The important point here is that this tradition of public television debates was not a Bengali innovation. Hindi news channels like Zee TV and STAR News had run numerous such events in various constituencies during national and state elections across North India in the preceding five years. This is what STAR Ananda emphasized, along with the long Bengali tradition of public culture, *adda* and political activism that goes back to the Bengal renaissance of the 19th century.[30]

The public appeal to democratic principles and Bengali-ness worked and the political violence ceased within two weeks. Many localities in Kolkata began to invite the channel to hold similar debates between contesting candidates and that single event turned STAR Ananda into a market leader in the Bengali news sphere. Following this success, a year later two more Bengali news channels started from Kolkata in 2006 in the run-up to the West Bengal assembly election. These two, Zee's 24 Ghanta and Kolkata TV, both followed similar programming formats of public debate and developed these even further.

Bengali television shows how news television feeds off, and into, liberal democratic values, which themselves are rooted in a long heritage of argumentation and debate. In this context, I have argued elsewhere.[31] That news channels tap into strong oral traditions and heterodox structures of social communication that Amartya Sen has labeled "the argumentative tradition of India".[32] For Sen, these traditions are an important support structure for the sustenance of Indian democracy.[33] Indian television thrives on programming genres that marry older argumentative traditions with new technology and notions of liberal democracy to create new hybrid forms that strengthen democratic culture. Argumentative television fits into broader cultural patterns but the very nature of the medium is such that they mutate

---

[30]Ibid

[31]Mehta, 2008, pp. 230–273.

[32]Sen, 2005, p. 14.

[33]Sen, 2005, p. 12.

into newer forms when mediated by television. In separate analyses of the uses of video technology for religious purposes in India, John T. Little[34] and Philip Lutgendorf[35] suggest that new electronic presentations are not overwhelming traditional religious performance genres. Instead, a new layer of interpretation is being added to what is likely to remain a vibrant and multi-vocal cultural tradition. Precisely, the same thing is happening in the arena of politics with news television's focus on politics and civic life.

The advent of 24-hour news necessitates a fresh look at what happened to the politics–television equation after the rise of news channels. Twenty-four-hour news introduces the element of permanent publicity and forces politicians to adapt to new forms of electronic mediation. First, 24-hour news makes politicians visible on a daily basis. The kind of high publicity that politicians desire during election campaigns is now thrust upon them on a daily basis. The daily television camera symbolizes the scrutiny of public opinion. Even if that public is a "phantom" one, the politician has to behave as if it is always there. The demands of 24-hour news force politicians to be on the campaign trail all the time. Anyone who has followed television reporters on their daily rounds of party offices in Delhi knows that it is often the insatiable drive of news channels to "take the story forward" that induces party spokespersons to "react" to the latest political controversy. Twenty-four-hour news leads to 24-hour politics.

3. Political Parties, Regional Languages and Television

Satellite networks have taken different meanings in different regions and in different languages. By the 2006 Tamil Nadu assembly election, for instance, it had become so important that the DMK made the free allotment of color television sets to every family a key plank of its election manifesto. It is a promise the DMK has begun to fulfill since winning back political power. As Maya Ranganathan writes, "not only had the DMK catapulted "television" into a premier position in the electoral discourse but also granted the status of an essential commodity on par with subsidized rice

---

[34] 1995, pp. 254–283.
[35] 1995, pp. 217–253.

and reservation in jobs . . . for the first time ever, television viewing moved to be part of the political discourse. . ."[36]

Similarly, Tamil television is very different from television in say, Chhattisgarh[37] where broadcast journalists encountered a very peculiar kind of censorship during the run-up to the 2003 state election. Every time any of the news channels broadcast a news item that was even mildly critical of then Chief Minister Ajit Jogi, it was blanked from the air. Chhattisgarh viewers watching that particular broadcast would suddenly find their television sets going blank and the pictures would return only fifteen minutes or so after the offending news story was over. This unannounced censorship would happen only within the territorial boundaries of Chhattisgarh and television viewers in the rest of India did not encounter this problem at all. This was because supporters of the Chief Minister, had set up a state-wide private television network — Akash (Sky) TV — that bought over, or took control of, cable distribution networks across Chhattisgarh and this provided an easy mechanism for controlling the broadcast of national news channels within the state's borders. The national networks could be turned off each time their product did not suit the ruling establishment. It was an ingenious form of censorship: It was not officially announced, it technically did not come from the state and there was nothing any of the channels could do about it.[38] The uses, or misuses, of Akash Television became an important part of the BJP's electoral campaign against Jogi in 2003 and within hours of his losing power on December 4, its television studios were taken over by a triumphant crowd of the party's supporters.[39] Anecdotes like these reveal the complexity and the centrality of news television across India's regions.

Like the Congress in Chhattisgarh, the ruling Akali Dal has been accused of forcibly capturing cable TV operations in Punjab. In August 2007, the Cable Operators Federation of India complained to the Ministry of Information and Broadcasting of physical threats and arrests of cable operators in the state. Like Jogi in Chhatisgarh, Sukhbir Singh Badal [President, Akali Dal]

---

[36]Ranganathan, 2006: 4949.

[37]Chattisgarh is a predominantly tribal state in central India, created in 2002.

[38]Interview with Sanjeev Singh, Principal Correspondent, STAR News. New Delhi: 25 Jan, 2004.

[39]Ibid.

denied the charges, but the parallels were undeniable. Many cable operators in the state were forced to replace the popular Punjab Today channel with the new Akali-friendly channel PTC on their prime frequencies soon after the Akali Dal came to power. As one cable operator from Patiala said after being released from prison on charges of violence, "This is state terror being used against us and the police are being used freely and scores of false cases are being filed".[40] Congress MPs, now on the back foot, even planned to approach the National Human Rights Commission on the issue and whichever side one chooses to believe in this dispute, it is undeniable that across India political parties are taking private television seriously.

In 2008, when the Ministry of Information and Broadcasting decided to investigate the ratings system of the television industry, arguing that it was lop-sided, many argued that the move was rooted in the fact that channels supported by the Congress Party and its allies were not doing well in the existing ratings and therefore not drawing enough advertising.[41] As such, the Ministry was accused of wanting to change the goalposts.

What is interesting is that, by 2008, numerous channels were openly owned or aligned with political parties. Doordarshan continued to be a state controlled enterprise. In Tamil Nadu, the DMK has shifted patronage from Sun TV to Kalaignar TV while the AIADMK controls Jaya TV. Makkal TV is considered close to the PMK while ETV has long had close tied with the TDP. In Karnataka, Kasturi TV is identified with JD (S) while the CPI (M) patronizes Kairali TV in Kerala. The Congress has recently backed Jaihind TV in Kerala while Akash Bangla in West Bengal is controlled by the CPI (M).[42] These networks with political patronage co-exist with many other independent ones, all competing for the same markets.

4. Stories from the Field: Indian News in the South Asia Context

What does all this mean for South Asia in particular? Anecdotal evidence indicates that the impact has been quite significant. Three 24-hour news

---

[40]Chakraborty, Aug 8, 2007.

[41]Raman, May 12, 2008.

[42]Raman, 2008.

networks operate in Bengali out of Kolkata, and the heads of all three agree that their biggest viewership is in Bangladesh. For the Bengali TV CEOs, the only concern is that "they haven't found a way of tapping into Bangladeshi advertising",[43] but the fact remains that Indian Bengali channels have now have huge cultural currency in Bangladesh.

I was in Nepal in 2001, covering the assassination of the royal family for NDTV and within two days of the killings, the Nepalese government banned Aaj Tak, the largest Hindi news network from India, because some of its broadcasts questioned the official versions of the assassination. NDTV, the BBC and CNN raised speculative questions about that version as well, but because we were broadcasting in English, they let us alone — it was the Hindi networks that were banned because that was the language the Nepali street understood. Nepal and India have an open border but the relationship has always been an uneasy one and the skeptical reports from Aak Tak and Zee News fed into a history of tenuous fear about an overbearing India. The anger against the reports was such that most Hindi reporters from India were physically roughed up by grief-stricken Nepali mobs and other Indian TV reporters started taking off their channel logos from their microphones so that they could not be identified as Indian. My own camera crew experienced much of this anger and purely as a defense mechanism, every time we were asked where we were from, we began saying, Bangladesh TV.

In Kathmandu that month, Indian reporters, coming from a different political culture, were seen as breaking Nepali conventions about reporting about the royal family. A typical comment that my own crew got a number of times was, "We don't need you Indians here. Go back." We were not the only foreign reporters in Kathmandu, but we got the sense that people were used to the Western agencies talking about them; Indian reporting, however, was a new experience and had a different connotation. Popular anger at time of public grief became mixed with an older history of what has been seen as Indian insensitivity.

Perhaps, the most significant South Asian ramification of the growth of Indian satellite television is for the India–Pakistan relationship. In 2004, when the Pakistan government granted 39 licenses to private broadcasters,

---

[43]Interview with Uday Shankar, CEO and Editor, Star News and Star Ananda. Shanghai: 22 Aug 2005.

many of them made overtures to Indian channels for technical cooperation just as the Indian channels had looked to Western consultants when they themselves had started.[44] When an Indian parliamentary delegation went to Pakistan in 2003, the newly launched Geo TV got a visiting Indian journalist, NDTV's Rajdeep Sardesai, to anchor its special coverage programming in a joint-production with NDTV. This was uncharted territory and a gesture that symbolized the increasing people-to-people contact between the two countries. Pakistani satellite television was still in a nascent stage but the decision to put an Indian TV journalist on air as a co-anchor was reflective of the respect news teams on both sides of the border regarded each other with. Journalists were forging links that were far ahead of the bilateral relationship. Geo TV was later at the forefront of the pro-democracy movement in Pakistan that finally contributed to the stepping down of General Musharraf as President. Most Indian and Pakistani channels now have reciprocal agreements wherein they share video footage free of cost and provide visiting television teams from either side with free studio facilities.

During the Kashmir earthquake in 2005, a special broadcast that emerged from this kind of cooperation resulted in a live television audience from both sides of the LOC talking to each other. In an especially poignant moment during this programme, a family from the Indian side actually discovered people in the audience on the Pakistani side, who knew some of their missing relatives in Pakistan and were informed on live television that their relatives had died in the earthquake.[45] It was a coincidence, but it resulted in the Indian government granting a rare visa to the one surviving child from that family to come to India.

Indian and Pakistani entrepreneurs have long cooperated in matters of commerce, in areas like the sugar industry. But television is different because it is a cultural product and it creates its own social dynamic. Pakistani channels have followed the model set by Indian private channels which got around tough Indian broadcast regulations in the early years by broadcasting into India from foreign soil.[46] Similarly, a number of Pakistani channels

---

[44]Interview with Rahul Kulshreshtha, Technical Producer, TV Today. New Delhi: 22 Jan, 2005.
[45]We the People, 2005.
[46]Fateh, 2005.

broadcast from Dubai in the early years. Geo TV, for instance, had plans to shift its news production to Dubai during its tense stand-off with General Musharraf's regime in its last months when it faced the threat of shutdown. But the antagonism between television and the state came later. When the networks started, the then Pakistani government, under a military dictatorship, was largely supportive because it needed Pakistani news channels, possibly as a response to Indian television's powerful cultural influence.

The story of the 2001 Agra summit between then Prime Minister Vajpayee and then President Musharraf sums up how seriously the Pakistani establishment takes Indian private television. This was a summit that was touted as one that one would break the post-Kargil war chill between both countries and herald a breakthrough in bilateral relations. There were still no Pakistani satellite networks and Musharraf landed in India in a blaze of round-the-clock publicity on the new Indian networks. On the second day of the summit, when everything seemed to be going well, General Musharraf met Indian newspaper editors for an off-the-record breakfast meeting. It was off-the-record and the only camera that was allowed in was a Pakistan TV crew, ostensibly for archival purposes. At that meeting, contrary to the atmospherics of that summit, Musharraf reiterated the Pakistani hardline on Kashmir, referring to militants "freedom fighters" and justifying the Kargil war as revenge for Siachen. This was usual diplomacy as long as it remained off-the-record, but as soon as the meeting got over the General's staff decided to leak the PTV recording to NDTV's Prannoy Roy.

The story goes that Prannoy, who was among editors at the breakfast meeting, walked up to Pakistan TV officials as soon as it finished and asked if he could get a copy of the tape. They asked him to approach the General who said yes. Roy ran out with the tape to his broadcast centre and the minute it was played on television, the entire dynamic of the summit changed. What was meant to be an off-the-record briefing was now on live television and Indian viewers saw a Pakistani head of state stating a no-compromise position on television in the middle of what was meant to be an ice-breaking summit. From that moment, the Agra summit could only have failed. But, it also allowed Pervez Musharraf to project himself as a tough leader of the Pakistani cause for his domestic audience.

We must be careful not to exaggerate the influence of television and the summit failed for a variety of complex reasons but the crucial point is how Musharraf used Indian television to project the Pakistani view. Even Pakistan Television, whose crew had recorded the breakfast meeting, did not have a copy of that recording and had to poach it off NDTV's broadcasts. When Musharraf dashed back to Islamabad in the middle of the night, the Indian side, which was still in traditional diplomacy mode, did not come out with a statement for another 24 hours. But the Pakistani Army spokesperson, Major General Rashid Qureshi, within minutes of his President's departure, was on Aaj Tak and in a live thirty minute interview pinned the whole blame on "hardline elements" within the Indian side. If Musharraf's breakfast meeting had projected him as the uncompromising defender of Pakistan, the Aaj Tak broadcast painted him as the peacemaker, thwarted by Indian hardliners. Such a platform for the Pakistani government in India would have been unthinkable just ten years ago, in the era before private television. The result was that, for the first two days after Musharraf flew back home, the entire media discourse of the summit revolved around the idea of sabotage and divisions within the Indian negotiators.[47] Soon after the Agra summit, General Musharraf gave the green light to Pakistani private networks and perhaps it was no accident.

The case of Indian television seems to validate the view that globalization is not just about the crass spread of capitalism, it is also about *new complex ways of communication.* As Thomas Friedman.[48] Points out: "The iron law of globalization is simple: If you think it is all good, or you think it is all bad, you don't get it. Globalization has empowering and disempowering, homogenizing and particularizing, democratizing and authoritarian tendencies all built into it. It is about the global market, but it is also about the internet and Google." It is also about Musharraf on NDTV and discovering that your family is dead on live television, across a border that has been fortified for over sixty years.

5. Challenges and Prospects

It is not my claim that satellite television's influence impact on India has always been positive. Television performs many of its transformations

---

[47]For more on the politics of the Agra broadcast see Kang, "Breakfast TV".
[48]2006: 510.

"subliminally". Simply by being there, available for viewing, for debate and for participation, it has effected changes in the way Indians operate in and interact with society. The capitalists who led the move towards private satellite broadcasting in India did not do it for altruistic reasons — their objective was to make money — but their efforts have led to the creation of newer modes of public action and publicness. Television has been adapted by Indian society — by its entrepreneurs, by its producers and by its consumers — to suit its own needs. Looking to create markets for advertisers, Indian producers and entrepreneurs searched for publics and, as purveyors of identity, they tapped in to, but also altered, existing social nodes of identity and communication. This has not always been rational or "positive", but it is fundamentally different from the past when television was nothing more than a governmental tool. Television has opened up avenues that previously did not exist and brought many more people into the public arena. This is why Rajdeep Sardesai (2006) has argued that:

> "The television picture and sound-bite has been one of the most dramatic political developments in the last sixteen years ... mutually competitive 24 hour news networks are almost direct participants in public processes: Not only do they amplify the news, they also influence it".

Measuring the political effect of television is, however, an inexact science. Television does not explain every social and political change in contemporary India. To make such a claim would be an overstatement. It is my argument, however, that it is impossible to imagine, or explain, modern India without reference to television, that it just would not make sense without it.

What now of the future? First and foremost, fifteen years after the Supreme Court's historic judgment that freed the airwaves from government monopoly, India is still waiting for a comprehensive new law that covers all aspects of broadcasting, including reasonable content guidelines and cross-media ownership laws. India remains the most unregulated television market in the world and while this suits the owners and the editors in their no-holds barred quest for revenues, the grey areas inherent in the legal structure underpinning Indian broadcasting are responsible for much of the current frustration with content issues. The problem is that, any discussion of broadcast reform in India gets stuck between two poles: The controlling impulses of a state always looking to turn the clock back and take back lost control and the need to maintain the independence of news television. The fear has always been that, any attempt at regulation risks throwing the baby out with the bathwater.

Yet, what we have in the form of oversight today in news television is tall promises of self-regulation that are given with seeming sincerity, but always fall prey to the weekly tyranny of ratings. There is still no overarching regulatory body to oversee broadcasting issues and compared to other developed television markets, Indian broadcasting exists within a highly confusing maze of overlapping controls. Such a state of affairs, at a time when India is fast emerging as a new global media capital cannot be sustainable.

In a sense, Indian television has continued to operate in a legal framework that is more akin to that utterly untranslatable North Indian word: jugaad. Jaipal Reddy's Broadcasting Bill of 1997 was based on British law after studying the broadcasting systems of six countries — USA, UK, France, Germany, Italy and Australia — and sought to create a new legal structure for broadcasting but disappeared into oblivion when the Gujral government fell. Priyaranjan Dasmunshi's draconian version of such a Bill is now on the backburner. Since the 1995 Cable Networks Regulation Act (which has limited uses), Parliament has only managed to pass one major broadcasting-related bill — the 2007 Act on mandatory sharing of sports feeds. And, that only passed because of the immense drawing power of cricket. The Ministry of Information and Broadcasting has periodically tried to fill the regulatory vacuum with draft legislation and summary executive directives/notifications.

Figure 1 charts out the battles over every legislative bill and most policy measures that the Ministry has tried to enact since 1994. It has often given the appearance of trying to put the genie of broadcasting back into the bottle and the lack of consensus on a new Broadcasting Bill means that the legal framework underpinning private broadcasting still remains a minefield. A recent industry move to add more teeth to its self-regulation mechanism, with backing from the Ministry, is still untested.

Second, we have already noted in the previous sections, there are issues over political control of regional language networks and the stranglehold of cable operators over distribution networks in most states. This is an area

LEGISLATION/ GUIDELINE	PROBLEM/STATUS	REASON/RESOLUTION
Cable Networks (Regulation) Act, 1995	Largely focused on distribution	Broadcasters based overseas & difficult to control
Broadcasting Bill, 1997	Introduced in Parliament but lapsed	Collapse of United Front govt.
Communications Convergence Bill 2001	Lapsed	Collapse of 13th Lok Sabha
Cable Networks (Regulation) Amendment Act, 2003	Withdrawn in 2004, being introduced in 3 metros after court order	Political agitation by cable operators supported by Delhi BJP
News Channel Uplinking Guidelines 2004	Changed repeatedly	Pressure by TV networks
The Sports Broadcasting Signals (Mandatory Sharing with Prasar Bharti)	Legislated to ensure telecast of Cricket matches on state network	Cricket nationalism
Broadcasting Services Regulation Bill, 2006	Draconian powers of news networks. Plans to introduce in Parliament dropped for fresh consultation	Public and media outcry Pressure by broadcasters

Fig. 1.   By fits and starts: Indian broadcast regulation.

that has so far been neglected in academic studies of Indian television and the latter problem of delivery platforms, in turn, is directly at the heart of the business model of Indian television. Not having control over their own distribution, leads to TV networks being inordinately dependent on advertising and greater relative expenditure on paying off cable operators just to be visible in viewer homes. Eventually, it has an adverse impact on content as ratings become even more important as a measure of viewership. This structural problem in many ways is at the center of the crisis of content that Indian television is currently facing. Progress on digitization and newer technologies that could change the current balance between networks and their distributors has been slow.

The other big question is one of expansion and what Indian television means for global flows of information. India's Zee TV is already a global satellite empire with 17 international and 25 domestic channels.[49] It had always been available in the Middle East, but by 2004 it was available in more than 120 countries on all continents. The international audience contributed 25% of its total revenues and of a total of 962,000 subscribers,

---

[49] Kamath and Venkat, 2006.

338,000 were in the Americas, 171,000 in Europe, 49,000 in Africa and 404,000 in the Asia-Pacific.[50] Significantly, roughly 70% of the content on these overseas channels consists of Indian programming, which is recycled, but the remaining 30% comprises local programming produced locally, including local news. Much of this focused on the diaspora, but Zee is now beginning to expand into foreign languages. By 2006, Zee had become confident enough to start dubbing its content into four foreign languages, starting with new services in Indonesia and Malaysia.[51] Its 24-hour channel in Bahasa Indonesia started in March 2006; a Russian entertainment channel, with Indian films dubbed in Russian, followed[52]; and Middle Eastern viewers have access to Zee Aflam, with programming in Arabic.

As a senior Zee executive in says, "Our demographic surveys show that the subtitling in local languages is very important for the diaspora as their children can then understand Indian programming. This is a big component of our strategy there."[53] This expansion is being driven partly by the fact that Indian channels can tap into the immense cultural capital of Bollywood. From the 1950s, the popular culture of Bollywood has always been popular in vast areas from Russia, to the Middle East to the Far East. For instance, in 2002, one of the most popular television events in Indonesia was Bollywood actor Shahrukh Khan live in concert.[54] It is not surprising therefore, that Indian television industry has begun to enter new markets by riding on the openings created by Bollywood.

By 2009, Zee had become aggressive enough to launch a mainstream and non-diasporic television network in the United States. Its fully owned Veria TV has not been acquired from another company, but was built from the

---

[50]Zee began operations in Africa in 1996 and the U.S. in 1998. Figures from "Zee Telefilms Limited: India's Leading Media and Entertainment Company", Zee TV Presentation at CLSA Investors' Forum. (Hong Kong, Sep. 2004), http://www.zeetelevision.com/Pdf/Presentations/Zee_Corporate_Nov_2006.pdf. [Accessed April 21, 2004].

[51]Subhash Chandra interview with Sanjay Pugalia on CNBC TV 18's Hindi news channel *Awaaz* (March 17, 2006), Transcript reproduced on http://www.indiantelevision.com/interviews/y2k6/executive/subhash_chandra.htm [Accessed April 15, 2006].

[52]Kamath, Venkat, 2006.

[53]Personal conversation with a senior Zee Asia-Pacific manager, Sep. 6, 2009.

[54]A.C. Nielsen Media Research figures quoted in Rachmah, 2006.

ground up as health and wellbeing TV network. Its broadcasts are supported by on-ground initiatives in the U.S. such as 120 wellness centers and spas, a medicine and supply chain network and a wellness helpline. Apart from its ownership pattern, there is nothing identifiably diasporic or Indian about it, like its other ventures. This is what makes Veria TV so unique. It is still too early to pass judgment on Veria TV, but its very existence is a reflection of the expanding muscle of Indian television overseas.

Zee is not the only Indian network spreading its wings overseas. In June 2006, NDTV partnered with Astro, a leading South East Asia media group, to jointly launch a 24 hour news, infotainment and lifestyle channel called "Astro Awani" in Indonesia. Broadcasting primarily in Bahasa Indonesia and distributed throughout Indonesia on PT Direct Vision's platform, this is the first channel launched by NDTV's outside India. It is also the first news channel in Astro's bouquet of channels and the deal is simple: NDTV has set up the entire infrastructure, because it is already running similar channels in India, and Astro provides the content. This is the first instance of an Indian company launching a news and infotainment channel outside India in partnership with an international media company. NDTV's chairman is clear on the implications of this deal for the future of his company: "We regard this as one our most exciting new ventures and look forward to launching many more channels outside India in the future." (Media News, 2006). NDTV's Indian channels themselves are now available across North America and all over South-East Asia. Just as India emerged as a major platform for outsourcing of game designs and cartoon animation and NDTV's venture in Indonesia indicates that the same process is underway with television channels. NDTV and Zee's domestic news networks have long been available on existing satellite platforms in North America and Europe, but these have been primarily watched by for viewers of Indian origin. We are now seeing a new trend which has implications far beyond the diaspora.

At a time when China is significantly expanding its global media footprint, this discussion raises the prospect of one of the great might-have-beens of Indian television. Robin Jeffrey (2008) has argued that an alert, well-funded public broadcaster could have given India a global media presence like the BBC, long before the appearance of Fox, Al-Jazeera or even CNN. As he put it, the talents existed from the 1950s, as did Indian aspirations to lead the "non-aligned movement." But fears about the dangers of electronic media, and the temptations of media control, produced policies in the 1950s that Indian public broadcasting still struggles to modify. This could still be a great "might-be": An Indian version of the BBC World Service, sufficiently removed from government to be able to respond quickly and efficiently to demands of news and entertainment, emerging as an attractive transnational broadcaster.

India has many advantages: A tradition of media freedom, large numbers of talented English-speaking journalists, an expanding computer and electronics industry and a vast film industry with 70 years of experience. However, the private satellite networks are still too entrenched on the imperative of profit in a fast-fragmenting domestic market while All India Radio and Doordarshan are branches of government, too dependent on the whims and pressures of ruling governments.[55] The path that Indian private news television takes depends in part on the imaginations and the choices of the private interests that increasingly dominate India's electronic media but one thing though is certain. India is changing, it has changed.

Bibliography

Chakraborty, S. Akali Dal accused of "state terror" on cable ops in Punjab [internet] (8 August 2007). Available at: http://www.indiantelevision.com/headlines/y2k7/aug/aug105.php [Accessed August 9, 2007].

China Foreign Ministry, 2009. Spokesperson Jiang Yu's Regular Press Conference on 15 September. Available at: http://www.fmprc.gov.cn/eng/xwfw/s2510/t584510.htm. [Accessed September 20, 2009].

CNN-IBN, NSA says media hype on Chinese intrusions risky [internet] (19 September 2009). Available at: http://ibnlive.in.com/news/nsa-says-media-hype-on-chinese-intrusions-risky/101741-3.html [Accessed September 19, 2009].

Dreze, J and A Sen (1989). *Hunger and Public Action.* Oxford: Clarendon Press.

Fateh, S (2005). The geography of GEO. *Himal: South Asian,* 18(2), Sep–Oct. Available at: http://www.himalmag.com/2005/september/special_report_1.html [Accessed December 30, 2005].

Friedman, T (2006). *The World is Flat: The Globalized World in the Twenty-First Century.* Victoria: Penguin.

Ghose, B (2005). *Doordarshan Days.* New Delhi: Penguin/Viking.

---

[55] Jeffrey, 2008.

Gupta, S. Stop fighting the 1962 War (19 September 2009). *The Indian Express* [internet]. Available at: http://www.indianexpress.com/news/stop-fighting-the-1962-war/518975/0. [Accessed September 20, 2009].

Jeffrey, R (2003). *India's Newspaper Revolution: Capitalism, Politics and the Indian-Language Press.* New Delhi: Oxford University Press.

Jeffrey, R (2006). The Mahatma didn't like movies and why it matters: Indian broadcasting policy, 1920s–90s. In *Television in India, Satellites, Politics and Cultural Change*, N Mehta (ed.). London: Routledge.

Joshi, SR and B Trivedi (May 1994). *Mass Media and Cross-Cultural Communication: A Study of Television in India.* Report No. SRG-94-041. Ahmedabad: Development and Educational Communication Unit, Indian Space Research Organisation.

Kamath, V and A Venkat. Zee plans Russian channel foray (23 June 2006). *Business Line.* Reproduced on http://www.thehindubusinessline.com/2006/06/24/stories/200606240-1520500.htm. [Accessed Jun 24, 2006].

Kang, B. Breakfast TV (30 July 2001). *Outlook.*

Kumar, R. When news is just round the corner (2 May 2008). *The Hindustan Times* (New Delhi).

Lutgendorf, P (1995). All in the (Raghu) family: A video epic in cultural context. In *Media and the Transformation of Religion in South Asia*, LA Babb and SS Wadley (eds.). Philadelphia: University of Pennsylvania Press.

Malik, A. No longer out of focus (7 June 2009). *The Hindustan Times* [internet]. Available at: http://209.85.135.132/search?q=cache:keBLPfu8yNwJ:www.hindu-stantimes.com/No-longer-out-of-focus/H1-Article1-418970.aspx+ashok+malik+hindustan+times+kevin+rudd+television&cd=2&hl=en&ct=clnk&gl=ch [Accessed June 9, 2009].

Manuel, P (1993). *Cassette Culture: Popular Music and Technology in North India.* Chicago: Chicago University Press.

Media News, NDTV Astro channel launched in Indonesia (Mumbai, 19 June 2006). www.exchange4media.com. [Accessed June 19, 2006].

MIB (Ministry of Information and Broadcasting), 2009. Available at: http://www.mib.nic.in/ShowContent.aspx?uid1=2&uid2=84&uid3=0&uid4=0&uid5=0&uid6=0&uid7=0 [Accessed December 6, 2009].

Mehta, N (2008). *India on Television: How Satellite TV Has Changed the Way We Think and Act.* New Delhi: Harper Collins.

NRS (National Readership Studies Council), 2006. *NRS 2006 — Key Findings*, Press Release. 29 Aug, Mumbai: NRS.

Population Reference Bureau, *2006 World Population Data Sheet.* Washington: PRB.

PricewaterhouseCoopers, FICCI, 2005. *The Indian Entertainment Industry: An Unfolding Opportunity.* New Delhi: FICCI.

Rachma Ida, The Construction of the Television Audience in Indonesia. Paper at "Television in Asia" conference, La Trobe University (Melbourne: 12 December 2005).

Registrar General of India, 2001. *Projected and Actual Population of India, States and Union Territories, 1991.* New Delhi: Office of the Registrar General, India.

Rajagopal, A (2001). *Politics After Television: Religious Nationalism and the Reshaping of the Indian Public.* Cambridge: Cambridge University Press.

Raman, A. Down for the count (12 May 2008). *Outlook.* New Delhi

Ranganathan, M (2006). Television in Tamil Nadu politics. *Economic and Political Weekly*, 41(48), 2 December.

Rao, BV. Madam Minister, please read the NBA's unwritten code of collective silence (25 September 2009). Available at: http://www.exchange4media.com/e4m/news/fullstory.asp?news_id=35997&section_id=6&pict=5&tag=31896 [Accessed Sep 26, 2009].

Sainath, P (2005). When farmers die: India's agrarian crisis, farmers, suicides and the media, July 13. Melbourne South Asian Studies Group Seminar, Australian Volunteers International.

Sardesai, R. Prime time reservation (29 May 2006) [internet]. Available at: http://www.ibnlive.com/blogs/rajdeepsardesai/1/11708/prime-time-reservation.html [Accessed May 30, 2006].

Schudson, M (1995). *The Power of News.* Cambridge: Harvard University Press.

Sen, A (2005). *The Argumentative Indian.* London: Penguin.

Sen, A (2002). *Rationality and Freedom.* Cambridge: Belknap Press.

STAR Ananda (n.d.), *Kolkata Municipal Election* tapes, STAR Archives.

Thompson, JB (1995). *The Media and Modernity: A Social Theory of the Media.* Cambridge: Polity Press.

Wade, M. No longer cricket for Australians in India (25 September 2009). *Sydney Morning Herald.* Available at: http://www.smh.com.au/opinion/society-and-culture/no-longer-cricket-for-australians-in-india-20090924-g4o7.html. [Accessed Sep 30, 2009].

Wade, M. Serious damage as "racist Australia" airs in India (4 July 2009). *Sydney Morning Herald.* Available at: http://www.theage.com.au/world/serious-damage-as-racist-australia-airs-in-india-20090703-d7u4.html. [Accessed Sep 30, 2009].

We The People, Oct 2005. [television programme] on NDTV 24 × 7.

Chapter 6

Economic Challenges for South Asia

*Jaspal Singh Bindra**

1. Introduction

Strong domestic demand, policy support and a post-conflict rebound (in Sri Lanka) defined a floor and thus enabled a quick recovery in South Asia post the financial crisis. Indeed, while it is true that growth slowed by 3% points between 2007 and 2009[1] in this region, it was the least pronounced amongst all developing regions, compared with the decline of 13% for emerging economies, 8% for Latam and 5% for East Asia. On a more positive note, it is widely expected that the region would reach its precrisis growth levels soon as several major economies still struggle to propel economic activity. Whilst such rates of change give us reasons to be optimistic on the outlook for this region, it is useful to keep a tab of the economic challenges which needs to be addressed to unleash the true potential. In this context, I would like to focus on three interlinked areas — (i) reduce vulnerabilities exposed during the financial crisis, (ii) enable growth and (iii) and ensure a human face to the overall growth story.

*Jaspal Singh Bindra is the Group Executive Director and a member of the Board of Standard Chartered PLC and is based in Hong Kong as Chief Executive Officer, Asia.
[1]IMF estimates.

2. Reduce Vulnerabilities Exposed During the Financial Crisis

This requires three action points viz. compress fiscal deficit, develop domestic financial market and increase regional integration.

First, as the downturn in economic activity was not overly pronounced in the region, the need to maintain an expansionary fiscal policy for long was not felt. In fact, economies like India and Bangladesh embarked on an exit strategy in H2 2009. However, had the crisis prolonged further, these economies would have been forced to provide more fiscal policy support, much beyond their capacity. The region as a whole has always lived beyond its means. Persistent fiscal deficit and high public debt constraints it from pursuing counter cyclical polices without choking investors' confidence which in turn can negate the stimulus effect. For economies like Pakistan and Sri Lanka, adhering to fiscal deficit targets is crucial because the IMF aid is tied to them. Also, recurrent government borrowing from the market crowds out private sector investment and deters development of domestic financial market, especially the debt market.

More importantly, had higher capital or developmental expenditure been at the root of such persistent deficits, it could have been still comfortable. However, recurrent expenditures like huge salary payment, interest payment and subsidies leave little room for such expenditures either during the normal or crisis period. Thus there is an imperative need to widen space on this front to provide better fighting muscles to any future crisis.

Can this be achieved? Most probably yes. As mentioned before, the region as a whole has ascended on a higher growth trajectory, indicating that higher revenues generation is more probable than a decade before. Also, tax reforms like implementation of Goods and Services Tax say in India can reduce distortions by removing cascading effects of several taxes existing now. In other economies, introduction of value added tax can be important.

Expenditure management is also critical. The proposed elimination of the continued losses due to inefficient administration in seven large state-owned enterprises in Sri Lanka through a strong reform program is one of such initiatives. Subsidies can be next. However arguments in favor of continuation of subsidies might be valid as the region is still developing. Still, better targeting is extremely important to avoid leakages. In this context, India's new initiative to better identify its citizens through the

Unique Identification (UID) programme is noteworthy as it cuts down on the layers of various intermediaries. Privatization is yet another way as it cuts down on recurrent expenditures like salary payments while improving efficiency simultaneously. Governments can use this as a useful mechanism to fund developmental projects without resorting to fresh borrowings. India is again a good example in this context.

Indeed, steps to increase public participation in the government owned companies can help in the development of the financial markets as equity markets will gain further depth while lower government borrowing needs in turn will provide breathing space for the development of corporate debt market. This brings me to the second action point viz. development of financial markets for financial stability of the region as a whole. The financial crisis demonstrated this as slower capital flows increased the dependency on the banking sector. Lack of vibrant corporate debt markets left these corporates with little option but to borrow from the banks. For instance, India Inc funded close to 50% of its borrowing needs from the banking sector during the crisis unlike the recent average of 30%. This obviously can exert pressure on the banking channel. Thus, while dependence on foreign capital cannot be eliminated, resilient domestic markets can provide greater flexibility in times of crisis.

Also, as the slow-down in the developed countries is expected to stay for longer, it underscores the need for South Asian economies to focus more on regional cooperation and trade in order to enhance their resilience to future global shocks. South Asia remains the least-integrated region in the world. Intraregional trade amounts to a little more than 1% of the regional GDP in South Asia compared to almost 2.7% in the Middle East and North Africa, 3.7% in Sub-Saharan Africa, 7% each in Latin American and East Asia, and 16% in Europe and Central Asia.[2]

According to one of the recent studies by IMF, there is a need to enhance South Asia's Look East Strategy. Their estimates indicate that integration with East Asia can be as large as some U.S. $450 billion of increased trade while trading closely within the region can result in some U.S. $50 billion worth of additional trade. However, increase in trade will not be

---

[2]World Bank, 2007.

possible without an improvement in infrastructure — both institutional and physical — and this brings me to the second major point of my presentation.

3. Enable Potential Growth to Unleash and Sustain

The region has attained strong growth rates essentially driven by the services sector. However, services-led growth that bypasses physical infrastructure cannot be an answer for the region's sustainable growth story. This is so as it over jumps the labor-intensive manufacturing growth needed for creating millions of new jobs for the increasing working population. The region is expected to add XX million people in the next 10 years through to 2020 to its labor force against the addition of 20 million by China in the same period.

More importantly, under investment in infrastructure facilities has prevented the region from realizing its economic potential. According to a 2009 study by McKinsey, delayed implementation of infrastructure projects will cost India as much as U.S. $200 billion by 2017, assuming an average GDP growth rate of 7.5% between 2008 and 2017. This is on top of an estimated U.S. $160 billion in losses arising from lost industrial productivity and 30–35 million lost jobs, which could have reduced the unemployment rate and potentially moved almost 4% of the country's population above the poverty line. While the study acknowledges that there is no conclusive approach to estimating the impact on productivity, a lack of adequate infrastructure is clearly a major hurdle to India's ability to achieve its potential growth rate. Other countries in the region are no exception. According to the World Economic Forum's Global Competitiveness 2010–2011 ranking Sri Lanka ranks 70 followed by India at 86 while the other countries are even further behind when assessed on infrastructure facilities.

The biggest gaps are in energy, transport, ports, and urban development. According to ADB, firms face rising power shortages throughout South Asia, and some 40% have standby generators; in Bangladesh, they face frequent power cuts (the peak gap between demand and supply of power is close to half of its generating capacity). In Pakistan, the debilitating power crisis has cost the economy 2.5% of GDP, according to government estimates. Electricity losses during transmission and distribution (T&D) further worsen the situation. It is estimated that almost 27% of the electricity generated in India in FY08 was lost during the T&D process.

Transport is choking everywhere and several investment climate surveys have pinpointed it as a sore point. While national highways comprise only 2% of India's road network, they carry 40% of total road traffic. According to one study, lack of adequate road network results in U.S. $6 billion of economic losses each year. In Pakistan, over half the national highways network is in poor condition and truck operating speeds on the main corridors are only 40–50 kph for container traffic, half the truck speeds in Europe. In Sri Lanka, while the end of three decades civil war has helped the government to step up its investment, the journey has just started. Similarly, port congestion and erratic water supply also need urgent attention in the region. However, funding needs might be huge and high fiscal deficit restrict significant government participation. This makes private participation via public private partnership (PPP) inevitable if infrastructure spending has to be stepped up in the region.

India plans to double infrastructure investment to U.S. $1 trillion for the five-year period through to 2017, from U.S. $500 billion in the 2007–2012 period with 50% to be funded by the private sector. Bangladesh has also embraced the PPP model, and Sri Lanka has accelerated its infrastructure development. The emphasis in Sri Lanka is on petroleum exploration, road development, ports and agriculture, with "mega-projects" underway at an estimated cost of U.S. $5.6 billion — nearly 12.5% of projected 2010 GDP. The massive multi-million rupee development projects on the five ports in Sri Lanka which are currently being carried out will generate over 250,000 direct and indirect employment opportunities within the next five years with over U.S. $1.7 billion being spent by the government on such development projects. That said, the government is expected to maintain public investment largely for infrastructure development at 6%–7% of GDP in 2011.

While acknowledgment of the growing role of private sector in developing infrastructure is encouraging, efforts to make such investments attractive for the private sector are extremely important. This brings me to the second related point — the need for effective governance. Even as most of the south Asian economies today have electoral democracies, albeit with varying degree of sustainability, high level of corruption, cumbersome bureaucracy, lack of accountability and transparent policy framework has deterred sufficient private interest. Trust in politicians is limited and weak property rights along with inflexible labor laws permeate the business environment. According to the ease of doing business ranking,[3] South Asia ranks 118 on ease of doing business, much behind 89 for China and 95 for Latin America and Caribbean economies. Efforts from policymakers are visible. Bangladesh implemented a modern electronic company registration system, cutting the time by almost a month. In Pakistan, thanks to an e-services project and the introduction of digital signatures, new companies can register and file tax returns online.

However, these are baby steps and reform in this segment has a long way to go, more over as the threat of terrorism has increased significantly in the past few years. Pakistan has been hit by a severe bout of terrorism; the deteriorating security environment, along with record-high inflation and a debilitating power crisis, has eroded the political capital of the ruling PPP government. While Bangladesh's political situation is much quieter than in previous years, demonstrations against the ruling Awami League on rising prices and a perception that economic policy is dictated by multilateral agencies rather than domestic needs has kept political tensions high. Recent terror attacks by Maoist groups in eastern India have attracted domestic and international attention; they are mild in comparison with the domestic conflicts elsewhere in the region. Sri Lanka, on the other hand, is reaping the post-conflict peace dividend. Human rights issues and war crimes allegations still haunt the country, but strong political will and support from agencies like the IMF are positives.

4. Ensure a Human Face to Economic Growth

For the first time in its long history, the people of South Asia have the chance of sharing gains amongst a larger section of the population as it has ascended on a higher growth trajectory. The approach, however, has to be two pronged — preserve the purchasing power of the population and pull more and more people out of poverty.

The broad demand–supply mismatch as growth moves to a higher trajectory in the region while investment in agriculture sector remains inadequate has created a persistent inflation problem, irrespective of commodity price shocks. Though inflation rates vary within the region

---

[3]A global ranking conducted by the World Bank.

(mid-single digits in Sri Lanka and Bangladesh and high single digits in India and Pakistan), structural changes flag the need of urgent policy measures to revitalize agriculture sector. Indeed, there is a need for a green revolution in this region if food inflation is to be controlled.

Also, as the regions depend on imports to meet its energy needs, vulnerability to price shock is high. Energy security is thus no longer merely a catchphrase, but an indisputable reality for vital economic development throughout South Asia. Here, attempts to diversify sources of fuel supply and improve the distribution will be important to ensure some lid on the prices.

Simultaneously, steps are needed to pull out the mass majority of people who live below the poverty line. While the world lauds the rise of the middle class especially in India, high incidence of poverty in the region continues to be a dark spot. India houses 462 million poor, according to the recently defined national poverty line; poverty in Pakistan is estimated to have increased sharply in the last three years, to 40% of the population in 2010. Besides the slow pace of poverty reduction, human development has not kept up with the pace of income growth, either. There are more than 250 million children in South Asia who are undernourished, and more than 30 million children who do not go to school. Over one-third of adult women are anemic.

Though there is no universal "fix" in economic development, it is imperative to find a solution. While simply directing financial resources to lagging regions or sections of population might help in some cases, the menace of leakages needs to be watched. Understanding what makes people poor is equally important to tailor policies for eradication of poverty. Thus, more emphasis on job creation, skill development and education is important. India's effort to promote schemes like National rural employment guarantee programme (guarantees 100 days of work to one member of rural household every year) has helped households on the margin to avoid falling into a poverty trap. Better social safety nets should also be a core element of the strategy to lower income inequality. Human development through increased public private partnership can be important too. Increased social responsibility amongst corporates is already an emerging trend. Further efforts are needed to encourage this. Social stock exchanges can be important in this context. The Social Stock Exchange is a Fund Raising initiative — first time launched by BOVESPA in the second half of 2003, which brings together nonprofit organizations that require funds and social investors (donors) willing to support their programs and projects. Just as it happens in the Stock Market, the nonprofit organizations build strength and pays back the investment as social profit.

5. Conclusion

In a nutshell, each of the challenges as discussed above are daunting. However, complacency is not an answer to it. We need to remember that most of these problems are manmade and if not possible to eliminate, can be ameliorated by increased coordination. The shift of balance of power from west to east provides an excellent opportunity, but the choice now rests with all stakeholders.

Chapter 7

Moving Up, Looking East — Prospects for South Asia's Integration After the Global Crisis

Dipak Dasgupta* and Nihal Pitigala[†]

1. Introduction

This paper examines regional integration prospects and policies for South Asia — with East Asia and between countries within the South Asia region — in the context of expected global rebalancing after the recent crisis and the expected shifts of global growth towards a more multi-polar world. Growing trade between South and East Asia, and that within the region — supported by an increasing number of regional trade agreements — makes this a matter of increasing reality.

South Asia is recovering well after this crisis, barring a few countries still severely affected by conflict and/or natural disasters. Future growth prospects of the region may well depend to a significant extent on how well the region continues to integrate with the rest of the world and with each other. Looking east, a process of faster integration with East Asia has already begun. With Asia growing fastest after the recent crisis, and the traditional industrial markets in North America and Europe slowing, the prospects are correspondingly better for this look east pattern of trade

---

*Principal Economic Adviser, Ministry of Finance, Government of India and was the Lead Economist (2009–2010) for the World Bank's South Asia region.
[†]Consultant at the International Trade Department of the World Bank.

and investment integration to accelerate. At the same time, this will be helped considerably by faster trade and investment integration within South Asia itself — offering greater opportunities for trade and scale economies. Policies to accelerate such patterns of trade and investment integration will therefore be essential to crowd in the private sector initiatives that are already well underway. The paper is in three parts. The first is on the implications of a "new normal" and global rebalancing for South Asian integration strategy. The second is a look at past patterns of growing trade and investment links with East Asia and possibilities for the future. The third is on prospects for growing integration within South Asia itself. This paper examines regional integration prospects and policies for South Asia — with East Asia and between countries within the South Asia region — in the context of expected global rebalancing after the recent crisis and the expected shifts of global growth towards a more multi-polar world. Growing trade between South and East Asia, and that within the region — supported by an increasing number of regional trade agreements — makes this a matter of increasing reality. The challenge for the South Asia region is to make its growth recovery from the recent crisis more durable, inclusive, and sustained in the medium-term. Part of that will require policy makers to reposition the region's trade and investment integration strategies after this crisis to a "new normal" in the global economy.[1] The ongoing global recovery will likely involve a fundamental restructuring of the economic order, where industrial country growth will be hesitant and slow to recover, whereas that in emerging markets will be much stronger. South Asia will correspondingly need to shift its market integration strategy, as developed countries start to save more and spend less and grow more slowly in North America and Europe, and as the East, especially Asia and emerging markets, overall look to become bigger drivers of global growth. In that setting, the South Asia region faces three interrelated challenges, as well as opportunities: to enhance its

---

[1]The "new normal" anticipates several fundamental shifts: muted growth (1%–2%, not 3%) with a shift away from the G-7 to emerging markets; slower consumption with debt-laden consumers and governments; financial markets facing greater regulatory burdens; banking being a shadow of its old self; a longer path of unemployment; and rising inflation expectations, currency, and sovereign risks (El-Erian, 2009; Davis, 2009; Galston, 2010). Many agree on a global recovery led by emerging markets, while households and governments struggle with higher debt and unemployment.

Look East strategy, looking to integrate faster with East Asia (the gains are potentially large, some U.S. $450 billion of increased trade annually); to find opportunities among countries in the region to integrate more closely with each other (the gains also are potentially big, some U.S. $50 billion of additional trade); and to maintain its traditional links with industrial markets, which will continue to be important for labor-intensive exports and for the demand and supply of high-value services, capital, know-how, and foreign direct investment, in sectors (from manufacturing to infrastructure, finance, and logistics) that remain crucial to South Asia's growth. The first section begins with an overview of the ongoing shift of global demand after this crisis to Asia and other emerging regions, and the relative decline of industrial country markets, and its implications for South Asia's trade prospects. The second section then analyzes the opportunities of expanding trade and investment links with East Asia. With a combined GDP of U.S. $6 trillion, it is South Asia's fastest-growing natural trade partner. Given complementary economic structures and specialization possibilities, trade and investment integration would not only help expand South Asia's services trade, but also its domestic manufacturing base, as East Asia looks to shift out of labor-intensive sectors. Although there remains some skepticism about the gains from such faster regional integration for faster growth in South Asia, analysis suggests that the gains could be substantial. Exports and trade would rise in sectors important for South Asia, and benefit growth, jobs and productivity. And among the most important side benefits for South Asia, in particular, would be a reduction in large behind-the-border barriers, especially in trade related services, transport, and logistics, that would benefit growth in the region's economies as a whole. These gains will be even bigger if countries in South Asia succeed in integrating more closely with each other which is examined in the third section. A bigger and integrated regional market will attract greater investment, improve scale economies and efficiency in manufacturing, allow the development of more efficient services, and lower real trade costs within the region. Private investment is likely to lead the way. India, the largest economy, has a vital role to play help carry its smaller regional neighbors with it, even as it grows faster and looks East, and as its neighbors respond.[2] Growing bilateral hub-and-spoke

---

[2] Kumar and Singh, 2009; Francois *et al.*, 2009.

trade, manufacturing specialization, logistics, and private investment flows offer the most promising prospects to increase such intraregional trade — as recent successes and potential suggest (as in the case of Bhutan–India, Sri Lanka–India, and emerging possibilities for Bangladesh–India trade and investment, including transit trade arrangements with Nepal, Bhutan, and India's Northeast). The strengthening of intra-regional trade will facilitate the growth of South-Asian–East Asian integration as trade barriers within the region are lowered. There are also similar opportunities for Pakistan–India trade, regional trade with the Middle East, and improved regional energy trade and transit arrangements (Central Asia–Afghanistan–Pakistan–India, hydropower potential in Nepal and Bhutan, and in the East with Myanmar), as power shortages are a rising and critical bottleneck to growth. A repositioning of trade and investment externally, that is, based on an accelerated regional and intra-regional integration can therefore be an important part of the adjustment in South Asia to the "new normal" in the global economy, in two important ways. First, as an instrument by which to achieve lower real trade costs, both at and behind the border, which will benefit producers and consumers throughout the economies, and overall trade more generally. Second, as a way to attract into South Asia accelerated investments in manufacturing and services and allow the region to specialize in particular niches and become more integrated with global value chains. The two are related: Lower trade and input costs (including of services) are critical for improved competitiveness. The policy challenge will be to design regional cooperation and initiatives in ways that achieve these twin objectives.

2. Global Rebalancing and the Rise of Asia

2.1. *Global rebalancing after the crisis*

Global rebalancing has two distinct connotations: one, the rebalancing of current account deficits between surplus and deficit countries; the other, the longer-term process whereby emerging countries are gaining much larger weights in the global economy as they grow faster. The concern with global rebalancing in this section is primarily with the latter process — although the former is also accelerating the latter after this crisis, as deficit developed countries such as the United States and others in Europe start to slow down and reduce their consumption, even as surplus countries, often developing ones such as China and India, grow faster from domestic sources after this crisis.

Forces were at work well before the crisis to increasingly question the sustainability of rising global current account imbalances. The global crisis has now sharply hastened the processes, marking a decisive change to a "new normal" — with the contraction of growth in advanced countries, an unwinding of global current account imbalances, and a shifting of centers of economic activity. Countries with large current account deficits, such as the United States, are now reducing imports because of depressed domestic demand and are seeking to raise exports by improving competitiveness and shifting to new export markets, and countries with large surpluses have stimulated domestic demand, raising imports and reducing their surpluses. As a consequence, the contribution to global GDP growth of developing countries, including China, India, Brazil, and other big emerging markets, has risen — with Asia the fastest growing region of the world — whereas that of high-income countries has diminished sharply, as their economies were the epicenter of this crisis. This process is expected to continue, as the high-income countries grapple with the long-lasting effects of the current crisis and with the recovery in capital flows to developing countries, as investors seek to raise returns by investing in countries with stronger fundamentals and growth outcomes.

By 2020, Asia could become the largest center of economic activity, with its share of world GDP projected to reach close to 35%. Correspondingly, the share of the United States and NAFTA would shrink from 35% posted in the wake of the East Asian crisis in 1998 to 27% in 2020 (see Fig. 1). Driving this change is the projected increase in weights of China and India, but also of other emerging markets. Indeed, under this scenario, by 2020, the share of all large emerging market countries in the global economy would account for close to one-half of the global economy.

2.2. *Global merchandise import-demand is shifting to China, East Asia, and other emerging markets*

Over the past few decades, the import share of China in world merchandise imports has increased rapidly, whereas the share of the United States

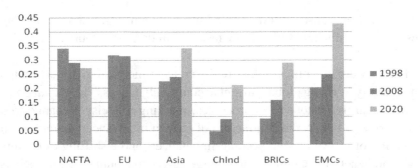

Fig. 1.   The growing role of emerging markets (share of world GDP, in current U.S. $).
Source: Authors' estimates, extrapolated from IMF, *World Economic Outlook to 2020*.

has fallen — a consequence of differing growth rates and relocation of manufacturing. The secular decline in the share of world imports in high-income countries such as the United States has accelerated during this crisis and has been matched by the rise in import shares of emerging markets in Asia, such as China. This is also reflected in the relative importance of South Asia's main export markets: During and after the crisis, East Asia has become the biggest merchandise trade export market for South Asia, supplanting the markets in advanced countries. Together, developing countries currently account for close to 70% of South Asia's total merchandise exports, reversing the picture that prevailed only a decade ago in 2000.

2.3. *In South Asia*

As can be seen in Fig. 2, bilateral trade between India and China has been on the rise and has surpassed the bilateral trade between India and the United States since 2008. Furthermore, trade between India and China held up during the crisis, whereas that between India and the United States showed a declining trend. This provides initial evidence that South-South trade is becoming more important now (see Box 1) and has recovered much faster than South-North trade. There is similar evidence from other South Asian countries. Share of exports from Pakistan to the United Arab Emirates plus Afghanistan, for example, has surpassed the corresponding share from Pakistan to the United States. It is also worth noting that all the top four importing countries from Pakistan are developing countries or

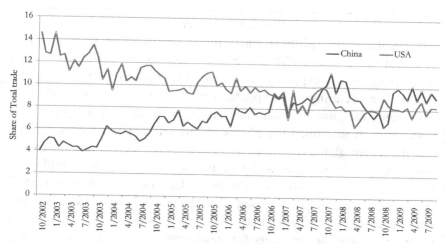

Fig. 2.   Share of India's bilateral trade with China and the United States.

Middle Eastern countries. Similarly, for Bangladesh and Sri Lanka, China, and India are the two most important trading partners, accounting for 30% of their total imports for both countries.

Box 1. Global rebalancing effects on developing country exports after the crisis

Two recent papers provide some analysis of the likely effects of global rebalancing on developing country exports after the crisis. The first (Canuto, Haddad and Hanson, 2010) suggests that a protracted contraction in final consumption in the United States and Europe, in the light of global rebalancing after the crisis, will hurt exports from low-income developing countries, especially in labor-intensive exports such as garments. However, South-South trade could play a powerful offsetting role. Such imports had been growing strongly even before this crisis, especially in the BRIC countries (Brazil, Russia, India, and China). After this crisis, these countries will play an increasingly important role, exceeding the contribution of the United States and Europe. These middle-income countries could also drive export diversification over time, with low-income countries occupying labor-intensive manufacturing niches as higher middle-income countries shift out of these sectors, diversify, and specialize.

Box 1. (*Continued*)

A second paper (Milberg and Winkler, 2010) looks more closely at global value chains (GVCs). It first analyzes the rapid growth in developing country exports and trade prior to this crisis, driven in part by GVCs and cutting up the production chain. It goes on to attribute, like others, the large downturn in world trade to the increasing role of GVCs, which magnified the effects of this crisis. The paper suggests that the recent global downturn in trade has been deeper and different from previous downturns and that it will likely lead to significant shifts — especially consolidation in "buyer-led" global chains, but also to "greater diversity" in producer-led global chains. The former will reduce opportunities, but the latter may well create others. It concludes that there are promising prospects for rapid growth in South-South trade after this crisis, especially if there are closer production ties between developing countries and regions, but that the prospects are more limited if consolidation in global value chains dominates.

2.4. *East Asia represents the greatest potential for growth in merchandise trade for South Asia*

Using an augmented gravity model, postcrisis medium-term estimates (with revised partner GDP growth estimates through 2014) of India's global merchandise trade potential, for example, suggests that the increase in India's trade potential will be highest with the Asia-Pacific region, followed by the European Union and NAFTA, and then by South Asia (De, 2010).[3] Potential for expansion of India's trade in the postcrisis period is highest with countries such as China and ASEAN-6. However, India's trade has remained unrealized with other large parts of the world, which presents further opportunities for expanding trade, despite a slowdown in global demand. The estimates of the gravity model suggest that trade with developing

---

[3]The paper estimates trade potential between India and its partner countries for (i) the precrisis and (ii) the postcrisis periods, using an augmented gravity model (Anderson–van Wincooop type), where bilateral trade is expected to be proportional to the product of economic sizes of country pairs and inversely related to the distance between them, among other factors.

East Asia has the potential to increase 32% per annum by 2014 (or an incremental U.S. $360 billion in exports by 2014, compared to an actual of U.S. $126 billion in 2008). This is twice as high as the potential increase in trade with the EU-25 group (15% per annum growth potential and an incremental gain of U.S. $190 billion), and three times as large as with NAFTA (21% annual growth potential and an incremental export potential of U.S. $120 billion). Trade within South Asia also has strong potential to grow and is complementary to the above. If regional markets grow, it will attract greater trade and investment, and improve scale economies and efficiency, especially in manufacturing. Estimates suggest fast potential of about 36% annual growth — the fastest for all of India's trade partners — although the absolute incremental gain in exports would be relatively small (U.S. $50 billion annually), given the small starting base.

2.5. *High-income countries remain important for global services trade*

In contrast to merchandise trade, high-income countries in the European Union and North America will continue to play much bigger roles in world trade in services. There are several fundamental reasons: Higher incomes that generate greater demand for services, higher wages and the shift to knowledge-intensive activities in reflection of differences in relative skills and factor endowments, and demographics that favor the demand for services. Europe, for example, still accounts for about 50% of global service imports, followed by Asia with about 25% (of which Japan is a big contributor) and the United States with some 17%. The United States remains the primary market for India's service exports to the OECD countries, accounting for 51% of total Indian exports to these markets, and an even larger 60% share of its exports of IT and IT-enabled services. With service exports constituting about one-third of South Asia's exports — with information technology, business process outsourcing, and tourism and travel playing large roles — the potential markets in high-income countries remain the biggest, even as rising incomes in East Asia and elsewhere provide new, albeit smaller, sources of growth and dynamism. Services trade imports (and FDI) are also crucial for South Asia as it seeks to upgrade its own domestic manufacturing and services sectors, in transport, logistics, and financial services, among others. As a result, a nuanced approach will be useful: With merchandise trade shifting to neighboring Asia, the traditional high-income countries will remain important markets and sources of service sectors. Enhancing and opening FDI into service sectors are important to facilitate this process.

2.6. *The gains to growth and welfare from faster regional integration with East Asia*

A formal analysis using CGE modeling confirms that a broader South Asia–East Asia integration would provide large gains to exports and trade for South Asia and to overall welfare (Francois and Wignaraja, 2008). Compared to a baseline scenario, exports from Bangladesh would be higher by 52%, for India by 23%, and between 6% and 7% for Sri Lanka and Pakistan. Sectorally, much of the gains from South Asia are in services, because no change is assumed for South Asia's potential for rising manufacturing exports. The aggregate welfare gains would also be significant, between 2% and 4% of base income. Typically, as with all such CGE models, these static gains considerably understate the growth impacts because of limited dynamic effects of higher cross-border investment decisions that follow the static gains. Conversely, the CGE modeling result also suggests most crucially that it is India's participation that provides most of the gains to East Asia. For the South Asian economies themselves, countries other than India gain significantly *only if* India carries its neighbors in South Asia with it. In its absence, the India–East Asia integration scenario produces significant trade and welfare losses for India's neighbors. The paper also models the impact of a subregional FTA within South Asia itself. The results suggest that India gains modestly from a South Asian subregional FTA, compared to that from a larger trade agreement targeting East Asia, even as the gains are bigger for its neighbors — again suggestive of the argument that South Asia–East Asia trade gains provided South Asian countries also open their markets to each other.

2.7. *Gains to growth from reduced behind-the-border barriers*

The results above are only illustrative of the possible directions of static gains of trade. Dynamic gains from cross-border investment flows in support of trade would be much bigger. Moreover, the effects of such opening would potentially raise the economy-wide productivity and scale economies of domestic firms and industries, as suggested earlier. Finally, the biggest specific gain from a regional trade deepening with East Asia and within South Asia may well be to lower what are currently very high trade-related service, transport, logistics, regulatory, and institutional barriers, with impacts on economy-wide domestic growth in South Asia. Regional trade agreements by themselves would do little to address these constraints, because such trade agreements are limited to shallow tariff reductions, with often large nontariff barriers and restrictive rules of origin. Instead, the true gains would emerge if the Look East and related initiatives induced improved policies and institutions in individual South Asian countries through unilateral and accelerated liberalization of trade and investment within the context of a regional framework. Behind-the-border barriers are important: high freight costs, delays in customs, slow port processing, transport bottlenecks, and bureaucratic and regulatory bottlenecks. Not only do they impede trade, but they work backwards throughout the economy and are one of the important reasons for the "missing middle" in South Asian manufacturing.

2.8. *Gains to growth from exploiting niches and potential in global value chains*

As suggested in a recent paper,[4] unlike East Asia, South Asia has failed to insert itself into global manufacturing supply chains, processing trade supply chains, and other ICT supply chains other than in textiles and garments. One of the principal reasons is such behind-the-border constraints. Regional services and cross-border investment in services can be a powerful engine for easing these constraints endogenously. The effects can be as powerful as increasing trade impacts by a factor of two or more.[5] East Asia, in particular, has developed specific expertise — its cost to export (in U.S. $ per container in 2006–2007) was 773, versus 1180 for South Asia, for example — and it would provide competition and learning gains to South Asia.[6] The lowering of trade costs is one of the reasons why East Asia has become closely integrated and has been able to capitalize on its manufacturing potential in

---

[4]Sally, 2010.
[5]Hoekman and Nicita, 2008.
[6]Brooks and Stone, 2010.

global value chains. South Asia might be able to do the same by integrating faster with East Asia, and a lowering of barriers would help generate the investments that are needed for countries and locations to specialize more in niches and product varieties and to become more integrated in the global value chains.

2.9. *Repositioning South Asia's trade and investment*

The overall picture for South Asia's strategy for repositioning its trade and investment integration after this crisis and with global rebalancing thus suggests three major priorities: a shift to closer integration with East Asia as its fastest-growing trading partner; still important trade and investment links with high-income countries, especially in services trade (and also as a source of longer-term capital flows and know-how in domestic services and man-ufacturing); and closer integration among the countries in its own region.

3. South Asia Looking East

Against this setting, increasing trade with East Asia is becoming important (see Fig. 3). East Asia is now home to the third-largest regional market, with a combined GDP of U.S. $6 trillion (versus South Asia's combined GDP of U.S. $1.5 trillion). It has already become the biggest partner for South Asia. We examine first the past performance and its drivers, and then turn to future prospects and policies that will help determine future trade.

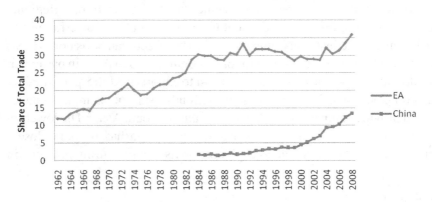

Fig. 3.   South Asia's rising trade with East Asia.
Source: World Trade Indicators.

Table 1.   South Asia trade expanding fastest with East Asia.

	1977–1987		2002–2008	
	Imports	Exports	Imports	Exports
All	11.6	8.5	27.1	21.4
East Asia	16.8	10.7	29.8	27.5
European Union (25)	13.8	7.6	21.9	20.2
South Asia	4.3	5.7	21	19.6
United States	7.1	17.2	26.5	11.3
Rest of the World	4.3	1.2	27.9	27.3

Source: Authors' calculations using UN Comtrade.

3.1. *Merchandise trade is growing rapidly*

As its natural trading partner,[7] East Asia's importance to South Asia (and the reverse) has grown since the 1970s, and especially in the past decade, even without formal preferential agreements.[8] By 2008, East Asia constituted the largest trading partner, accounting for approximately 36% of South Asia's merchandise trade. Total merchandise trade grew from U.S. $25 billion to U.S. $148 billion (still a small share, 2.5%, of East Asia's world merchandise trade) (Table 1). There were no apparent displacement effects, as South Asia's trade with other regions continued to expand rapidly (and faster than East Asia's).

---

[7]Richard Lipsey (1960) and Larry Summers (1990) have put forward the hypothesis of "natural trading partners," suggesting that a regional agreement is more likely to raise welfare effects the higher is the proportion of trade with the region and the lower the proportion with the rest of the world.

[8]East Asia is now home to the world's third-largest free trade association (FTA), with the launch of the ASEAN-China Free Trade Area (ACFTA) in 2002, and its full implementation since 2010. With its Look East policy, India also signed a free trade agreement with ASEAN in August 2009, which promises to expand the FTA further and deepen South Asia's trade with East Asia. Two prominent early RTAs were the Bangkok Agreement in 1975 by India, Bangladesh, Sri Lanka, Korea, and Lao PDR, and the Bay of Bengal Initiative for Multi-Sectoral Technical and Economic Cooperation (BIMSTEC) — comprising Bangladesh, Myanmar, India, Sri Lanka, Thailand, Nepal, and Bhutan — in 1997. Neither have provided significant market access due to unresolved issues with regard to "negative lists," rules of origin, and dispute-settlement procedures (Pursell *et al.*, 2001).

3.2. *Complementarity of South Asian and East Asian exports*

Is the faster growth of South Asia trade with East Asia a result of being displaced in third-country markets, particularly in the United States and European Union? The answer seems to be no, as South Asia continued to export strongly to third-country markets and capture larger market shares of merchandise trade. And South Asia's exports to the rest of the world continued to diversify to industrial processed goods and parts and components, even as its industrial primary exports to East Asia rose. Following Freund and Ozden (2006), we more formally test for these effects,[9] looking at the relationships between South Asia's exports and East Asia's exports in the same import markets.[10] Results are reported in Annex Table 1. It allows a test of whether East Asia is affecting South Asian countries negatively or positively in third-country markets. The results suggest that South Asia's exports grew more slowly than the total imports in these markets (the export supply coefficient for all South Asian countries was lower than 1, around 0.4). This suggests losses in market share in third countries other than East Asia, which is partly to be expected, given that such market shares in goods include nonfuel commodities, where South Asia does not have a strong comparative advantage. By contrast, the positive coefficients on East Asia's specific exports to these same third-country markets suggest strong complementarities in manufacturing — India's export growth is higher when East Asian exports are large and growing. This is also true for Pakistan, Bangladesh, and Sri Lanka, whereas the impact

---

[9]Estimating the following regression equation:

$$dexports_{ijkt} = \alpha_{it} + \beta_0 dimports_{jkt} + \beta_1 dEastAsia_{jkt} + \varepsilon_{ijkt}$$

where $dEast\,Asia_{jkt}$ is growth of East Asia's export in country j in sector k. The advantage of this specification is that we are exploiting both cross-section and time-series variation to estimate how South Asian countries are affected by East Asia. If East Asia has roughly the same effect on all exporting countries, then the coefficient yielded from the regression on imports will be close to 1, and the coefficient on East Asia will be 0. A negative coefficient on East Asia indicates that East Asian export growth is correlated with a decline in South Asian export growth in a given industry. We estimate this equation using data from 1990 to 2008, with the four-digit classification.

[10]Only nonfuel products are included; we also distinguish between industrial products (technology-intensive, skilled labor-intensive, unskilled labor-intensive) and nonindustrial products (agricultural products, minerals, raw materials).

is not significant for Nepal. Over time, the positive impact diminished during 2000–2008, except for in India — suggesting the emergence of some competition at the margin (e.g., as in the case of Bangladesh). This also highlights the importance of maintaining the competitiveness of export sectors (and real exchange rates), and reducing real trade costs at or behind-the-borders.

3.3. *Shifting composition of trade*

The growing trade between East Asia and South Asia is also enlarging the possibilities for domestic manufacturing. The composition of exports from South Asian countries to East Asia has, however, shifted toward industrial primary goods (see Fig. 4) — reflecting growing demand by China and other East Asian countries for such products in their manufacturing. They also reflect the effect of much higher trade costs in South Asia that prevent it from integrating with global value chains, as well as possible competitiveness issues. The major exports were metals, ores, and minerals (including petroleum products from India). The latter therefore requires closer attention and the discovery of possible ways to increase South Asia's ability to deepen its manufacturing trade potential with East Asia. The intensive margins (existing exports) still dominate for all major South Asian countries' exports to East Asia, although Sri Lanka, Pakistan and Bangladesh have experienced limited success in extensive margins in industrial primary and processed goods.[11] Conversely, the composition of imports by South Asia shifted toward industrial processed goods, especially capital goods and machinery and parts. Evidence points to a significant impact on productivity improvements.[12]

3.4. *Rising services*

Services trade for South Asia has been growing rapidly during the past decade. But this trade with East Asia so far has been relatively small.

---

[11]The intensive margin is typically thought to be more important for growth in exports between countries at similar levels of income (Brenton and Newfarmer, 2007; Amurgo-Pacheco and Pierola, 2008).
[12]Topalova, 2007; Nataraj, 2009.

2000   **2008**

INDIA

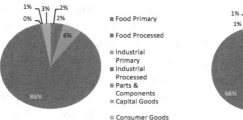
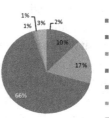

PAKISTAN

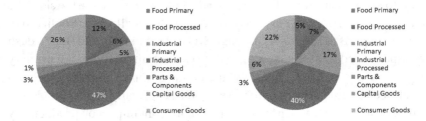

BANGLADESH

SRI LANKA

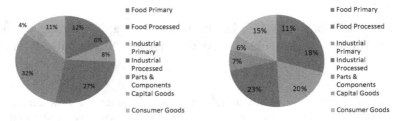

Fig. 4.   South Asia's composition of exports to East Asia.
Source: World Integrated Trade Solution (WITS).

Bilateral data flows are dominated by Indian exports (exports of U.S. $2.4 billion in services to Japan, Singapore, Hong Kong and China, equivalent to 16% of its total, in 2007). Transportation services, professional services, IT, financial services, and insurance services follow. The rest of South Asia's exports were in the traditional segments, mainly transport services. Sri Lanka shows a surge in exports as an emerging transshipment hub between the East and West.

3.5. *Tourism: The brightest spot?*

South Asia's overall tourism receipts have grown at 13.5% per annum between 2002 and 2007, compared to 8.1% in all developing countries. The impact reaches beyond direct expenditures on lodging, restaurants, entertainment, and retail, to include indirect impacts[13] (ranging from 5.3% of GDP in India to as much as 66.6% of GDP in Maldives). East Asia now accounts for a significant and growing share of South Asia's tourism. East Asian arrivals account for 26.5% of tourism arrivals in Nepal, 24.2% in India, 19.8% in Bangladesh, and 18.5% in Maldives (see Table 2), and they are growing.[14]

4. Prospects for Deeper Integration

Given the size of the East Asian region and South Asia, the faster growth prospects in both, and the increasing trade with each other along with mutual benefits, major gains are clearly to be realized from deepening trade and investment. Such trade would be complementary to each one's strengths and changing development patterns, and the evidence for this is suggested next. East Asia is exporting capital-intensive manufactures; is beginning to shift out of labor-intensive manufacturing and is exporting transport, logistics, tourism, financial, health, and other services to South Asia; even as South Asia is exporting more industrial products, gaining in third-country markets, and is expanding its service exports, especially in tourism, transport, IT,

---

[13]The World Travel and Tourism Council utilizes satellite accounting and input-output modeling to capture both direct and indirect impacts of travel and tourism.
[14]Data from India show that arrivals from East Asia grew 37% per annum between 2001 and 2006.

Table 2.   South Asia tourism, economic contribution and role of East Asia.

	Share of GDP (2006)	Share of Exports (2006)	Share of Tourism Arrivals	
			East Asia	South Asia
South Asia	5.5	5.4	n.a.	n.a.
Bangladesh	n.a.	n.a.	19.8	35.4
India	5.3	4.7	24.2	5.5
Maldives	66.6	65.9	18.5	4.5
Nepal	8.2	22.6	26.5	31.9
Pakistan	n.a.	n.a.	9.2	n.a.
Sri Lanka	9.6	14.9	10.4	36.4

Sources: Share of GDP and share of exports from World Travel and Tourism Council; share of tourism arrivals derived from available national tourism statistics (2006 for India and Pakistan, 2007 for others).

and business processes. The pace of growth and the size of benefits are clearly large. Underpinning the prospects are fast-expanding cross-border investments, as well as formalization of free trade agreements (FTAs).

4.1. *Rising merchandise-trade complementarity*

Trade has greater potential to grow if neighboring regions start growing trade in similar product lines — as they deepen their production relations. One way to assess this is by measuring so-called complementarity indexes, which correlate the countries' exports in similar products. These indexes for the two regions suggest that trade complementarity is growing (see Fig. 5).[15] Current South Asian values with respect to East Asia are similar to those for countries such as the original European Union (6) members at the time of the formation of the European Economic Community — suggestive of the scope for further gains.

---

[15]The trade complementarity, TC, between countries k and j, is defined as

$$\text{TC}_{ij} = 100 - \text{sum}(|m_{ik} - x_{ij}|/2)$$

where x_{ij} is the share of good i in global exports of country j, and m_{ik} is the share of good i in all imports of country k. The index is 0 when no goods are exported by one country or imported by the other and 100 when the export and import shares exactly match. As such, it is assumed that higher index values indicate more favorable prospects for a successful trade arrangement between countries.

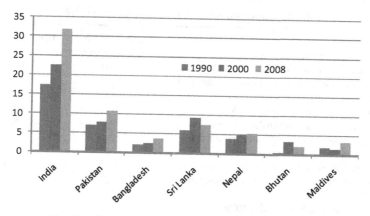

Fig. 5. Growing trade complementarity with East Asia.
Note: Complementarity index correlates exports of South Asian countries with imports of East Asia at the HS-6 disaggregated level — with increasing values suggesting strong positive matches of the two over time. Intra-industry trade indexes could reinforce the qualitative conclusions here, but we choose TCI as a more relevant measure.
Source: Authors estimates, World Bank. 2010.

4.2. *Supportive comparative advantage*

An alternative measure of trade potential is the so-called revealed comparative advantage (RCA), which calculates the share of one region's exports to another partner region, relative to total world exports. If this is greater than unity, it means greater comparative advantages in the other's market. Table 3 summarizes the picture on calculated RCA indexes for East and South Asia, where they have such advantages, based at a disaggregated product level.[16] The results again suggest strong complementarities. The key categories, where either region has a comparative advantage, comprise as many as 2843 products, or 64% of total trade, suggesting strong prospects for trade between East Asia and South Asia. Drilling down further to identify where South Asia's comparative advantage lies suggests that (i) South Asia has outright comparative advantages in food, organic and inorganic materials,

---

[16]At HS-6 level. However, RCA growth at country level and relative compositions may be more informative than levels. It is important to note, however, that the RCA index, as a measure of comparative advantage, does not discriminate between "inherent" comparative advantages and policy-induced comparative advantages. Any attempt to apply the concept of RCA to South Asian countries must therefore acknowledge the influence of distortions created by their policy regimes.

Table 3.   Revealed comparative advantage favorable (2008).

	Category	Number of Lines	Percent of Lines
1	Both East Asia and South Asia have positive RCA, but RCA in East Asia is greater than RCA in South Asia	540	12.3
2	Only East Asia has positive RCA	846	19.3
3	Both East Asia and South Asia have negative RCA, but RCA in East Asia is greater than RCA in South Asia	800	18.3
4	Both East Asia and South Asia have positive RCA, but RCA in South Asia is greater than RCA in East Asia	637	14.5
5	Only South Asia has positive RCA	820	18.7
6	Both East Asia and South Asia have negative RCA, but RCA in South Asia is greater than RCA in East Asia	740	16.9
		4383	

Source: Authors' calculations.

textiles, and metal products, and (ii) the products where both region's share positive revealed advantages in each others' markets, but where South Asia has greater advantages than East Asia, are apparel, yarn and textiles, and other labor-intensive manufactures (footwear, parts, jewelry). Ultimately, the drivers of such advantages stem from relative factor endowments — and their changes over time. Similar analysis[17] supports growing differences in factor intensities between the two regions as one factor in trade driving this, and hence driving growing complementarity.

A more detailed look at China's imports from South Asia shows that products in which South Asia has both a comparative advantage, as defined by RCA, and a growing market share in China numbered some 166 (out of a total 1594 products at Standard International Trade Classification five-digit level, exported by South Asia to China). Although small in number, those products together accounted for more than 47% of South Asia's merchandise exports to China. This finding bodes well for further export penetration. The exports remain concentrated in industrial primary products, with the exception of textiles.

---

[17]UNCTAD, 2009.

4.3. *Large production-sharing potential*

Beyond the static comparisons of complementarity and revealed comparative advantage are, however, the much greater potential for South Asia to integrate with global manufacturing (and services) value chains, by driving down real trade costs and trade and transport logistics barriers. The drivers of such trade go beyond relative factor endowments, to factors such as complementary use of information and communication technologies and natural geographies (clustering, agglomeration, and scale effects). Manufacturing production sharing (or vertical specialization) is a key characteristic in East Asia's regional integration and export dynamism.[18] So far, there has been a limited engagement with South Asia, but it is starting. Production-sharing in apparel and textiles is well established (Bangladesh and Sri Lanka with East Asia). India and Korea show greater production-sharing in automobiles and steel. A few projects in Sri Lanka supply truck parts, optical parts, telecommunications parts, and electrical parts manufactures that are exported to Japan, Korea, and Malaysia (Board of Investment, Sri Lanka). However, evidence suggests that the proportion of parts and components that constitute major activity in East Asia is only a small part of South Asia's trade with the East. By the same token, the room for growth is large if policies start to address the fundamental drivers, such as lowering the trade costs in South Asia.

4.4. *Rising foreign direct investment*

Asian outward FDI is playing an important role in promoting South Asia's extraregional and interregional trade (see Table 4). East Asian FDI was earlier key in transforming Bangladesh and Sri Lanka to labor-intensive textile and apparel exports. It is likely to prove equally important in fostering the shift to other sectors. The recent rise in FDI is already starting to do this. Time-series data of bilateral FDI flows (or stocks) between Asian economies is not readily available, but the data presented below provide some insights. First, the sources of FDI are diversifying: China, Malaysia, and Thailand joined traditional high-income countries, such as Hong Kong, China; Korea; Japan; and Singapore. Second, service sectors are assuming increasing

---

[18]Yeats, 2008; Kimura, 2006.

Table 4.   FDI inflows from East Asia.

	India (2008)		Pakistan (2007)		Bangladesh (2005)		Sri Lanka (2008)	
	Flow (U.S. $ millions)	Rank	Flow (U.S. $ millions)	Rank	Flow (U.S. $ millions)	Rank	Flow (U.S. $ millions)	Rank
Cambodia	—	—	—	—	—	—	—	—
China	50.5	35	101.4	6	0.9	21	101.2	3
Hong Kong, China	493.7	19	156.1	5	47.4	9	—	—
Indonesia	72.9	29	—	—	5.4	15	—	—
Japan	3481.1	6	74.3	10	22.8	10	26	8
Korea, Rep.	513.3	15	2.3	13	53.9	7	—	—
Lao PDR	240.9	24	—	—	—	—	—	—
Malaysia	3.2	75	—	—	44.5	12	162.6	1
Myanmar	1.4	80	—	—	—	—	—	—
Philippines	0.7	90	—	—	0	26	—	—
Singapore	9146	2	—	—	35.9	13	20.6	10
Taiwan, China	33.2	37	—	—	2.4	19	—	—
Thailand	55.5	34	—	—	0.1	25	—	—
Vietnam	0.1	100	—	—	—	—	—	—
Total	102, 058.7	—	3, 719.9	—	792.4	—	888.9	—

Sources: India: Ministry of Finance; Pakistan: Board of Investment 2010; Sri Lanka: Board of Investment 2010; Bangladesh: Board of Investment.

importance, helped by framework agreements, such as the Comprehensive Economic Cooperation Agreement (CECA) between India and Singapore; as a result, Singapore has climbed to become the second-ranked source in 2009, and India's service exports to Singapore have increased; there has also been a temporary movement of workers. Third, inflows of FDI are opening new sectors and directions. These are notable in sectors such as automobile manufacturing in India from Korea and Japan; electronics in India from Korea; Taiwan, China; and Singapore; infrastructure in India, Pakistan, Bangladesh, and Sri Lanka from China, Malaysia, and Singapore; and tourism and related aviation and freight and transshipping services across the region.

FDI outflows to East Asia, in services and overall, were minimal prior to 2004. By the end of 2005, more than 300 Indian IT companies had set up software development operations in Singapore. There are around 1500

Indian companies currently based in Singapore; on average, approximately 150 Indian companies set up base in Singapore every year.[19] Anecdotal evidence also indicates that much cross-border investment from East Asia to South Asia has been in services (under Mode 3 of GATS). Recent trends also point to opportunities in transport services, including recent heavy investment by China in Pakistan's transport infrastructure following the implementation of their own bilateral agreement.

Findlay *et al.* (2009) point to a number of other growing opportunities to expand service exports from South Asia to East Asia, including health services (India), travel (Nepal), telecoms (Pakistan and Sri Lanka), financial services (Sri Lanka), and transport (Sri Lanka and Pakistan), among others. An established network of support services and a pool of trained workers (promoting agglomeration), along with lower-cost service links (to support fragmented activities), are crucial if South Asia is to encourage links "eastward".[20]

Box 2. Improved logistics: A critical precondition
The World Bank's Logistics Performance Index (LPI) provides assessment of logistics performance of countries. In the latest 2010 index, India, Bangladesh, and Pakistan scored better than new low-income members of ASEAN (Lao PDR, Myanmar, and Cambodia), but much lower than ASEAN original members Malaysia, Thailand, and the Philippines, as well as China. Sri Lanka scored marginally lower than Lao PDR, Maldives, Bhutan, Cambodia, and Myanmar, all low-income countries. If South Asian countries are to exploit the marginal advantage of the transportation costs or wages to Europe and the east coast of the United States, improving logistics performance will be critical, given the increasing time sensitivity of vertically linked production networks, including higher value-added apparel, and there will be spillover benefits to promote trade more broadly.

---

[19]India Brand Equity Foundation, CII, http://www.ibef.org/artdispview.aspx?art_id=4267 &cat_id=400&page=3 (Accessed July 15, 2009).
[20]Carruthers *et al.*, 2003; Arvis *et al.*, 2007.

4.5. *Lowering real trade costs*

A critical link to the success of a Look East trade integration strategy for South Asia will thus be to attract sizeable investments from East Asia and the rest of the world to the Region to become integrated into global production chains in both manufacturing and services. But in order to do so, the Region will also need to improve its trade logistics and lower substantial barriers at and behind the borders. Indeed, high trade costs are the biggest deterrent to expanded integration (see Box 2). Increased integration strategy with East Asia will help to attract these complementary investments (where East Asia has a decided comparative advantage) provided entry into services and trade logistics is encouraged by lowering policy and institutional barriers.

At the same time, closer intra-regional integration within South Asia will be another critical instrument to enlarge market size and attract more investment, and lower the substantial within-region trade costs — given a long coastline that surrounds a very large geographic hinterland and the difficulties of land-locked countries and cross-border trade within South Asia. A review of trade facilitation and transport logistics in the region illustrates weakness of South Asian countries in port and transport infrastructure, regulatory environments, and service-sector infrastructure.[21] Delays at seaports due to congestion and outdated infrastructure raise costs for exporters throughout the region. Furthermore, landlocked countries in the region confront additional delays due to congestion in road and transit caused by the poor road infrastructure and networks.[22] The study finds that very large gains from improved trade facilities are possible — much of which will accrue from intra-regional efforts at and gains from lower trade costs. Continued reform in regulation and harmonization of standards, accelerating the diffusion of technology to lower transactions costs, and promoting efficiency in customs regimes within the region are thus needed. The next section discusses the complementary approach to accelerate intra-regional integration as a critical instrument to lower these real trade costs within the region.

---

[21]Wilson and Ostuki, 2007.

[22]De, Chaturvedi and Khan, 2007; Roy and Banerjee, 2007.

5. Boosting Intraregional Trade in South Asia

While the fast-expanding trade with East Asia (and with other regions) will open new avenues for South Asian countries individually, they are likely to gain even more by expanding trade and cross-border investments with each other — enlarging the South Asia market. A larger South Asian integration, if policies and institutions needed to do so can be improved, could also provide an important platform to reduce real trade costs and behind-the-border barriers in the region, which would then attract greater investment and integration with East Asia — enlarging dramatically the gains. In a similar vein, more closely integrated South Asian markets would improve the scale economies of domestic firms, especially in manufacturing (where the small size of domestic markets has been one big constraining factor[23]); would increase competition, and hence efficiency; and would facilitate skills and technology spillovers.[24] A process that is already starting in sectors such as IT and business process outsourcing. Industrial structures that are similar across the region (for example, apparel and textiles) would also gain from greater specialization and intraindustry trade, helping to strengthen comparative advantages with the rest of the world. Services, too, would gain, such as tourism, transport, energy, and shipping, with scale economies and competition. Such a bigger regional market would, in turn, attract greater trade and investment from East Asia (and the rest of the world), making the likelihood of gains even stronger. In reflection, quantitative studies.[25] Find consistently that the gains from greater trade integration for South Asia are much bigger and benefit all country members

---

[23] Evidence across the world suggests that exporting plants overwhelmingly tend to be larger, to have higher levels of productivity and shipments, and to be more capital intensive and technologically more sophisticated (Wagner, 2001), even if this is not true of all industries. In assessments of firm size and performance in South Asia, this appears to hold. Scale effects are consistently positive in exporting, whether in (i) highly clustered network industries such as garments (Cawthorne, 1995) or (ii) vertically integrated and R&D-intensive sectors such as IT and pharmaceuticals (Pradhan, 2002). Evidence from China also suggests that scale economies are strong, with exporting firms distinctly larger, even after controlling for sectoral, regional, and ownership factors (Kraay, 1997).

[24] Kumar, 2009.

[25] Francois *et al.*, 2009.

more, if countries of the region also trade more with each other, even as they integrate faster with East Asia and the rest of the world.

The potential for such intraregional trade is large — the current levels of about 5% share of intraregional trade, in total, could quadruple to about 20% with such supportive policies, by some estimates. The more likely and faster way to do so is by expanding bilateral trade and investment relations — helping support the eventual goal of formal intraregional trade cooperation arrangements (the SAPTA and its transition to SAFTA[26]). The latter has had some difficulties in reducing binding barriers to intraregional trade and in producing results because of political-economic and other constraints to obtaining significant reciprocal concessions across member states. At the bilateral level, however, the pace of liberalization can be much faster, can help build confidence, and can induce competitive spillovers across the region. Some of the reasons why such bilateral agreements work better and faster include the practical aspects of the broader scope of liberalization in such bilateral FTAs, less restrictive rules of origin, bigger and faster cuts in tariff and nontariff barriers, and features such as asymmetrical concessions (especially by larger countries to smaller ones) in the political-economy setting of the region.[27] And, as the subsequent trade and business climate improves sharply in the wake of such bilateral trade, so do cross-border investments, helping to drive further gains faster and to build greater private-sector and business support. Sector-level agreements, as in energy, are another possibility, if they induce similar specificity and rapid mutual gains in confidence and cross-border investments.

There are signs that such bilateral trade and cross-border investment is starting to show greater vitality in South Asia — particularly in the post-2000 period, a time that saw key developments in growing trade relations between India and other member countries, and with East Asia. The latest developments in Indo–Bangladesh trade relations and Indo–Bhutan economic cooperation, along with the growth in Sri Lanka–India trade (and cross-border investment) and the potential for energy trade with neighbors, are some examples and possibilities described in Boxes 3 to 6.

---

[26]SAPTA became operational in 1995, 10 years after the first SAARC summit, and it transitioned to SAFTA in 2004.

[27]Aggarwal and Mukherji, 2005.

6. Raising the Game: Policy Directions

In positioning the South Asia region in the "new normal" of the global economy, as highlighted in this chapter, the region needs to redirect its market integration strategy. What does this imply in terms of the changes in the direction of policies?

Box 3. Bhutan–India cooperation

Bhutan is well endowed with mountainous, glaciated peaks that feed its four main rivers with potential hydroelectric power — generating capacity estimated at 30,000 megawatts (MW), of which about 26,000 MW are commercially viable. Bhutan and India signed a series of four agreements in 2009 that include energy, educational, and vocational needs. The four agreements are for the preparation of detailed project reports for 10 hydropower projects. Of the 10 projects, six will be financed through an intergovernmental model, whereby India will supply 40% of the cost as grants and the remaining 60% as loans. A free trade regime exists between Bhutan and India that expired in March 2005 but has been renewed for 10 years. Bhutan experienced a notable rise in its exports to India.

Box 4. India–Sri Lanka free trade agreement (ISLFTA)

Sri Lanka's regional trade, particularly with India, has undergone a significant increase compared to others. Sri Lanka's share of intraregional imports rose from 11% in 2000 to 23% in 2008, while its export share rose proportionately faster from a very low 2.7% in 2000 to 8.5% in 2008.[28] Traditionally, Sri Lanka's exports to India have been relatively small, but since ISLFTA, Sri Lanka's bilateral exports have soared compared to the other nonlandlocked countries, and relative to growth levels of Indian overall imports.

The reasons behind the success are (i) the ISLFTA, although principally an agreement in trade in goods, provided a boost to services trade and FDI — in air travel (the "open skies" agreement brought in

---

[28]Pitigala, 2010.

Box 4. (*Continued*)

several new carriers), in transshipment (70% from India), and in FDI (India joined the top five investors, with cumulative investment of U.S. $2.5 billion); (ii) the scope of product coverage was enhanced through a "negative list" approach; (iii) a faster pace of implementation was used — for example, duty-free access was granted by India within three years of signing on 81% of the agreed items, and similar reciprocity was pursued by Sri Lanka; and (iv) rules of origin were simplified.

Box 5. Bangladesh–India cooperation

Bangladesh and India have a long history of agreements to facilitate trade and economic cooperation. Although bilateral trade between the two countries has been growing steadily, exports from India far outweigh imports from Bangladesh, resulting in a wide and growing trade gap. Bangladesh and India signed a series of new agreements in January 2010 to address some of the barriers to bilateral trade through new trade and transit provisions:

- *Greater market access for Bangladesh.* India has extended duty-free access beyond its South Asian FTA commitments, broadening the scope of goods to benefit from duty-free access to India, with the aim of narrowing the large trade gap.
- *Promotion of transit links between Bangladesh and India.* India also agreed on transit rights for goods from India's northeastern state of Tripura to Chittagong, including a new rail link. The new links will benefit both countries by reducing transport costs for Indian exporters in the border regions and by gaining greater revenues for Bangladesh from transit and port fees.
- *Regional trade facilitation.* India also agreed to a long-pending request from Bangladesh to allow rail transit from Bangladesh to Nepal and Bhutan, thereby benefiting all three of India's regional trade partners as India expands its demand for underused port facilities and services, and as Bangladesh's, Bhutan's and Nepal's landlocked regions gain greater market access for their exports.

Box 5. (*Continued*)

Other agreements signed at the January meeting include India's extension of an infrastructure credit facility at highly preferential rates and new energy supplies to meet Bangladesh's shortfalls.

Box 6. An energy ring trade for South Asia

Bangladesh, India, Pakistan, and Sri Lanka have a demand for energy that is in excess of their domestic capacity to varying degrees, and the gap will only become larger with future growth. Conversely, Bhutan and Nepal in the South Asia region; the Islamic Republic of Iran and Qatar in the Middle East and North Africa region; Kyrgyzstan, Tajikistan, and Turkmenistan in the Central Asia region; and Myanmar in the East Asia region have resource endowments considerably in excess of domestic demand.

The benefits from energy trade in South Asia can be enormous: The most obvious direct benefit would be in alleviating the energy constraint to growth for the potential energy-importing countries, India and Pakistan. In addition, transit countries would earn large fees, and grids could improve efficiency of supply and could attract private investment with better services, while potentially improving the environment. In India, the volume of unmet demand for electricity in 2007 is estimated to have been 55 terawatt hours (TWh), which can be valued at U.S. $12 billion on the basis of the short-term marginal cost in the Indian grid. The value of the forgone industrial value added would be considerably more. In Pakistan, unmet energy in 2007 is estimated to have been 18 TWh. When valued at the Pakistan system's average incremental cost of about U.S. $0.07 per KWh, the direct cost of shortages is of the order of U.S. $1.9 billion. In Bangladesh, electricity shortages are forcing garment exporters to ship orders through chartered flights, while stoppages of production are reducing exports.

6.1. *The Look East strategy*

The most important policy initiatives would be to accelerate the lowering of tariff and nontariff barriers with respect to East Asia and the rest of the world, and then to expand to the opening of services and foreign direct investment.

Individual South Asian countries are already relatively well positioned and are making good progress, as far as formal trade agreements are concerned. India, for example, has already signed an FTA with ASEAN, while bilateral agreements with member states are enlarging the scope and pace of its trade and investment integration. Others, too, have similar bilateral and regional agreements, although not as encompassing as India's. Although theory suggests that a single trade arrangement encompassing both South and East Asia may provide the optimal strategy within broader Asian integration, this is unlikely to happen, and a "noodle bowl" phenomenon of overlapping bilateral and regional agreements, with multiple rules of origin and market access provisions, is therefore likely to stay.

To lower trade and transactions costs within this setting, South Asia would benefit by lowering trade barriers to levels similar to East Asia (Annex Table A.2) and extending them to all countries to reduce the potential for trade diversion. This would accelerate its South-South trade potential, in light of the global rebalancing. Relatively higher nominal tariffs above 15% still prevail; countries could decide to unilaterally reduce them closer to the norm in East Asia of below 9%(the rate that all developing countries face incidentally in high-income markets). Nontariff barriers, however, account for even bigger protection, and "para-tariffs" are often large. Import restrictions have often increased after the crisis. Liberalizing such non-tariff protection unilaterally could be an even more important component of such open regionalism,[29] including cutting import restraints, protracted customs clearance processes, and often complicated and redundant documentation requirements. Complementary and similar approaches would be needed to boost intra-regional trade within South Asia.

South Asia could also more aggressively liberalize services trade and investment. Such liberalization should not be limited to more visible champions, such as IT and BPO sectors, but should also extend to backbone

---

[29]In principle, reducing barriers at a multilateral level reduces negotiation costs, minimizes the risk of trade diversion, permits countries to reap gains from trade with the rest of the world, increases transparency for exporters and importers, and gives recourse to the enforcement mechanisms of the multilateral system (e.g., dispute settlement).

services — in finance, domestic transport, wholesale distribution, and other professional services — permitting entry on an MFN basis and encouraging competition. Indeed, the success stories emerging from the agreements between India and Singapore, Pakistan and China, and Sri Lanka and India may have been triggered by the "credibility" of their FTAs, but they are largely a consequence of such unilateral measures.

Improvement of *trade logistics* will be especially crucial for South Asia to better exploit its manufacturing potential and may prove decisive in tapping into East Asia's global production sharing. South Asian countries, as a result, needs to fast-track East Asian investment into the logistics chain: trucking, customs, brokerage, freight forwarding, shipping, aviation, port and airport operations, and others.

6.2. *South Asia's intra-regional integration*

The acceleration of bilateral trade and investment arrangements will be central, where India plays an important role, and private-sector cross-border investments will be key.

Similar considerations, as in the case of South East Asian trade, apply regarding why bilateral trade and investment integration will lead the way. How might this come about? The challenge will be for the region's largest and fastest-growing economy, India, to extend quickly such bilateral benefits of closer trade and investment with all its neighbors and to ensure that implementation is faster. But these agreements can go only so far, and a key role will need to be played by *private-sector, business-to-business transactions*, in expediting and enlarging such intra-regional trade, leveraging such bilateral agreements.

In a similar vein, within South Asia, too, *services complementarity* is expected to be greater than in just merchandise trade, such as in transport, travel, health, education, and other sectors, which will carry immediate and more visible benefits to people. Trade liberalization within the region might also start to consider agriculture, which remains untouched despite its potential, as well as energy trade, given the constraints across the region.

Given the landlocked nature of some countries in the region, *facilitating transit trade* will also be critical. The new agreements between India and Bangladesh, signed in January 2010, suggest a promising breakthrough, and they will benefit the neighboring landlocked countries of Nepal and Bhutan (as well as the northeastern border regions of India). Much more can be done. A quantitative test (De, 2010) supports the above: A 10% reduction in the ad valorem price (transport and tariff), for example, would raise trade within South Asia by as much as 6%, a larger impact than the effects of standard reduction of at-the-border tariffs.

6.3. *Maximizing opportunities in high-income and other markets*

The main imperative will be, again, services liberalization. The high-income markets will continue to provide critical markets for outsourced services (IT, BPO) and labor-intensive exports from South Asia, even if at a slower pace than in the past. Increasingly, the high-income countries will also provide bigger sources of longer-term capital and know-how — from manufacturing to critical to South Asia's domestic growth. For both reasons, South Asian countries should accelerate liberalizing services on an MFN basis with all, including high-income countries, even as they pursue multilateral approaches in formal trade negotiations and agreements. While pursuing such market opportunities in high-income countries, South Asia would also do well to keep its trade and investment open to the rest of the world — to an increasingly multipolar world — including other regions and emerging markets that continue to be important, given long-standing and growing ties: the Middle East, Central Asia, Sub-Saharan Africa, and Latin America. Leveraging regional integration with these markets could also offer promising opportunities, as in energy, manufacturing, and services.

7. Annex

Table A.1.   Displacement versus complementarity of South Asian and East Asian exports: Regression results.

	Export India		Pakistan		Bangladesh		Sri Lanka		Nepal	
Export supply effect (*dimports*)	0.4347a (89.89)	0.4347a (89.89)	0.3284a (26.98)	0.3286a (26.99)	0.4185a (15.59)	0.4199a (15.63)	0.4009a (22.12)	0.4012a (22.13)	0.2648a (7.28)	0.2649a (7.29)
East Asia	0.0430a (20.94)		0.0511a (8.66)		0.0752a (5.1)		0.0439a (4.7)		0.0015 (0.09)	
Export effect (*dEastAsia*)										
East Asia		0.0400a (9.94)		0.0585a (5.39)		0.1101a (3.92)		0.0550a (3.07)		0.0132 (0.38)
Export effect: 1990–1999										
East Asia		0.0441a (18.48)		0.0481a (6.87)		0.0621a (3.6)		0.0398a (3.65)		-0.0026 (0.12)
Export effect: 2000–2008										
Constant	0.1162a (53.1)	0.1162a (53.07)	-0.0065 (1.46)	-0.0063 (1.42)	0.0635a (8.48)	0.0642a (8.56)	0.0185a (3.47)	0.0186a (3.49)	0.0451a (4.93)	0.0452a (4.94)
Observations	591566	591566	166350	166350	61239	61239	113481	113481	35656	35656
R-squared	0.19	0.19	0.28	0.28	0.33	0.33	0.31	0.31	0.32	0.32

Source: Staff calculations.

Note: The regressions include two-digit product, importers, and year effects. The estimates thus rely entirely on cross-market variation in East Asian import penetration in a given product. Robust *t*-statistics are shown in brackets. The symbol *a* denotes significance at the 1% level.

Table A.2.   Tariff barriers in Asia: 2007*.

Country/Region	Binding Coverage	Simple Mean	Weighted Mean	Primary	Manufactured
India	73.8	16.4	10.4	25.2	15.9
Pakistan	98.7	14.9	11.4	14.2	15
Bangladesh	15.9	14.5	11	15.2	14.4
Sri Lanka	38.1	11	7.1	17.8	10.6
Nepal	...	12.6	13.7	12.4	12.7
Bhutan	...	18.2	17.8	43.7	15.5
Maldives*	97.1	21.4	21.1	18.1	22.2
Cambodia	...	12.5	10	14.8	12.1
China[†]	100	8.9	5.1	9	8.9
Hong	45.6	0	0	0	0
Indonesia	96.6	5.9	3.9	6.6	5.8
Korea,	94.6	8.5	8	20.8	6.6
Lao	...	5.8	8.3	9.9	5.3
Malaysia	83.7	5.9	3.1	2.8	6.5
Myanmar	17.4	4.1	3.9	5.8	3.9
Philippines	67	5	3.6	6	4.8
Singapore	69.7	0	0	0.2	0
Thailand*	75	10.8	4.6	13.6	10.4
Vietnam	...	11.7	10.6	14.5	11.3
Lower Middle Income	88.7	2.9	1.8	12.9	8.9

Source: World Bank, WDI.

Notes: *Available for 2006, Primary products are commodities classified in SITC revision 3 sections 0–4 plus division 68 (nonferrous metals).
[†]Manufactured products are commodities SITC revision 3 sections 5–8 excluding division 68 classified in.

Bibliography

Aggarwal, Vinod and Mukherji, R (2005). The Emerging Institutional Architecture of Trade in South Asia, Conference Paper "Asia's New Institutional Architecture: Managing Trade and Security Relations in A Post 9/11 World," Berkeley APEC Study Center, University of California at Berkeley, California.

Ahmed, S and E Ghani (2010). Making regional cooperation work for South Asia's poor. World Bank Working Paper, World Bank, Washington, DC.

Ahmed, S, S Kelegama and E Ghani, ed. *Promoting Economic Cooperation in South Asia Beyond SAFTA*, Sage Publications and World Bank, New Delhi and Washington, DC.

Amurgo-Pacheco, A and MD Pierola (2008). Patterns of export diversification in developing countries: Intensive and extensive margins. World Bank Policy Research Working Paper 4473. Washington: World Bank.

Arvis, J-F, G Raballand and J Marteau (2007). The cost of being landlocked: Logistics costs and supply chain reliability. World Bank Policy Research Working Paper 4258 (June). Washington: World Bank.

Baldwin, R (2009). The great trade collapse: What caused it and what does it mean? (27 November 2009). *VOX*. http://www.voxeu.org. Processed January 28, 2010.

—— (2004). "The spoke trap': Hub and spoke bilateralism in East Asia." Korea Institute for International Economic Policy, CNAEC Research Series 04-02.

Ballard, C and I Cheong (1997). The effects of economic integration in the pacific rim: A computational general equilibrium analysis. *Journal of Asian Economics* (forthcoming).

Bandara, JS and W Yu (2003). How desirable is the South Asian free trade area? A quantitative economic assessment. *World Development*, 1293–1323.

Bhattacharya, D (2005). Bangladesh's experience with foreign direct investment. In *Foreign Direct Investment: High Risk, Low Reward for Development*, pp. 51–66. Bonn: Church Development Service (EED).

Blanchard, O and G Miles-Ferretti (2009). Global imbalances: In mid-stream. International Monetary Fund (IMF) Staff Position Paper (December), Washington: IMF.

Brenton, P and R Newfarmer (2007). Watching more than the discovery channel: Export cycles and diversification in development. World Bank Policy Research Working Paper 4302. Washington: World Bank.

Brooks, D and S Stone (2010). Accelerating regional integration: Issues at the border. Asian Development Bank Institute 200 (February).

Business Outlook. The "New Normal" vs. "The New Mix." *Business Week* (March).

Canuto, O, M Haddad and G Hanson (2010). Export-led growth v2.0. World Bank, PREMnotes 148 (March). Washington: World Bank.

Carruthers, R, JN Bajpai and D Hummels (2003). Trade and logistics in East Asia: A development agenda. World Bank, Working Paper 3. Transport Sector Unit, infrastructure department, East Asia and Pacific region (June). Washington: World Bank.

Dasgupta, Dipak, Mustapha Nabli, Christopher Pissarides and Aristomene Varoudakis (2007). Making trade work for jobs. In *Breaking the Barriers to Higher Economic Growth: Better Governance and Deeper Reforms in the Middle East and North Africa*, M. Nabli (ed.). Washington, DC: The World Bank.

Davis, I (2009). The new normal. *McKinsey Quarterly* (March 2009).

De, Prabir (2010). South Asia: Trade integration after the global crisis. Background paper. Washington: World Bank.

De Prabir, S Chaturvedi and AR Khan (2007). Transit and border trade barriers in South Asia. In *Promoting Economic Cooperation in South Asia Beyond SAFTA*, S Ahmed, S Kelegama and E Ghani (eds.). New Delhi and Washington: Sage Publications and World Bank.

Dowling, M and T Chia (2000). Shifting comparative advantage in Asia: New tests of the "Flying Geese" model. *Journal of Asian Economics*, 11, 443–463.

El-Erian, Mohamed (2009). A New Normal. Secular Forum, PIMCO.

Engen, E and R Glen Hubbard (2004). Federal government debt and interest rates. NBER Annual Conference papers.

Francois, J and G Wignaraja (2008). Economic implications of deeper Asian integration. Centre for Economic Policy Research 6976.

Freund, C and C Ozden (2006). The effect of China's exports on Latin American trade with the world. Background paper for the Office of the Chief Economist for Latin America and the Caribbean Regional Study: Latin American and the Caribbean's Response to the Growth of China and India. Washington: World Bank.

Galston, W (2010). The new normal for the US economy: What will it be? Brookings.

Govindan, K (1994). A South Asian preferential trading arrangement. Draft.

Hoekman, B and A Nicita (2008). Trade policy, trade costs, and developing country trade. World Bank Policy Research Working Paper 4797. Washington: World Bank.

Hummels, D, J Jun and K-M Yi (2001). The nature and growth of vertical specialization in world trade. *Journal of International Economics*, 54, 75–96.

Hummels, D and P Klenow (2005). The variety and quality of a nation's exports. *American Economic Review*, 95(3), 704–723.

IMF (International Monetary Fund) (2010). *Regional Economic Outlook: Western Hemisphere taking Advantage of Tailwinds*. Washington: IMF.

Kelegama, S and I Mukherjee (2007). India–Sri Lanka bilateral trade agreement: Six years' performance and beyond. RIS Discussion Paper 119.

Kimura, F (2006). International production and distribution networks in East Asia: Eighteen facts, mechanics, and policy implications. *Asian Economic Policy Review*, 1, 326–344.

Kojima, K (2000). The "Flying Geese" model of Asian Economic development: Origin, theoretical extensions, and regional policy implications. *Journal of Asian Economics*, 11, 375–401.

Kraay, A (1997). Exports and economic performance: Evidence from a panel of chinese enterprises. World Bank (August).

Kumar, R and M Singh (2009). India's role in South Asia's trade and investment integration. ADB Working Paper Series on Regional Economic Integration 32.

Lipsey, R (1960). The theory of customs unions: A general survey. *Economic Journal*, 70, 498–513.

Milberg, W and D Winkler (2010). From crisis to recovery: Hysteresis and restructuring of global value chains. Draft.

Mohanty, S and S Pohit (2007). Welfare gains from regional economic integration in Asia: ASEAN+3 or EAS. RIS-DP 126, Research and Information System for Developing Countries (RIS). New Delhi (September).

Mohanty, S, S Pohit and S Roy (2004). Towards formation of close economic cooperation among Asian countries. RIS Discussion Papers 78, Research and Information Systems for the Non-Allied and Other Developing Countries, Delhi.

Mukherjee, IN (2005). Regional trade agreements in South Asia. In *South Asian Year Book of Trade and Development*, CENTAD, 363–392.

Nataraj, S (2009). *The Impact of Trade Liberalization on Productivity and Firm Size: Evidence from India's Formal and Informal Manufacturing Sectors*. Berkeley: University of California.

Ng, F and A Yeats (2003). Major trade trends in East Asia: What are their implications for regional cooperation and growth? Policy Research Working Paper 3084. Washington: World Bank.

—— (2001). Production sharing in East Asia: Who does what for whom, and why? In *Global Production and Trade in East Asia*, LK Cheng and H Kierzkowski (eds.), pp. 63–109. Boston: Kluwer Academic.

OECD Economic Outlook No.87, May 2010.

Ozawa, T (2003). Pan-American-led macro-clustering and flying-geese-style catch-up in East Asia: Mechanisms of regionalized endogenous growth. *Journal of Asian Economics*, 13, 699–713.

Page, J (2010). India's "manufacturing problem." The Brookings Institution and World Bank, mimeo.

Pham, C and W Martin (2007). *Extensive and Intensive Margin Growth and Developing Country Exports*. Washington: World Bank.

—— (2007). Extensive and intensive margin growth and developing country exports. Draft. DECRG World Bank, Washington, DC.

Pigato, M, C Farah, K Itakura, K Jun, W Martin, K Murrell and TG Srinivasan (1997). *South Asia's Integration into the World Economy*. Washington: World Bank.

Pitigala, N (2008). *Vertical Specialization in Developing Countries: Gravity and a Panel Data Analysis*. Ph.D. dissertation, University of Sussex.

Pursell, G and N Pitigala (2001). Trade Agreements in the South Asia Region. Draft. Washington: World Bank.

Rana, P (2006). Economic integration in East Asia: Trends, prospects, and a possible roadmap. Working Paper Series on Regional Economic Integration 2, Asian Development Bank, Manila.

Reuters (2010). Global Imbalances to Avoid New Crisis — King (January).

Roy, J and P Banerjee (2007). In *Connecting South Asia: The Centrality of Trade Facilitation for Regional Economic Integration*, Ahmed, Kelegama, and Ghani, op. cit.

Sally, R (2010). Regional economic integration in Asia: The track record and prospects. ECIPE, London School of Economics, Occasional Paper 2/2010.

Schiff, M (2001). Will the real "natural trading partner" please stand up? *Journal of Economic Integration*, 16(2).

Sengupta, N and A Banik (1997). Regional trade and investment: Case of SAARC. *Economic and Political Weekly*, 32(November 15–21), 2930–2931.

Srinivasan, TN and G Canonero (1995). *Preferential Trading Arrangements in South Asia: Theory, Empirics and Policy*. Unpublished manuscript. New Haven: Yale University.

Steinbock, D (2010). How not to correct global imbalances. *China Daily*.

Taneja, N, M Sarvananthan and S Pohit (2003). India–Sri Lanka trade: Transacting environments in formal and informal trading (July 2003). *Economic and Political Weekly*, pp. 19–25.

Topalova, P (2007). *Trade Liberalization and Firm Productivity: The Case of India*. Washington: World Bank.

UNIDO (2009). *Industrial Development Report 2008/9: Breaking in and Moving Up: New Industrial Challenges for the Bottom Billion and the Middle Income Countries*. Geneva.

Wagner, J (2001). A note on the firm size-export relationship. *Small Business Economics*, 17, 229–237.

Weerakoon, D and J Thennakoon (2007). *India–Sri Lanka FTA: Lessons for SAFTA, CUTS*. Jaipur.

Wilson, J and T Ostuki (2007). Cutting trade costs and improved business facilitation in South Asia. In *South Asia Growth and Regional Integration*, S Ahmed and E Ghani (eds.). Macmillan and World Bank.

World Bank (2010). *World Bank East Asia Economic Update 2010*. Vol. 1, May. Washington: World Bank.

World Development Indicators (2010). World Bank, Washington: World Bank.

World Economic Outlook. IMF 2010 updates.

WTI (World Trade Indicators). 2007.

Zhang (2006). Towards an East Asia FTA: Modality and road map. A Report by Joint Expert Group for Feasibility Study on EAFTA, ASEAN Secretariat, Jakarta.

Chapter 8

South Asia's Economic Future with or without Economic Integrations

*Shahid Javed Burki**

1. Introduction

The structure of the global economy is changing rapidly. The centre of gravity of economic activity is moving from the Atlantic toward the Pacific. China, the world's fastest growing large economy, is already the world's second largest. It overtook Japan earlier in 2010. A number of other East Asian economies — in particular those that were called the "miracle economies" in a report published by the World Bank in 1993[1] — played the catch up game with the more advanced economies preceded China in terms of registering spectacular growth rates. China not only ranks higher of these fast growing economies, it has now begun to pull them around its orbit. Because of these developments, it has become normal to label the 21st century as the Asian century.

But that description does not usually imply South Asia. That was certainly the case until the beginning of the century when the Indian rate of economic growth picked up significantly. The recent Indian performance poses a number of questions with respect to South Asia. One, is the country's recent high rates of growth sustainable? Two, would India also become the

---

*Former Finance Minister of Pakistan and Vice President for Latin American and the Caribbean at the World Bank.
[1]The World Bank (1993). *The East Asian Miracle: Economic Growth and Public Policy.* New York: Oxford University Press.

engine of growth for the rest of South Asia as China is now for many countries in East Asia? This paper attempts to provide some answers to both questions.

This brief presentation is centered around two propositions. One, that the major economies of South Asia by giving less attention to human and capital accumulation have followed a growth model that has produced spectacular results in East Asia; and two, that this region can climb on to a higher growth trajectory by increasing greater economic integration among the countries belonging to the area.

However, before touching upon these two aspects, I will make one general observation about the growth strategies pursued in the South Asian region. India is the only country that has followed one particular approach with reasonable consistency, but that was only in the last quarter century. In the mid-eighties, the country began to wean itself away from the model that placed enormous faith in the ability of the state to lead the economy toward accelerated growth and development. Under Jawaharlal Nehru, the country's first Prime Minister, and his early successors, the country put the state on the commanding heights of the economy. That resulted in what the late economist Raj Krishna called the "Hindu rate of growth". Beginning in the mid-eighties, the country began to free the private sector of control by the state. From 1991 on, the "license raj" began to be dismantled. The results were spectacular, producing the rates of growth that were once considered unachievable in the cultural, social and political contexts of India.

But consistency was not the case for South Asia's other major economies. Over the last several decades, Pakistan has tried many different approaches to speed-up development. Sometimes, it relied on public sector to take the lead; at other times, it placed its faith in private enterprise. As we know from the experience of other developing countries, policy consistency is an important factor contributing to growth and development. If Pakistan is to interrupt the current downward slide in its economy and stop it before it reaches the point at which recovery will become exceedingly difficult, it will need to put in place a well thought out strategy and stay with it for several years.

Bangladesh, largely account of the political roller-coaster it has ridden since gaining independence in 1971, has also not articulated a consistent approach to economic development. It has done well in part because of the remarkable work done by some of the large NGOs — in particular BRAC and the Grameen Bank — and in part because of the extraordinary growth of the ready-made garment sector. I would suggest that, policy consistency could come to South Asia by encouraging regional cooperation — a subject I will take up in detail in a later section of the paper.

2. Sources of South Asian Growth

It is always helpful to look at history to develop ideas for the future — to learn lessons from it. In this context, we might analyze the sources of growth by borrowing from the work done in recent years by some economists using what they call "growth accounting". Susan Collins of the Brookings Institution in Washington is one of the several economists who have done work in this area. She has applied this methodology to study 84 industrial and developing economies. Four of these — Bangladesh, India, Pakistan and Sri Lanka — are in South Asia. Growth accounting "provides a means for decomposing increases in output per worker into the contributions from accumulation of physical and human capital (per worker) and a residual measure of the change in total factor productivity", she wrote recently in an essay contributed to a book published by the World Bank.[2]

What was South Asia's growth experience in the past several decades? According to Collins, average annual GDP growth rates for India and Bangladesh increased by 2% points in the 1980–2003 period compared to the two decades between 1960 and 1980. For India, the rate of national income increase went up from 3.5% to 5.7%; for Bangladesh from 2.4% to 4.4%. The trend in Pakistan was in the opposite direction. It declined from 5.9% to 4.9%. In the three countries, the share of investment in GDP declined; in the case of Pakistan, the decline was the sharpest, from 22.1% to 19.5%.

The first thing to be noted about the pattern of growth in South Asia, therefore, is that while it was impressive for the region as a whole, it was not so much the result of accumulation of capital as was the case in East Asia where investment as a proportion of GDP was about twice as high as in South Asia. In none of the South Asian states, investment rates approached the 30% to 40% typical for East Asian economies during their rapid growth periods.

---

[2]Collins, SM (2007). Economic growth in South Asia. In *South Asia: Growth and Regional Integration*, S Ahemed and E Ghanni (eds.), pp. 45–60. Delhi: Macmillan.

Does this mean that if capital accumulation was a relatively unimportant contributor to growth in South Asia in the past it can, perhaps, remain that way in the future. Such a conclusion would be important for Pakistan since its savings rate is much lower than other economies of Asia. Collins argues that it would be wrong to reach that conclusion. Countries in South Asia will need to increase their rates of investment so as to accumulate both physical and human capital more rapidly if they are to achieve their desired rates of income increase going forward. This has already begun to happen in India and to some extent also in Bangladesh. Pakistan, however, is falling behind with every passing day.

A country's per capita income can be decomposed into productivity, the proportion of domestic income that accrues to the country's residents and labor force as share of the total population. For India, productivity and living standards both doubled from 1980 to 2003. The former increased by 130% from U.S. $2705 to U.S. $6144 in the 23 year period. The latter increased from U.S. $1185 per head of the population to U.S. $2721. Pakistan's increases were much less impressive: Labor productivity increased by 81%, from U.S. $2916 when it was higher than that of India to U.S. $5277 when it fell below that of the country's large neighbor. Gross domestic income per head of the Pakistani population increased by only 68%, almost one half that of India's. It went from U.S. $1148 to U.S. $1927. Pakistan's relatively poor performance is in part due to the low rate of labor participation which remains close to one third of the total work force. This, in turn, is because only a small proportion of women work outside their homes for remuneration. The rate of worker participation increased by only one percentage point, growing from 37% to 38%. It remained steady at 44% in the case of India. In Bangladesh, there was a two percentage points increase with the participation rate going up from 49% to 51% of the work force. This happened because of the increase in the employment of women in the ready-made garments industry.

Collins' work provides estimates of the contribution made by various sources of growth to the South Asian economies. Again, comparisons of the trends in India and Pakistan are instructive. In the more recent period examined by her — from 1990 to 2003 — output per worker in India increased by 3.99% a year. Factor productivity contributed almost one-half to this increase with capital accumulation providing another 37%. The remaining 13% came from education. In the case of Pakistan, output per worker grew by only 1.08%, about one-fourth of that of India's increase. Factor productivity contributed 64% to this increase and capital accumulation another 43%. The contribution of education was negative, taking away 7% from the increase in worker productivity. For Pakistan to have its economy grow at a faster pace, it must invest in education. In 2000, for population in the working age — for people over 15 years — average years of schooling was only 3.9 compared to 5.1 for India.

The perspective that capital accumulation matters goes hand-in-hand with the extensive and convincing new findings by development economists linking positive growth experience with strong domestic institutions such as contract enforcement and protecting property rights. Empirical work done at the World Bank shows strong links between the structure, efficiency and efficacy of the legal and judicial systems for promoting development. All major South Asian countries are weak in this respect; Pakistan probably the weakest of all. Growth accounting, therefore, points to some of the elements that must receive attention in the design of a growth-oriented public policy. These include large increases in the rates of public and private investment, increased participation of women in the work-force, increased investment in education and skill development, greater attention to improving the technological base of the economy, and reform of the legal and judicial systems. Including all these in a growth strategy may help the country to join the ranks of the fast growing economies of Asia. But these elements in the growth strategy are largely internal; what would be exceedingly rewarding for the region will be closer cooperation in economic matters. That is the subject to which I will devote the rest of the paper.

3. Accelerating Growth by Better Regional Integration[3]

Disregarding the current problems in Europe, the fact remains that regional integration helps countries achieve the rates of economic growth that would not be possible if they acted alone. Size matters in both trade and economics, a conclusion reached by Adam Smith two centuries ago. This is the case in

---

[3]This part of the paper draws upon an earlier work by the author for the Institute of South Asian Studies. See Burki SJ, Institute of South Asian studies, South Asia's Economic Future With or Without Economic Integration. Working Paper No. 110, 14 July, 2010.

particular in South Asia where economic progress, India's remarkable performance in the last couple of decades notwithstanding, is being held back by intra-regional conflict. This is where the European experience becomes relevant. The initial European dream was to create a political structure that will also have strong economic foundations. With such a working organizational structure, future conflict would become practically impossible. The dream was realized. Although some historians tell us that scholars should "never say never", it does seem unlikely that Europe will ever see a conflict on its soil of the type that twice devastated the continent in the last century. Economic union has played a large part in realizing this level of comfort.

This was also the dream that drove Ziaur Rehman, Bangladesh's second president, to convince the heads of state in the South Asian region a quarter century ago to work toward greater regional cooperation, this was the spirit behind the creation of the South Asian Association of Regional Cooperation. But the potential of SAARC has yet to be realized in part because the countries of the region are not convinced that this is the way to go but sometimes, simple mathematics helps to clear the mind and this is what is attempted here. The purpose is to develop a simple macreconometric model to make the case that there are enormous economic rewards available by improving trade and economic links among the eight countries of the SAARC region. Before providing the results of some simple calculations, the paper takes a slight detour. This will provide a quick overview of the current economic situations in India and Pakistan; indicate how the global economy is evolving and what could be South Asia's role in it; and suggest what India and Pakistan could do to take advantage of the opportunities that are opening in the global economy. This detour sets the stage for the main part of the analysis which is focused on the gains to be made by increasing trade among South Asian neighbors.

4. The Future of the Indian and Pakistani Economies

After a slight slowdown in economic growth as a result of the Great Recession of 2008–2009, the Indian economy has gone back to the growth trajectory it has followed over the last decade and a half. The quick recovery was the consequence of two factors. One, the country's economy is not as integrated with the West as that of East Asia. In the case of the latter, the impact of the global slowdown was much more severe. Two, the government was effective in stimulating the economy by the judicious use of fiscal stimulus aimed at reducing the impact on the level of employment of some slowdown that did occur.

India today is the fastest growing economy in South Asia with rates of growth close to those achieved by the "miracle economies" of East Asia in the quarter century between 1975 and 2000. Those growth rates structurally transformed those economies. From essentially rural economies, they became industrial powerhouses. The incidence of poverty was also dramatically reduced and the quality of human resource markedly improved. Even though India is now achieving comparable rates of GDP growth, the social and economic transformation will be slower. This is for several reasons. Among them the more important ones are the size of the population, concentration of the high growth areas in essentially one region of the country, and the contribution of few economic sectors to growth. In other words, the Indian model of growth is less inclusive than those followed in East Asia.

Trade other than the exports of the IT sector — and now of the sector of health services — has been less of a contributing factor in the Indian growth model than was the case for the miracle economies of East Asia. This will have to change for India to sustain the rate of growth into the future. But the emphasis on trade should include refocusing it on the countries in the immediate neighborhood. Regional integration could play an important part in pushing the sustainable rate of growth even higher. But for that to happen, Pakistan, the second largest economy in South Asia, will need to pull out of its current economic slump.

Pakistan today is passing through an extremely difficult period because of a perfect storm that has gathered around it. The country is dealing with extremism and terrorism that have stubbornly persisted and have continued to take a heavy toll on the economy and the society. Several shortages have developed in such vital goods and services as electricity, natural gas and water that are hurting industrial and agricultural output. The quality of governance has deteriorated to the point where people have lost faith in the state's ability to provide even for their most basic needs.[4] All these developments have affected the state of the economy. Last year, the GDP growth rate was only 1.2%; this year it will probably not be more than 4%.

---

[4]For an analysis of Pakistan's current economic situation, see Institute of Public Policy, Beaconhouse National University, Lahore, *State of the Economy: Pulling Back from the Abyss*, Lahore, 2010.

These rates are about a third to one-half of the rates of growth being currently recorded by India. But that has not been the case always. From 1947 to 1988, a period of 41 years, Pakistan's GDP increased at an average rate of 5.5% year, a percentage and a half points more than that of India's growth rate. As Surjit Bhalla estimates in an essay contributed to a volume honoring Montek Singh Ahluwalia,[5] the average industrial growth rate in Pakistan in 1965–2005, a period of 40 years, was 6.5% a year compared with India's 5.3%. Pakistan achieved a maximum of 10.4% increase in industrial output during this period. India's maximum was only 6.9%. The point of making these comparisons is that nations and economies have their ups and downs; there is nothing permanent about the trends they show at any given time.

If Pakistan manages to navigate out of the perfect storm, it could see acceleration in its rate of growth to 8% by 2025 provided it could settle its relations with India. Peace with India and strong economic ties with the large neighbor could add almost U.S. $200 billion to Pakistan's gross domestic product, increasing it from U.S. $375 billion in 2007 to U.S. $571 billion a year. This translates into an increase of U.S. $850 in per capita income by 2025. The Indian GDP could increase by U.S. $1.5 trillion and its GDP per capita by U.S. $1140.

Pakistan has potential in many areas. It has a large and young population which could become an economic asset rather than a social and political liability depending upon the choices made by those who make public policies. A large population can deliver considerable benefits in a world which is seeing populations rapidly ageing. Then there is the large and well endowed agriculture sector which is working way below its considerable potential. It is not always recognized that Pakistan has the largest contiguous irrigated area in the world which could produce significant amounts of high value added exports if there are right sets of public policies in place with respect to the efficient use of water, development of marketing infrastructure and development of appropriate technologies.

Pakistan also has some well-honed skills that could be used to produce parts and components for the large industrial sectors of China and India.

---

[5]Bhalla, S (2010). Indian Economic growth, 1950–2008: facts and beliefs, puzzles and policies. In *India's Economy: Performance and Challenges*, S Acahrya and R Mohan (eds.). New Delhi: Oxford University Press.

Finally, there is Pakistan's geographic location which could turn the country into the hub of international commerce provided relations improve with some of the neighbors, in particular with India and Afghanistan. This potential could be realized if South Asia could begin to work as a cohesive regional economy.

5. Global Economic Changes

Analyzing the on-going changes in the global economy is a vast subject on which much has been said and written. The world is passing through another period of what economic historians call the "catching-up" phenomenon. Asia is catching up with the more advanced regions of the world and the center of gravity of the global economy is shifting from the Atlantic to the Pacific.[6] In this change, China is in the lead; it has been able to improve its position in the global economy by taking the right set of decisions to deal with the situation created by the Great Recession of 2008–2009. China's lead in the global economy is partly the result of the active role it has played in developing the new structure of industrial production which builds on the Japanese "just in time" system, but has been taken much beyond the original design. In producing finished products, China imports parts and components mostly from the countries in its neighborhood. The large Japanese manufacturers such as Toyota Motors relied mostly on smaller domestic producers for parts and components. China's different approach has meant developing strong trading and economic relations with the countries in which the suppliers are located. South Asia does not have such a system of production but it could develop it if its economies get better integrated.

The other major change occurring in the global economy is related to demography. As already indicated, the populations in developed countries are ageing rapidly; their demand for services is increasing. These have to be supplied by mostly younger people. Overtime, these countries will begin to rely heavily on the more populous parts of the world. Some of these are in South Asia. India has already carved out a niche for itself in the service

---

[6]The author developed this argument in some detail in a two-part working paper issued by ISAS in April and May 2010. See Burki, SJ. Asia in 'Catch-Up Game', Part 1. Working Paper No. 106. 9 April, 2010 and Asia in the "Catch-Up" Game: Part 2. ISAS Working Paper 107. 10 May, 2010.

sector and Bangladesh in the ready-made garments sector. Some of the other countries of South Asia could follow their example.

6. The Roles India and Pakistan can Play in the Changing World Economy

In indicating the roles India and Pakistan could play in the changing world economy, focus should be on at least two things. First, Pakistan has to change its stance from being a competitor to India to becoming a collaborator with its large neighbor in many fields. Economics — particularly trade — is one of the more important areas in which it should be prepared to work with India. It has to recognize that India is South Asia's anchor economy which, at this time, accounts for 82% of the total regional product. At the same time India has to realize that it can only gain the status of an economic superpower if it works with the countries in its immediate neighborhood. It should not be tempted to leap-frog over them to form distant associations with groups such as the ASEAN and the European Union. No large economy has succeeded without first developing strong regional associations. This is as true for the United States, China and South Africa as must and will be the case for India.

If India and Pakistan could work together in the field of economics and trade, they will see considerable and palpable impacts on the structures of their economies. This will be more true for Pakistan than for India which is to be expected since the size of the former's economy is only one-eighth of the latter's. Some fundamental changes in the structures of both agriculture and industry in Pakistan can be expected as these two sectors begin to supply the larger and rapidly growing Indian markets. The Pakistani motorway system, currently more advanced than that of India's, would get integrated with India's planned system of highways called the "golden quadrilateral". The electrical grids will get connected with trade in power becoming an integral part of interstate commerce. The two countries may finally be able to build the gas pipelines connecting them to the Middle East and Central Asia.

7. Benefits from Regional Association in Commerce

In spite of the efforts made over the last quarter century to bring about more meaningful economic integration of the South Asian region, not much has been achieved. Regional trade as a proportion of the total has increased a little but compared to other world regions, it remains almost insignificant. How much is the area losing out by not focusing sufficient amount of political attention to integration and cooperation? One way of answering this question is to use trade as the driving force for accelerating economic development. Using trade as the basis and historical GDP-trade elasticities for making projections, it is possible to develop some scenarios for the future. This is done purely for illustrative purposes in this paper not for establishing firm targets. The three scenarios presented here are based on assumptions about the extent of integration as well as the degree of reorientation of trade with significantly more trade going to Asia in general (Scenario II) and South Asia in particular (Scenario III).

According to the first scenario in Table 1, the countries in the region continue to focus the direction of international trade and its content on distant trading partners. This is the base case. For India, the United States and the European Union remain the most important markets for its exports and the most important sources of its imports. The same is true for Pakistan. Even though China–India trade is likely to grow at a faster rate than overall trade, increasing Beijing's share in New Delhi's international trade, India does not become a partner in the China centered system of production that is taking shape. According to this scenario, the growth of India's GDP is sustained at the rate of 7% a year in the 18 year period between 2007 and

Table 1.   Scenario I (The base case).

	GDP (U.S. $ Billion)		Population (Million)		Per capita income (U.S. $)	
	2007	2025	2007	2025	2007	2025
Bangladesh	68	195	159	195	431	1000
India	1177	3978	1125	1382	1046	2878
Nepal	10	24	28	38	357	632
Pakistan	143	375	162	230	883	1630
Sri Lanka	32	78	20	22	1600	3545
Total	**1430**	**4650**	**1494**	**1867**	**957**	**2491**

Note*: The base case assumes the following GDP growth rates: Bangladesh, 6%; India, 7%; Nepal, 4.8%; Pakistan, 5.55%; and Sri Lanka 5%.
Note**: 2007 is the base year.
Source: The author's calculation based on the data for 207 from The World Bank, *World Development Indicators*, The United Nations World Population Prospects. Same sources are used for Tables 2 and 3.

2025. This is well below the 10% growth target Finance Minister Pranab Mukherjee set for the country in his budget for the year 2010–2011. The size of the Indian GDP increases more than three-fold and income per capita grows 2.75 times. India's share in the combined GDP of the region increases from 82% to 86%.

Bangladesh will be the second most rapidly expanding economy according to this scenario with the rate of increase in GDP averaging 6% a year. Nepal does the least well with the rate of growth at 4.8%. Pakistan's performance lies somewhere in between that of India and Nepal. Growing at 5.5% a year, the size of its GDP increases 2.6 times but its share in the South Asian total output declines from 10% in 2007 to only 8% in 2025.

The second scenario is based on the assumption that the South Asian countries take greater cognizance of the importance of international trade as a contributor to growth and also of the move in the center of gravity of the global economy to the Pacific from the Atlantic. What this means is that, the countries of the area pay greater attention to the changing structure of the global production system. This will be largely centered on China. New Delhi's policymakers, taking note of this, are already deeply engaged in building better economic relations with the ASEAN group of countries. They are also participating in the Asian Economic Summit, an arrangement that includes ten countries of the ASEAN region as well as Australia, China, Japan, New Zealand and South Korea. This change in strategy adds to the rate of growth of all South Asian countries. India's GDP is 12% higher compared to the base case scenario but its share in the regional GDP in 2025 remains the same at about 86%. (See Table 2.)

The third case builds on the second by assuming that South Asia manages to develop stronger economic contacts among the countries in the area. Compared to the status quo situation in the first scenario, the combined GDP of the region is considerably larger as is income per head of the population — both by as much as 40%. The incidence of poverty declines significantly and better services are provided to the citizenry. South Asia is also better integrated with the rest of Asia.

The impact on poverty and quality of life will be pronounced if the third scenario is played out. This is for the reason that economic structures will be profoundly different in this case, particularly in the countries on India's borders. Pakistan, for instance, will be able to develop the sector

Table 2.   Scenario II.

	GDP (U.S. $ Billion)		Population (Million)		Per capita income (U.S. $)	
	2007	2025	2007	2025	2007	2025
Bangladesh	68	202	159	195	431	1034
India	1177	4473	1125	1382	1046	3236
Nepal	10	25	28	38	357	658
Pakistan	143	445	162	230	883	1927
Sri Lanka	32	82	20	22	1600	3696
Total	**1430**	**5227**	**1494**	**1867**	**957**	**2800**

Note*: The scenario II assumes the following GDP growth rates: Bangladesh, 6.2%; India, 7.7%; Nepal, 5%; Pakistan, 6.5%; and Sri Lanka 5.3%.
Note**: 2007 is the base year
Source: See Table 1.

of agriculture to take advantage of the huge Indian market. This would have happened had the countries not severed their trade relations soon after gaining independence from the British rule. Then, close to two-thirds of Pakistan's imports came from India and about the same proportion of its exports went to that country. These proportions declined to about 5% when the two countries declared a trade war in 1949 on the issue of the rate of exchange between their currencies. This is where the proportions have remained in spite of the launch of the South Asia Free Trade Area (SAFTA) initiative in January 2004. With the rebuilding of economic and trade contacts, other sectors could also get aligned. Pakistan could become an important supplier of auto parts to the rapidly developing Indian automobile industry while India would become the main provider of iron ore to the steel industry in Pakistan. Both countries would buy chemicals from one another — India urea from Pakistan and Pakistan pesticides for India, for instance. Bangladesh could get integrated in the much larger textile sectors of the two larger economies, India and Pakistan, taking advantage of their better developed fashion industries. However, to realize the third scenario there will have to be exercise of considerable amount of political will which has been in short supply now for many decades.

Footnotes to Tables 1–3 provide GDP growth estimates based on these three scenarios for the five larger countries of South Asia. This represents, of

Table 3.   Scenario III.

	GDP (U.S. $ Billion)		Population (Million)		Per capita income (U.S. $)	
	2007	2025	2007	2025	2007	2025
Bangladesh	68	239	159	195	431	1223
India	1177	5551	1125	1382	1046	4016
Nepal	10	26	28	38	357	692
Pakistan	143	571	162	230	883	2479
Sri Lanka	32	88	20	22	1600	3957
Total	**1430**	**6475**	**1494**	**1867**	**957**	**3468**

Note*: The scenario IV assumes the following GDP growth rates: Bangladesh, 7.2%; India, 9%; Nepal, 5.3%; Pakistan, 8.0%; and Sri Lanka 5.7%.
Note**: 2007 is the base year.
Source: See Table 1.

Table 4.   GDP growth rates: 2007–2025, (percent per year).

	2007		
Scenarios	I	II	III
Bangladesh	6	6.2	7.2
India	7	7.7	9
Nepal	4.8	5	5.3
Pakistan	5.6	6.5	8
Sri Lanka	5	5.3	5.7

Source: Author's estimates.

course, some heroic assumptions that is why it is so important to emphasize the illustrative nature of this exercise. These rates are presented in Table 4. In terms of the rates of growth, the largest gainer is Pakistan followed by India. Pakistan's GDP growth according to the third scenario is 2.4 percentage points higher compared to the first scenario while India's is two percentage points better. In the case of Pakistan income per capita of the population in the third scenario is 52% higher while that of India is 40% greater.

It is also essential to underscore that, in identifying the determinants of growth for any economy, it is important to include a number of variables — to undertake what economists call multivariate analysis. The scenarios built for this exercise use only one variable as the driver of growth. This is international trade. Historical elasticities were used to gauge the quantitative impact on growth rates. But even if trade was to be the most important determinant, for it to play that role, it must be supported by a whole host of other developments. Trade economists now emphasize that, given the general lowering of tariffs across the globe, "trade facilitation" is a much more important contributor to growth than tariffs. Trade facilitation includes well functioning physical infrastructure — roads, railways and ports — that takes goods from the points of production to the points of shipping. Even today, in spite of the development of air cargo, 90% of trade moves by ships. Producers participating in trade must have a steady and reliable supply of water, electricity and other sources of energy. They must have access to capital at reasonable rates to expand their supplies; availability of human skills in order to be able to compete in international markets; labor laws that do not interfere with the hiring and firing of workers; and availability of information about the markets the producers and exporters are hoping to reach. There must also be good governance so that the rent seeking behavior on the part of those whose assistance is needed by traders does not eat into the profits they are hoping to make. To achieve all this means an active and well-intentioned state.

All this notwithstanding, some analysts have argued that of the many determinants of growth in the emerging markets that still have large sectors of agriculture — as is the case with all South Asian economies — weather may be one of the more important ones. India's Surjit Bhalla points out that "surprisingly, rainfall (lagged plus current) alone explains as much as 60% of the variation in the growth of agricultural output...the model for GDP growth also works well: 40% of the variation of GDP growth is explained by rainfall alone."[7] He goes on to suggest that the levels of rates of interest as administered by the Reserve Bank of India, the country's Central Bank, and the rate of inflation are much more important determinants of growth of the Indian economy than capital accumulation or the movement of workers from less to more productive parts of the economy.

---

[7]Surjit Bhalla, Indian Economic Growth, 1950–2008: Facts and Beliefs, Puzzles and Policies. in *India's Economy: Performance and Challenges*, S Acahrya and R Mohan, p. 42, Op. City.

8. Conclusion

Notwithstanding all the caveats mentioned above, easing of tensions among the countries of South Asia, especially between India and Pakistan, will have many positive consequences for the region. The simple model developed for this paper showed that trade alone will add about two percentage points to the rate of growth of the region. As the Europeans have discovered, easing trade restrictions produces a number of other beneficial consequences. They increase tourism and cultural contacts. They also contribute to knowledge accumulation as networking increases among the researchers working in various laboratories and research institutions. Some of the positive outcomes cannot be fully appreciated *ex ante*. That said, three of these are worth reflecting on.

Greater intra-regional trade in South Asia will have a significant impact on the structure of the economies of the smaller countries as they develop linkages with the large enterprises in India. This would lead to more labor intensive activities as producers in Pakistan begin to supply parts and components to India's large industries or as textile producers in Bangladesh get to work for India's (and Pakistan's) fast developing fashion industry. Second, the grant of transit rights by both Bangladesh and Pakistan to India — the former to provide better access to India's eastern provinces and the latter to allow Indian goods and people to travel to Afghanistan and beyond — will develop some components of the service industry. These include warehousing, servicing of vehicles, hotel business, insurance and other related activities needed to move goods and commodities over long distances. Third, by linking the various infrastructural networks such as electricity grids and gas pipelines, the countries in the region should be able to meet one another's occasional deficits while creating markets for electricity, gas and possibly water.

The positive economic consequences of opening up to one another will be enormously significant. There will also be positive outcomes on the political side as well, but that is an entirely different subject which those with greater competence in this area should analyze.

Chapter 9

Indian Trade Policy After the Crisis

*Razeen Sally**

1. Introduction

India has had a "good" crisis. The global financial crisis has induced a sharp divergence of economic performance between the West and emerging markets, particularly in Asia. China and India both enjoy roaring growth and are leading emerging markets out of the crisis. More than ever, India is seen as a rising regional and global power.

This is the broad backdrop for an assessment of Indian trade policy after the crisis. The next two sections flesh out the context. Section 2 is on post-crisis trends in the global economy, focusing on trade policy. Section 3 is on the post-crisis Indian political economy, focusing on economic policy. Section 4 concentrates on Indian trade policy.

2. The Post-Crisis Global Economy: Focus on Trade Policy

The crisis has induced both *divergence* and *convergence* between the West and emerging markets. Post-crisis economic performance has markedly diverged; but this has accelerated the long-run catch-up or convergence of emerging markets with the West.

---

*Visiting Associate Professor at the Lee Kuan Yew School of Public Policy and Institute of South Asian Studies (ISAS), National University of Singapore.

Diverging economic performance has its roots in the crisis itself. The West had a financial crisis. That translates into a deeper-than-normal recession and a slower-than-average recovery.[1] The picture looks very different in emerging markets, particularly in Asia. Unlike the West, Asia did not suffer a financial crisis; its banks and balance sheets (household, corporate, government and external) were reasonably solid. Rather it suffered a trade or delocalization crisis as the financial crisis, originating in the West, spread to the "real economy" and demand for exports collapsed. But Asia rebounded quickly — much more so than the West. China led the Asian bounce back, helping to lift other East Asian countries out of the crisis, and India recovered fast as well. China and India are expected to grow at more than 10% and just under 10%, respectively and developing Asia at over 9%, in 2010. Advanced economies are projected to grow at only 2.7%. Trade volumes for emerging and developing economies are expected to increase by over 13% in 2010, compared with an estimated 10%–11% increase for advanced economies. FDI to developing countries shrank much less than it did in the West in 2009. Inward and outward FDI for China and India remained buoyant in 2009 and are projected to increase significantly in 2010.[2]

What about post-crisis economic policies in Asia and the West? How do they compare?

So far, government interventions have been more evident in domestic economic policy than in trade policy. Domestic "crisis interventions" are bunched in two key areas: huge bailouts and associated subsidies, especially but not confined to financial services; and fiscal stimulus packages, usually combined with loose and unorthodox monetary policies. The former is concentrated in the West; the latter spread across the OECD and developing countries.

The post-crisis effects of these policies are likely to be far worse in the West than in emerging markets. The cost of financial-sector bailouts and Keynesian macroeconomic policies amounts to about 28% of OECD GDP in 2008 — akin to financing a world war. Both sets of policies

---

[1]This is the central lesson from perhaps the best book about the crisis, based on historical data on financial crises. See Reinhardt, C and K Rogoff (2009). *This Time is Different: Eight Centuries of Financial Folly.* Princeton: Princeton University Press.

[2]*IMF World Economic Outlook*, October 2010; UNCTAD, *World Investment Report* 2010.

leave oceans of public debt that portend higher taxes and real interest rates, in addition to inflationary threats (given governments' temptation to inflate their way out of debt repayments). The *microeconomics* and *politics* of financial bailouts and profligate macroeconomic policies are equally vexing. Intrusive financial regulation and bigger public expenditure portend arbitrary interventions by politicians and bureaucrats, wasteful pork-barrel spending, indiscriminate subsidies, long-term entitlements and rent-seeking. This will stifle private-sector incentives to save, invest and innovate; and it will restrict competition and raise costs for businesses and consumers. These could be the medium-term consequences of short-term crisis interventions and the return to Big Government.

The news is much better on international trade: The world has not hurtled into tit-for-tat protectionism. As the WTO notes, obvious protectionism — mainly border measures such as tariffs, quotas, import licenses and anti-dumping duties — have hardly increased; they affect just over 1% of international trade.[3] But this does not take account of nontraditional, non-border protectionism — mainly complex domestic regulations that spill over the border and discriminate against international trade. Many crisis interventions fall into this category: intrusive new financial regulations that affect cross-border finance; public-procurement restrictions; industrial subsidies; and onerous product and process standards (including environmental standards to promote renewable energy and combat climate change).[4]

Nontraditional regulatory protectionism in the wake of the crisis, especially on subsidies and standards, is worrisome. It is more opaque than traditional protectionism and much less constrained by WTO rules. The danger is that, if not contained, it will spread gradually to cover bigger swathes of international trade. That is what happened in the 1970s and

---

[3]Overview of developments in the international trading environment, *Annual Report by the Director-General*, World Trade Organisation WT/TPR/OV/12, 18 November 2009, pp. A18–19. http://www.wto.org/english/news_e/news09_e/wt_tpr_ov_12_a_e.doc. Also see European Commission, *Sixth Report on Potentially Trade-Restrictive Measures*. http://trade.ec.europa.eu/doclib/docs/2010/may/tradoc_146198.pdf; WTO, OECD and UNCTAD *Reports on G20 Trade and Investment Measures* (May 2010 to October 2010), 4 November 2010. http://www.oecd.org/dataoecd/20/56/46318551.pdf.

[4]For analysis that includes these regulatory measures and their impact on international trade, see Simon Evenett, Executive summary, in *Tensions Contained ... For Now: The Eighth GTA Report*. http://www.globaltradealert.org/sites/default/files/GTA8_exec_summary.pdf.

early 1980s: Rampant domestic interventions to combat external shocks led to creeping protectionism. The result: industrial overcapacity, and delayed global recovery and globalization.[5]

To sum up the global policy outlook: The medium-term consequences of domestic crisis interventions are likely to be far worse in the West than in emerging markets. The prevention of traditional protectionism is good news all-round. Equally, creeping nontraditional protectionism is worrying news all-round.

3. The Post-Crisis Indian Political Economy: Focus on Economic Policy

India has weathered the crisis well, buoyed by exuberant domestic consumption. The Government of India's response to the crisis was fiscal-stimulus packages amounting to about U.S. $60 billion — though, unlike China, in the context of deteriorating public finances, with the consolidated fiscal deficit climbing to above 10% in 2009 (more like 13%–14% of GDP if off-balance-sheet items like food and fuel subsidies are taken into account).

The May 2009, election delivered an unexpectedly strong mandate to the Congress-led UPA government; India has its most stable government in over twenty years, but this has not led to a new wave of market reforms. There have been a few mini-reforms, such as the partial removal of the Administered Price Mechanism on fuel and fertilizer subsidies (reintroduced by the UPA government a few years ago), and pending legislation to partially liberalize higher education. But reforms of the pensions and insurance sectors have stalled, a Generalized Sales Tax (GST) has been postponed to 2012, and delays continue to impede public–private partnerships for infrastructure development.

Relatively high levels of protection remain: agricultural tariffs and nontariff barriers (NTBs), peak industrial tariffs and restrictions in big-ticket services sectors (such as professional services, banking, insurance, retail and distribution, and aviation). There are even higher and largely unreformed

---

[5]On emerging protectionism since the crisis, its link with domestic crisis interventions and comparisons with 1970s, see Erixon, F and R Sally (2010). Trade, globalisation and emerging protectionism since the crisis. *ECIPE Working Paper* 2. http://www.ecipe.org/trade-globalisation-and-emerging-protectionism-since-the-crisis/PDF.

domestic regulatory barriers. These include extremely restrictive employment laws, reserved sectors for small-scale industries (though this list has been reduced), high and differing barriers between the states, repressed financial markets, extremely interventionist agricultural policies (subsidies, price controls and other internal trade barriers), domestic restrictions on services sectors, huge subsidies and price controls on energy, lack of rural property rights, and very inefficient, corrupt public administration. Public-sector reform has hardly begun.

Basically, reforms have stalled since Congress came back to power in 2004, and there are no signs of big change. Dr. Singh and his "dream team" have not proved to be genuine reformers in the past six years; and anti-market sentiment and vested interests remain strong in the Congress Party.[6] The opposition BJP has lost the reform impulse it had in government and is in disarray.

Nevertheless, a combination of stable government and roaring growth gives rise to exuberant optimism. India boosters claim that growth will soon exceed 8%–10% per annum, on the back of increasing rates of aggregate savings and investment (the latter approaching 40% of GDP).[7] Growth catalysts will be high-value services and manufacturing niches; and this can happen without a new wave of policy reforms. At the same time, India is rising to be a regional and global power.

This is India hype: It defies belief that India can boost growth above an annual 10% without further structural reforms. In terms of market reforms, India lags behind China and other parts of East Asia. It has higher protection against imports and inward investment. Its public finances, infrastructure and lower-education system are much weaker. It has more damaging restrictions that stymie domestic markets in agriculture, manufacturing and services — especially draconian employment laws that prevent firms from employing unskilled workers in large numbers. Government subsidies are more wasteful. Worst of all, India's unreformed, dysfunctional state — the Union government in Delhi, the state governments and other levels of

---

[6]Razeen Sally, Congress deserves to lose India's elections (April 15, 2009). *Financial Time*; and India after the elections. http://www.ecipe.org/blog/india-after-the-elections.

[7]Martin Wolf, India's elephant charges on through the economic crisis (March 3, 2010). *Financial Times*.

government — is the biggest obstacle to faster growth. Growth has come from capital- and skill-intensive sectors in manufacturing and services. It has primarily benefited the urban well-to-do and middle classes, but not flowed down as much as it has in East Asia to the poor in the rural areas.[8]

Absent further market reforms, India will not have what it desperately needs: East Asian-style, labor-intensive agricultural services and industrial growth. In particular, India needs its Industrial Revolution so that the impoverished in the countryside can move to (initially) low-wage work in mass manufacturing.[9] That has yet to happen and it demands regulatory reforms — not least in labor markets and the public sector — that remain politically very hard nuts to crack. Moreover, the combination of a barely-reforming government in Delhi and worse global economic conditions after the crisis might make it difficult to maintain current levels of growth.

That said, India has a silver lining: Policies, institutions and economic performance have been improving in a minority of Indian states, roughly in an arc from the south to the west, with a few outliers such as Bihar in the North. They set positive examples for other states to emulate.

No one can deny that India is a bigger player on the global stage. But, economically and militarily, it is still too small to be a pan-Asian, let alone a global, leader. It pales in comparison with China. Even within South Asia its leadership is diminished by testy relations with most of its neighbors, and disastrous relations with its biggest neighbor, Pakistan. Hence India, like Brazil and Russia, is a second-tier emerging power, well behind China. This is the present reality — though India's regional and global power may look different a decade or more ahead if it keeps growing at or just below 10% per annum.[10]

---

[8]Though high growth in the last two decades — the product of market reforms since 1991 — has lifted nearly 200 million people out of extreme poverty. Previous decades of much lower growth barely made a dent into overall poverty. See Jagdish Bhagwati, Indian reforms: Yesterday and today, *The Third Prof. Hiren Mukerjee Memorial Annual Parliamentary Lecture*, 2 December 2010. http://www.columbia.edu/~jb38/papers/pdf/Lok-Sabha-speech-FINAL-EXPANDED-Deceber-14.pdf.

[9]Panagariya, A (2008). *India: The Emerging Giant*. Oxford: Oxford University Press; Luce, E (2007). *In Spite of the Gods: The Strange Rise of Modern India*. London: Abacus.

[10]Wolf, M (2010). India in the world. In *India's Economy: Performance and Challenges*, S Acharya and R Mohan (eds.), pp. 387, 394–396. New Delhi: Oxford University Press.

4. Post-Crisis Indian Trade Policy

This section starts with India's trade and FDI patterns and their associated policy framework. It then looks at India's "multi-track" trade policy — through unilateral measures, the WTO and FTAs. Finally, it adds explicitly political observations on Indian trade policy.

4.1. *Trade and FDI patterns; the policy framework*[11]

India's retreat from the "license raj" — its equivalent of Soviet-style central planning — began halfheartedly in the 1980s; but its decisive opening to the world economy dates back to 1991. Most border NTBs have been removed, as have internal licensing restrictions. Nominal applied tariffs came down from an average of 100% in 1985 to 13% by 2008–09. The maximum tariff on nonagricultural goods, save for a few items, has come down to 10%. However, in agriculture, tariffs and NTBs remain much higher. The average applied tariff in agriculture is 32%. The maximum MFN tariff is 246%. India has bound 74% of its tariffs in the WTO at an average rate of 50% (Table 1).

These reductions have significantly narrowed the gap between Indian levels of trade protection and those of other developing countries. India is now much closer to ASEAN and Chinese levels of trade protection. Its trade-weighted tariff, at 6%, is lower than that of Brazil or Russia and not that far off Chinese and ASEAN levels (Table 1). Still, India's tariff structure remains more protectionist than those of East Asian countries. Intermediate inputs and consumer goods (e.g. cars, motorcycles, textiles and garments) face relatively high tariffs. The effective rate of protection for manufacturing, though it has decreased, remains high compared with East Asian countries. In addition, the Government of India operates an extremely complex, bureaucracy-ridden system of duty exemptions, special establishment and investment regulations, sectoral support programmes and

---

[11] This section draws on WTO, *Trade Policy Review: India*, 2008. www.wto.org; USTR, *National Estimate of Foreign Trade Barriers: India*, 2010. www.ustr.gov; Narayan, S (2009). Trade reforms in India. In *The Political Economy of Trade Reforms in Emerging Markets: Crisis or Opportunity?* P Alves, P Draper and R Sally (eds.). London: Edward Elgar; Hoda, A (2005). India in the WTO. In *India–ASEAN Economic Relations: Meeting the Challenges of Globalisation*, M Asher, N Kumar and R Sen (eds.). Singapore/India: ISEAS/RIS.

Table 1.   Bound and applied MFN tariffs (WTO 2010).

Country/Economy	Year	Tariff Binding Coverage in %	Simple Average Final Bound (All Goods)	Simple Average Applied Tariff (Manufacture)	Simple Average Applied Tariff (Agriculture)	Simple Average Applied Tariff (All Goods)	Trade Weighted Average (All Goods)	Maximum MFN Applied Duties
EU	08/09	100.0	5.2	3.9	13.5	5.3	2.9	166
U.S.	08/09	100.0	3.5	3.3	4.7	3.5	2.0	350
Japan	08/09	99.7	5.1	2.5	21.0	4.9	2.0	641
Brazil	08/09	100	31.4	14.1	10.2	13.6	8.8	96.7
Russia	08/09	—	—	10.1	13.2	10.5	10.3	357
India	08/09	73.8	48.5	10.1	31.8	12.9	6.0	246
Indonesia	08/09	95.8	37.1	6.6	8.4	6.8	4.1	150
China	08/09	100.0	10.0	8.7	15.6	9.6	4.3	65
South Africa	08/09	96.4	19.0	7.5	8.9	7.7	5.0	878

Source: WTO World Tariff Profiles (2010). http://stat.wto.org/TariffProfile/WSDBTariffPFHome.aspx?Language=E.

Special Economic Zones (SEZs) to encourage exports.[12] Also, India has become the world's most active user of AD duties, especially directed at Chinese imports.

FDI and services liberalization have proceeded alongside the liberalization of trade in goods. Manufacturing is fairly open to FDI. In terms of overall FDI regulatory restrictiveness, India is on a par with China, but it is more restrictive than Russia and Brazil (Fig. 1). Some services sectors, notably insurance, aviation, construction, retail and distribution, face especially high levels of protection. Restrictions include foreign-equity limits, the form of commercial establishment, and complicated and costly licensing procedures.

India is placed 134th overall in the World Bank's 2011 "ease of doing business" indicators — the worst of the BRICS and well behind China.

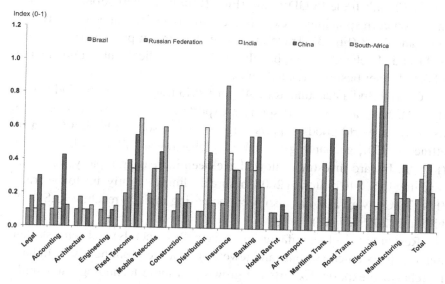

Fig. 1.   FDI regulatory restrictiveness by country and sector.
Source: Koyama and Golub (2006) OECD'S FDI Regulatory Restrictiveness Index: Revision and Extension to more Economies, Economic Department Working Papers No. 525, pp. 8–10.

---

[12]As indicated by even a cursory reading of Government of India, Ministry of Commerce and Industry, *Foreign Trade Policy* 2009–2014. http://dgftcom.nic.in/exim/2000/dn/ftpdnl/high0910-eng.pdf.

It is ranked 100th overall for "trading across borders", better than Brazil and Russia but well behind China (Table 2). These scores are reflected in the World Economic Forum's *Enabling Trade Index* (Table 3). Among the World Bank indicators, India scores particularly badly in starting and closing a business, dealing with construction permits, paying taxes and enforcing contracts. There is considerable variation among Indian states: If only the top ten performing states were counted, India would jump 55 places in the ease-of-doing-business rankings — roughly to where China is now. India's "hard" infrastructure is at least as bad as its "soft" regulatory infrastructure. It has appalling roads, airports and ports, and serious power shortages.

Trade and FDI liberalization have rapidly integrated India into the global economy. The trade-to-GDP ratio climbed to over 55% of GDP in 2008, before coming down to about 45% of GDP in the wake of the crisis — not far off China's trade-to-GDP ratio (Fig. 2). India's international trade has increased correspondingly; exports grew by about 20% annually between 2000 and 2008 (Fig. 3). Trade in services has grown particularly fast, led by IT and IT-related sectors, but also including medical, entertainment and a host of other business-related services.

Overall, India accounts for 2.4% of world trade — well behind China (Fig. 4). Its share of world services exports (4% of the total) is double its share of world goods exports (Fig. 5). It is also well behind China in attracting FDI, accounting for 1% of global inward FDI stock by 2009 (Fig. 6). Inward investment flows have been increasing rapidly, however, reaching U.S. $40 billion in 2008, before declining slightly due to the crisis (Fig. 7). Outward FDI has also been increasing rapidly, reaching U.S. $18 billion in 2008 (Fig. 8).

Resource-based manufacturing (especially minerals) and semi-skilled manufactures (such as gems and jewellery) feature prominently in India's merchandise exports. Exports are growing in more technology and skill-intensive (though still capital-intensive) products in chemicals, engineering, cars and car parts, and pharmaceuticals. But India continues to underperform badly in labor-intensive exports. Garments is the only unskilled labor-intensive product range in India's list of top six merchandise exports; but even its share of world exports is declining and pales in comparison with China's share. Bangladesh and Sri Lanka, both with much smaller populations, have garments exports as large as India's. Unlike China, India

Table 2. World ranking for ease of doing business (2011).

	Ease of Doing Business	Starting a Business	Dealing with Constr. Permits	Registe Ring Property	Getting Credit	Protecting Investors	Paying Taxes	Trading Across Borders	Enforcing Contracts	Closing a Business
Singapore	1	4	2	15	6	2	4	1	13	2
H-Kong	2	6	1	56	2	3	3	2	2	15
U.S.	5	9	27	12	6	5	62	20	8	14
Denmark	6	27	10	30	15	28	13	5	30	5
Korea	16	60	22	74	15	74	49	8	5	13
Japan	18	98	44	59	15	16	112	24	19	1
Thailand	19	95	12	19	72	12	91	12	25	46
Malaysia	21	113	108	60	1	4	23	37	59	55
Vietnam	78	100	62	43	15	173	124	63	31	124
China	79	151	181	38	65	93	124	50	15	68
Indonesia	121	155	60	98	116	44	114	47	154	142
Russia	123	108	182	51	89	93	130	162	18	103
Brazil	127	128	112	122	89	74	105	114	98	132
India	134	165	177	94	32	44	152	100	182	134

Source: World Bank Ease of Doing Business 2011. http://www.doingbusiness.org/rankings.

Table 3.   The enabling trade index (2010).

Country/ Economy	Overall Rank		Market Access		Border Administration		Transport and Communications Infrastructure		Business Environment	
	Rank	Score	Rank	Score	Rank	Score	Rank	Score	Rank	Score
Singapore	1	6.06	1	5.97	1	6.56	7	5.74	2	6
Hong-Kong	2	5.7	16	5.12	6	5.96	5	5.79	5	5.94
Denmark	3	5.41	95	3.76	3	6.22	8	5.71	3	5.96
Sweden	4	5.41	96	3.75	2	6.34	9	5.7	10	5.84
Switzerland	5	5.37	58	4.23	10	5.76	10	5.63	8	5.87
United States	19	5.03	62	4.17	19	5.6	11	5.49	37	4.86
Japan	25	4.8	121	3.2	16	5.65	14	5.45	34	4.91
China	48	4.32	79	3.87	48	4.53	43	4.13	41	4.74
Indonesia	68	3.97	60	4.21	67	3.99	85	3.28	60	4.42
South-Africa	72	3.95	87	3.78	53	4.25	65	3.64	79	4.11
India	84	3.81	115	3.42	68	3.98	81	3.34	58	4.48
Brazil	87	3.76	104	3.72	80	3.7	66	3.64	83	4
Russia	114	3.37	125	2.68	109	2.99	48	4	92	3.79

Source: The Global Enabling Trade Report 2010, pp. 10 & 11.

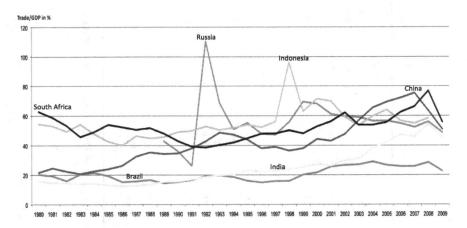

Fig. 2.   Trade (goods and services)/GDP in percentages for BRIICS (1980–2009).
Source: World Bank, World Development Indicators; WTO, International Trade Statistics 2010.

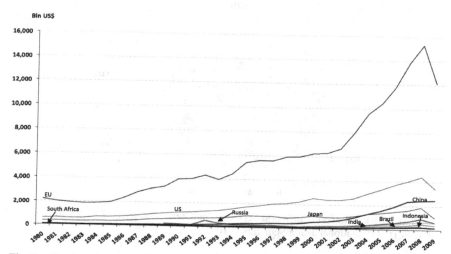

Fig. 3.   Total trade (goods and services) in billion U.S. $ for BRIICS, EU, Japan and U.S., incl. Intra-EU trade (1980–2009).
Source: World Bank, World Development Indicators; UNCTAD Statistical Handbook 2009; WTO, International Trade Statistics 2010.

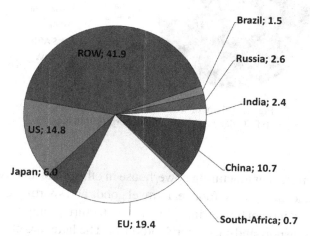

Fig. 4.   BRIICS, EU, U.S. and Japan share of world goods & services trade (2009: EU excl. intra trade).
Source: WTO, International Trade Statistics 2010. http://www.wto.org/english/news_e/pres10_e/pr598_e.htm; Eurostat and own calculations.

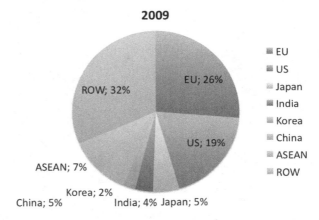

Fig. 5.   Share of exports in World Services Trade (excl. Intra-EU27 trade) 2009.
Source: WTO International Trade Statistics 2010.

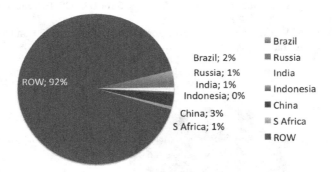

Fig. 6.   Share of world IFDI, BRIICS (2009).
Source: UNCTAD, FDI/TNC database. www.unctad.org/fdistatistics.

has not become a manufacturing powerhouse in other labor-intensive goods such as toys, leather goods, footwear, travel goods and sporting goods. Also unlike China, it has not broken into global manufacturing supply chains in IT and other "transport-and-machinery" products. The latter are characterized by "processing trade": Raw materials and components are imported for assembly and export of finished goods. Processing trade accounts for half of China's overall trade, but it is negligible in India. Last, FDI goes to India mostly to serve the local market rather than for export production.

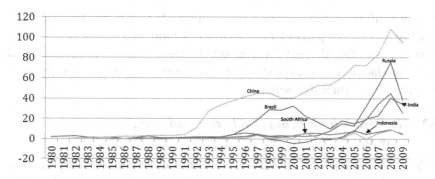

Fig. 7.   Inward FDI flows for BRIICS in billion U.S. $ (1980–2008).
Source: UNCTAD World Investment Report 2010 (WIR 2010). http://www.unctad.org/templates/WebFlyer.asp?intItemID=5535&lang=1.

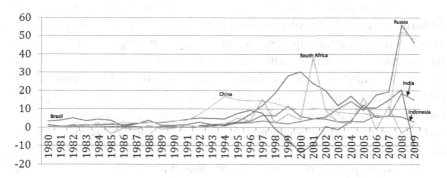

Fig. 8.   Outward FDI flows from BRIICS in billion U.S. $ (2000–2009).
Source: UNCTAD, FDI/TNC database. www.unctad.org/fdistatistics.

In contrast, in China and other parts of East Asia, much FDI is linked to processing trade to serve global markets.[13]

These patterns show that India is not exploiting its labor abundance and concomitant comparative advantage in labor-intensive exports, particularly in manufacturing. That goes some way to explaining why growth rates averaging over 6% since 1991, and 8%–9% in the last few years, have not delivered the employment, poverty-reduction and

---

[13]Panagariya, *op cit.*, pp. 264–268; Athukorala, P and H Hill (2010). Asian trade: Long-term patterns and key policy issues. *Asia-Pacific Economic Literature*, 24(2), 52–82.

human-welfare-improvement effect of comparable (or higher) growth rates in China and other parts of East Asia. Remaining protection and — even more so — high domestic regulatory barriers channel production and trade into labor-saving, capital and skill-intensive activities and away from unskilled labor-intensive activities.[14]

4.2. *Multi-track trade policy: Unilateral measures, WTO and FTAs*

India's trade and FDI liberalization has come about almost totally through *unilateral* measures — outside trade negotiations, whether in the WTO or FTAs. This happened mostly in two reform bursts, first in 1991–93 and then in 1998–2004, with "reform pauses" in 1993–1996 and after 2004.

External liberalization has stalled under the present Congress-led government, save for industrial-tariff reductions in annual budgets (until 2008) and marginal FDI reforms. Recent rule changes may allow companies to get round sectoral caps on foreign equity. One regulation allows an Indian holding company with up to 49% of foreign equity to invest in "downstream" companies without counting the holding company's foreign equity. Another allows FDI to be counted with different types of foreign portfolio investment. But both are incredibly opaque and baffling, and appear designed to maximize lobbying and special favors for well-connected companies.

Moreover, protectionist measures increased in the run-up to and during the global economic crisis, though not in a major way. First, there were new export restrictions on agricultural products in response to commodity-price inflation in 2007–2008. Other trade-restricting measures — higher import tariffs, licensing requirements, provisional anti-dumping and safeguard duties, and tighter standards restrictions — followed when the crisis hit. Iron, steel, aluminum, yarn and assorted agricultural products were affected. Many of these measures targeted Chinese imports. According to Global Trade Alert, India is a chief offender in terms of crisis-related protectionist measures, alongside the EU-27, Russia and Argentina (Table 5). However, these measures have not affected a big chunk of India's trade. Interestingly,

---

[14]Krueger, AO. India's trade with the world: Retrospect and prospect. In *India's Economy*, pp. 422–426, *op cit.*

Table 4. Countries targeted by crisis-era trade-restrictive measures.

Target	Number of Discriminatory Measures Imposed on Target		Number of Pending Measures which, if Implemented, would Harm Target too	
	November 2010	Increase since June 2010	November 2010	Increase since June 2010
China	337	55	129	4
EU27	322	56	88	8
USA	260	47	51	5
Germany	240	36	63	7
France	221	33	50	4
UK	214	33	48	4
Italy	211	36	53	3
Japan	192	24	50	4
Netherlands	191	21	45	3
Belgium	189	19	46	3

Source: Global Trade Alert (2010): *The 8th GTA Trade Report*, CEPR, London. http://www.globaltradealert.org/sites/default/files/GTA8_0.pdf.

China is not in the list of top ten offenders, but it is the prime target of others' crisis-related protectionism (Tables 4 and 5).

India, along with Brazil, is the most active developing country in the WTO. Its GATT and GATS commitments are weak. Nevertheless, Uruguay Round agreements have led to changes in national practice — most notably the abolition of import quotas on consumer goods on balance-of-payments grounds. India is active as both plaintiff and defendant in WTO dispute settlement. As a result of losing disputes, it has had to change domestic regulations on import quotas, patents, local-content measures, and internal taxes on wines and spirits. It may have to abolish remaining export subsidies if this issue is pursued in dispute settlement.[15]

India is a lead player in the Doha Round, but its defensiveness in the Uruguay Round has continued in the Doha Round. It is rigidly defensive in agriculture and rather defensive in industrial goods (in the nonagricultural market access — NAMA — negotiations). It was strongly opposed to the

---

[15]Hoda, A (2010). Enforcing WTO rights and obligations — India in the WTO disputes. *ICRIER Trade Policy Newsletter*, pp. 18–21.

Table 5.   Crisis-era trade-restrictive measures by country.

Rank	Ranked by Number of Measures	Ranked by the Number of Tariff Lines Affected by Measures	Ranked by the Number of Sectors Affected by Measures	Ranked by the Number of Trading Partners Affected by Measures
1	EU27 (166)	Viet Nam (926)	Algeria (67)	Argentina (174)
2	Russia (85)	Venezuela (785)	EU27 (57)	EU27 (168)
3	Argentina (52)	Kazakhstan (723)	Nigeria (45)	China (160)
4	India (47)	Nigeria (599)	Venezuela (38)	Indonesia (151)
5	Germany (35)	Algeria (476)	Viet Nam (38)	Algeria (476)
6	Brazil (32)	EU27 (467)	Germany (36)	India (145)
7	UK (31)	Russia (426)	Kazakhstan (36)	Russia (143)
8	Spain (25)	Argentina (396)	Russia (36)	Finland (132)
9	Indonesia (24)	India (365)	India (32)	Germany (132)
10	Italy (24)	Indonesia (347)	Ethiopia (32)	South Africa (132)

Source: Global Trade Alert (2010): *The 8th GTA Trade Report*, CEPR, London. http://www.globaltradealert.org/sites/default/files/GTA8_0.

inclusion of most of the Singapore issues, and remains in favor of strong special and differential treatment for developing countries. That said, India is not as militantly obstructive as it was in the GATT. Its main negotiating shift has been in services, where it has discovered offensive interests in the wake of the IT services take-off at home.[16]

Still, Indian trade policy appears somewhat schizophrenic: Domestic economic considerations have driven unilateral liberalization, but this has not translated into greater flexibility in the WTO (except to some extent in services). The domestic backlash against India's Uruguay Round commitments (negotiated by the Ministry of Commerce and Industry, largely without wider consultation or discussion) and messy coalition politics have combined to restrict the government's room for maneuver in the WTO. Hence, unilateral and multilateral trade-policy tracks seem disconnected.[17]

India has become very active with FTAs, in its South Asian backyard and beyond. It has 11 FTAs on the books and plans many more (Table 6). Its FTA activity is on a par with that of the other two major Asian powers, China and Japan.

---

[16]Hoda, India in the WTO, *op cit.*

[17]Narayan, *op cit.*

Table 6.   Recently established or proposed RTAs/CEPAs by India (2000–2010).

Trading Partners	Nature of Agreement	Status of Agreement 2010
Singapore	FTA	Agreement in force
Sri Lanka	FTA	Agreement in force
APTA	FTA	Agreement in force
Bhutan	FTA	Agreement in force
Nepal	FTA	Agreement in force
SAFTA	FTA	Agreement in force
Bhutan	FTA	Agreement in force
Canada	EPA	Proposed
Thailand	EPA/ FTA	Framework Agreement signed
ASEAN	FTA	Agreement in force
BIMSTEC	FTA	Framework Agreement signed
SACU	FTA	Framework Agreement signed
MERCOSUR	FTA	Agreement in force
GCC	FTA	Framework Agreement signed
New Zealand	FTA	Under Negotiation
Afghanistan	PTA	Agreement in force
Chile	PTA	Agreement in force
Russia	CEPA	Proposed
USA	FTA	Proposed
China	BIPA & FTA	Proposed
Korea	FTA & CEPA	Agreement in force
Mauritius	CEPA	Under negotiation
Japan	EPA/ FTA	Under negotiation
Colombia	FTA	Proposed
Australia	EPA/ FTA	Proposed
Egypt	PTA	Under negotiation
EU	FTA	Under negotiation
EFTA	FTA	Under negotiation
Indonesia	EPA/FTA	Proposed
Israel	FTA	Proposed
Turkey	FTA	Proposed
Uruguay	FTA	Proposed
Venezuela	FTA	Proposed
Nepal	FTA	Agreement in force
CEPEA/ASEAN+6	EPA/FTA	Proposed

Source: Asia Regional Integration Centre.

In South Asia, India has FTAs with Sri Lanka, Bhutan and Nepal, and is negotiating with Bangladesh. The strongest of these is the Indo–Lanka FTA, but even the latter is weak: Up to half of bilateral trade is excluded or restricted with carve-outs, tariff-rate quotas and stringent rules of origin (ROOs). Hitherto loose regional cooperation is supposed to be transformed into the South Asian FTA (SAFTA) by 2010, leading to a customs union by 2015 and economic union (whatever that means) by 2020. This looks unachievable in practice. For starters, SAFTA excludes Indo–Pakistani trade. Planned negotiations are only on goods; they do not cover services, investment and other non-border market-access issues. And over half of intra-regional trade is excluded through "sensitive lists", restrictive ROOs and assorted NTBs.[18]

India's approach to FTAs outside South Asia is mostly about foreign policy and is "trade light": Not much trade is actually liberalized. At best, tariffs are eliminated on close to 90% of products — though with often long transition periods and restrictive ROOs. But "WTO-plus" issues — nontariff and regulatory barriers in goods, services, investment and public procurement — are hardly tackled, with little advance on weak WTO disciplines. Indeed, India has the worst-quality FTAs of all major FTA players in Asia.

An FTA with ASEAN is planned for completion by 2011; and bilateral FTAs are also in place with Thailand and Singapore. ASEAN–India, India–Thailand and India–Malaysia negotiations have been bedeviled by India's insistence on exempting swathes of products and on very restrictive ROOs for products covered. Fear of Chinese competition is one of the main factors driving product exemptions and restrictive ROOs. India's recently concluded FTA with South Korea fits the pattern: Only 66% of Indian tariff lines are subject to duty elimination over an eight-year transition period; and agreements on services and investment are weak. In addition, India is part of the BIMSTEC group (the other members being Bangladesh, Sri Lanka, Nepal, Bhutan, Thailand and Myanmar) that plans an FTA by 2017. It has mini-FTAs — basically limited tariff-concession schemes — in force or planned with several countries and regions, for example Chile, SACU, Mercosur and IBSA.[19]

---

[18] Sally, R (2010). Regional economic integration in Asia: The track record and prospects. *ECIPE Occasional Paper* 2, p. 10. http://www.ecipe.org/publications/ecipe-occasional-papers/regional-economic-integration-in-asia-the-track-record-and-prospects/PDF.

[19] Sally, R (2006). FTAs and the prospects for regional integration in Asia. *ECIPE Working Paper* 1, pp. 12–13.

India's most serious FTA negotiation is with the EU. Both sides have committed to an ambitious agreement, with tariff elimination on more than 90% of goods trade and a strong GATS-plus agreement in services. Most of agriculture will be exempted by mutual agreement. Whatever the rhetoric, the EU will find it extremely difficult to tackle India's high trade-related regulatory barriers through an FTA, and specifically, to open up government procurement and some services sectors (for example professional services, financial services, retail and distribution). Given stalled policy reforms in Delhi, snail-like unilateral liberalization, WTO defensiveness and other trade-light FTAs, a "deepintegration" FTA with India is next to impossible.[20]

4.3. *Political economy of Indian trade policy*[21]

Now consider some explicitly political observations on Indian trade policy. The following treatment adopts a simple taxonomy of relevant factors: circumstances, especially crises; organized interests; institutions; and foreign policy.

First, circumstances — crises in particular. India's big burst of external liberalization, in 1991–1993, was linked to macroeconomic stabilization, both set against the backdrop of an extreme balance-of-payments crisis in 1991. India has seen stop-go reforms since 1993; and they have been more "stop" than "go" since 2004. Increasing and seemingly sustainable growth has clearly bred "reform complacency". The global economic crisis induced marginal protectionist backsliding rather than further liberalization.

Indian trade and FDI liberalization have also benefited from an East Asian "demonstration effect". Unilateral liberalization swept across Southeast Asia, and then China, in the 1980s and 1990s. China became the engine of liberalization for the wider region — sending ripple effects across to India. These concentrated policy-makers' minds in India; they felt they could not fall too far behind East Asian liberalization if they were to improve

---

[20]Sally, R (2007). Looking east: The European Union's new FTA negotiations in Asia. *Jan Tumlir Policy Essay* 3, European Centre for International Political Economy. http://www.ecipe.org/publications/jan-tumlir-policy-essays/looking-east-the-european-union2019s-new-trade-negotiations-in-asia-1/PDF.

[21]This sub-section draws on Sally, R (2009). Globalisation and the political economy of trade reforms in the BRIICS. Chapter 4 in *Globalisation and Emerging Economies: Brazil, Russia, India, Indonesia, China and South Africa*. Paris: OECD.

economic performance. However, unilateral liberalization has stalled in East and South Asia. It stalled in China from about 2006, corresponding with greater industrial-policy interventions.

Second, organized interests. India's culture of democracy has long accommodated lively and diverse interest-group activity. In trade policy, such activity sprang to life after the Uruguay Round. Trades unions remain very protectionist. Their fortress is extremely restrictive employment laws that make it unviable for firms to take on new workers beyond a certain size. Unions represent a tiny minority of workers in sectors that were long protected under the license raj. In manufacturing, there are only six million workers in the formal sector, in a total employable population of 450 million or more. State-owned enterprises, for example in power, energy, infrastructure, agriculture and financial services, are also bastions of protection.

India's private sector, in contrast, has been transformed since the opening of the economy from 1991. It was dominated by long-established conglomerates who benefited from the license raj. The two main industry associations, the CII (Confederation of Indian Industries) and FICCI (Federation of Indian Chambers of Commerce and Industry) were strong defenders of protectionism. Now the landscape is more varied. There remain influential protectionist interests in manufacturing. But India's leading business houses — some long-established, like the Tatas, Birlas and Mahindras, others newer on the scene, such as Reliance, Mittal and Bharthi — have restructured, expanded exports and are investing in production abroad. Many still lobby for protection, but in more muted form given their wider international interests. This is reflected in the changing positions of the industry associations — more pronounced with the CII, which represents the big firms, less so with FICCI, which houses more inward-looking medium-sized firms. Confederation of Indian Industries and FICCI, given the mixed interests they represent, tend to be defensive in trade negotiations, but somewhat more flexible on unilateral liberalization. Finally, India's stellar IT firms, notably in software and business-process outsourcing, are very open-economy oriented. They operate in a far less regulated policy environment compared with other sectors, have myriad links with foreign multinationals, and have fast-expanding exports and foreign investments. They are represented by NASSCOM.

The challenge is to harness open-economy interests to the wagon of further liberalization, and especially to domestic regulatory reforms. Their stakes in structural, microeconomic reforms are becoming ever clearer. Previous liberalization has spurred firm-level restructuring, export-orientation and overseas expansion. But firms remain hamstrung by high-cost domestic business environments, which they feel puts them at a disadvantage to foreign competitors with more salubrious business climates in their home markets. That also translates into defensiveness in trade negotiations. Structural reforms at home would lower business costs, boost the international competitiveness of local firms, make them less resistant to opening domestic markets to foreign competition, and translate into less defensive positions in trade negotiations.

Third, institutions. The complications of liberal-democratic politics — split policy competences between the centre and the states in a federal system, freewheeling interest-group activity, media scrutiny, public discussion, multiple "veto points" — makes it very difficult to pursue comprehensive reforms, including trade reforms. Also, trade policy is controlled by the Ministry of Commerce and Industry (MOCI). The Ministry of Finance was influential in liberalization in 1991–1993, but less so thereafter. Organized business and NGOs have become more active since the Uruguay Round. Interagency coordination on trade policy functions badly, and state governments are largely left out of the loop.[22] The MOCI remains defensive in trade negotiations and ambivalent about unilateral liberalization — rather at odds with the global integration of the Indian economy since 1991.

Thus, a combination of organized interests and defective institutions cramps further liberalization and structural reforms. But India's great advantage is its factor endowment — labor abundance. We know from recent economic history that the star developing-country performers are from East Asia. These countries had different starting positions, but, at a certain stage of development, labor abundance allowed them to break into labor-intensive manufactured exports, which became an engine of growth and in turn aided poverty reduction and human-welfare improvement. This is the shadow of South Asia's future. By plugging into global markets for manufacturing, and labor-intensive services too, South Asian countries can

---

[22]Narayan, *op cit.*

get on to sustainable growth paths. Labor-intensive exports attract FDI (and the technology and skills that come with it), feed quickly into poverty-reducing, welfare-improving employment, and, more gradually, into better infrastructure and institutions. This creates and strengthens a constellation of interests to support open trade and FDI policies. This bodes well for China, India and other labor-abundant countries in East and South Asia.

Fourth, foreign policy. The end of the Cold War and the collapse of the Soviet Union transformed Indian foreign policy. India looked west to a *rapprochement* and closer relations with the USA, and in the second instance with Europe. It also looked east, first to Southeast Asia and then to China. Closer engagement, looking east and west, started in the early 1990s, paused in the mid to late 1990s, and has been renewed and strengthened ever since. It corresponds with the timing of external liberalization. Arguably, India's foreign-policy shift is an important factor influencing its belated embrace of the world economy.[23]

To sum up: An economic crisis led to a big opening of the economy. India emulated successful liberalizing policies in East Asia — up to a point. New open-economy interest-group constellations emerged to counter traditional protectionist interests — though business interests still have mixed preferences and do not lobby vigorously for market opening. Liberalizing reforms have stalled; but a party-political and wider public consensus, supported by open-economy business interests, has gradually formed around existing reforms. This prevents reform reversal. Shifts in foreign policy have also encouraged external opening and greater cross-border commerce. Last, India's great good fortune is its labor abundance. This is the strongest medium-to-long-term factor to support further external liberalization and global integration.

5. Conclusion

India, like China, had a "good" crisis; both have spearheaded exuberant post-crisis recovery in emerging markets. A combination of stable government and roaring growth gives rise to predictions that India will hit annual growth

---

[23]Narayan, *op cit.*; Baru, S (2006). *Strategic Consequences of India's Economic Performance*. New Delhi: Academic Foundation.

rates of 10% or more. This is India hype. Reforms have stalled since 2004, with no prospect of big change. The combination of a barely-reforming government in Delhi and turbulent global economic conditions will make it difficult to maintain existing levels of growth. Geopolitically, India is a rising regional and global power, but it is still a second-tier emerging power, well behind China.

Turning to trade policy: India's cumulatively substantial trade and FDI liberalization has narrowed the gap with other developing countries. External protection is now much closer to Chinese and ASEAN levels. But that still leaves significant pockets of protection in agriculture, some industrial products and big-ticket services sectors. India also has high domestic regulatory barriers — much higher than the East Asian average — that are an even bigger obstacle to trade and FDI.

Indian trade and FDI liberalization have been overwhelmingly unilateral. But this has stalled since 2004. India is one of the worst offenders in terms of crisis-related protectionist measures, though this does not affect a big chunk of its trade. India is defensive in the WTO, as its Doha Round positions show. It is very active with FTAs, but these are "trade light", pursued more for foreign-policy than commercial reasons. Indeed, India has the worst-quality FTAs among major Asian FTA players.

To throw some explicitly political observations into the mix: Reform complacency cramps further liberalization and structural reform — more so in Delhi than in the better-performing states. But a party-political and wider public consensus, supported by open-economy business interests, prevents reform reversal. Foreign-policy shifts — notably India's "look west" and "look east" policies — cement cross-border commercial ties. India's most favorable endowment is its labor abundance. This is the most promising factor to support further external liberalization and global integration.

India's challenge is to stimulate further unilateral trade and FDI liberalization related to domestic structural reforms. That means tackling non-border, but still trade-related, regulatory barriers. These are "second-generation" reforms whose politics can be more challenging than the politics of "first-generation" reforms. The latter involve the reduction and removal of border barriers. This is relatively simple technically and can be done quickly though politically these measures are rarely easy. The former are all about complex domestic regulation. These reforms are technically and administratively difficult, and take time to implement. They demand a minimum of capacity across government, especially for implementation and enforcement. Above all, they are politically very sensitive, as they affect entrenched interests that are extremely difficult to dislodge. Nevertheless, the case should be made to take on these reforms so that they can be pushed through when political opportunities present themselves.

Index

List of Contributors

Mr. Teo Chee Hean is the Deputy Prime Minister, Minister for Home Affairs, Minister in charge of Civil Service and Coordinating Minister for National Security, Republic of Singapore.

Dr. Amitendu Palit is the Head (Development & Programmes) and Visiting Senior Research Fellow at the Institute of South Asian Studies (ISAS), National University of Singapore (NUS).

Mr. Rory Medcalf is the Program Director for International Security at the Lowy Institute for International Policy and a Senior Research Fellow in Indian Strategic Affairs at the University of New South Wales, Australia.

Mr. Ashley Townshend is a Joan Rydon Scholar in Government and M.Phil. Candidate in the Faculty of Oriental Studies at the University of Oxford. He coauthored this chapter during his time as a Research Associate in the International Security Program at the Lowy Institute for International Policy, Sydney.

Dr. Patrick Mendis, a former American diplomat and a Military Professor in the NATO and Pacific Commands, is an Affiliate Professor of Public and International Affairs at George Mason University. While serving as a visiting scholar in foreign policy at Johns Hopkins University's Nitze School of Advanced International Studies, he authored two books entitled "Trade for Peace and Commercial Providence: The Secret Destiny of the American Empire".

Professor Peter Mayer is the Associate Professor of Politics and Visiting Research Fellow at the School of History and Politics, University of Adelaide.

Dr. Sadiq Ahmed is the Vice Chairman at Policy Research Institute of Bangladesh.

Dr. Nalin Mehta is the Visiting Senior Research Fellow at the Institute of South Asian Studies and Asia Research Institute, National University of Singapore and Joint Editor, South Asian History and Culture (Routledge).

Mr. Jaspal Singh Bindra is the Group Executive Director and a member of the Board of Standard Chartered PLC and is based in Hong Kong as Chief Executive Officer, Asia.

Mr. Dipak Dasgupta is the Principal Economic Adviser, Ministry of Finance, Government of India and was the Lead Economist (2009–2010) for the World Bank's South Asia region.

Mr. Nihal Pitigala is a consultant at the International Trade Department of the World Bank.

Shahid Javed Burki is a former Finance Minister of Pakistan and Vice President for Latin American and the Caribbean at the World Bank. Mr. Burki is currently Chairman of the Institute of Public Policy in Lahore, Pakistan and Visiting Senior Research Fellow at the Institute of South Asian Studies (ISAS), National University of Singapore.

Dr. Razeen Sally is the Visiting Associate Professor at the Lee Kuan Yew School of Public Policy and Institute of South Asian Studies (ISAS), National University of Singapore.